Eliza Jessie Scott
from Edith L. S.
August 14th 1882.

P Ⅲ

¹9/9

SCORPIO AND OPHIUCHUS.

"Thou shalt bruise his heel."—Gen. iii. 15.

"I give unto you power to tread on serpents and scorpions, and over all the power of the enemy."—Luke x. 19.

PRIMEVAL MAN UNVEILED:

OR, THE

ANTHROPOLOGY OF THE BIBLE.

BY

THE REV. JAMES GALL.

"We ask, with musing wonder, Was this Satan's world once? . . . and do we find him, like a beast of prey, prowling round the habitation of its new possessor? Is it because of his original connection with our earth that he is still prince of the power of the air, disenthroned?"—*Dr. H. Bonar.*

"Now shall the prince of this world be cast out."—JOHN xii. 31.

SECOND EDITION.

LONDON:

HAMILTON, ADAMS, & CO.,

EDINBURGH: GALL & INGLIS.

MDCCCLXXX.

EDINBURGH :
PRINTED BY LORIMER AND GILLIES,
31 ST. ANDREW SQUARE.

PREFACE TO THE FIRST EDITION.

THE present work is a further development of views published in 1858 in a volume entitled "THE STARS AND THE ANGELS." A thousand copies only were published at the time, and it was soon out of print; but, in the mean time, Sir Charles Lyell's work on the "Antiquity of Man" appeared, having so important a bearing on the *locality* of Satan and his angels, that a second edition could not be issued without introducing the new element, and presenting the new light which it was capable of shedding upon Scripture history.

The present, work, however, is not a reprint of the former volume, being much more limited in its survey, and containing a large amount of matter altogether new. At the same time, it would not have been intelligible without the reproduction of at least a portion of the contents of the original work, although in a much more condensed form.

A prominent place has been given in this volume to an attempted solution of the problem of the person and history of Satan. The position which he occupies in Scripture is very remarkable, and has not hitherto been explained. The relations which he sustained to Christ and His mission, especially, cannot be accounted for on merely moral grounds, as if Satan were only a myth, the personification of sin and death, which Christ came to destroy. Satan is a real person, and the perplexing question arises, How was it that his attitude towards Christ, politically, was defensive, while yet personally it was aggressive? Our Lord, on the one hand, had to sustain the assaults of Satan against His person, and, on the other, to wage war politically upon his kingdom and power. In fact, His personal defensive victory was a political conquest, for it was through His obedience unto death that He destroyed him that had the power of death, that is, the devil.

There is evidently a legal standing conceded to Satan in Scripture as the sifter and accuser of the brethren, and the tempter of Christ; and the power which he claimed as the Prince of this World and the dispenser of its honours is rather acknowledged than denied. Besides all this, he is represented as an important personage connected with the work of Christ; and it is difficult to believe that the bruising of his head, and the destruction of his power over death, amounted to no more than disappointment at the salvation of man.

This legal and dynastic standing, so evidently conceded to Satan, seems to have misled some theologians of the early Church, who imagined that the death of Christ must have been a satisfaction, not to God, but to the devil; and it has also led many Christians into a vague sort of belief that Satan is a being of portentous power, whose province of evil is as universal as is God's province of good, and whose might could be encountered and counteracted only by the superior might of the Son of God.

It may be disappointing to some, but more satisfactory to others, to be asked to believe that Satan is merely a local personage, who never was in heaven, and that his claims to sovereignty are confined to this little planet and its inhabitants, and rest upon the rights, of primogeniture and dominion conferred upon him at his creation, and forfeited, when he fell, to his next unfallen successor. The interest which he had in the fall of Adam and the temptation of Christ, as well as his acknowledged standing as the accuser of the brethren, are more intelligible in a dynastic and legal, than in a Miltonic point of view. There may be, and probably are, other elements in the case, of which we are at present ignorant: but the general aspect presented in these chapters is, we venture to think, so consistent with reason, with Scripture, and with itself, that it is at least worthy of examination.

In connection with the present publication, and especially its title, the Author has to mention Mrs. Duncan's elegant and ingenious work, "Pre-Adamite Man," which he has only lately seen, and in which he was not only surprised but pleased to find that his theory of the physical constitution of Angels, as possessed of bodies, and that of Devils as the disembodied spirits of a previous race, has been adopted and advocated, not without acknowledgment. In other respects there is very little similarity between the respective views of the two authors.

In regard to that portion of the present volume which specially deals with theoretical Astronomy, the progress of scientific discovery since 1858, when the former work was published, has been very great; and it has been gratifying to the Author to find, year after year, that it has been entirely confirmatory of the views which were then presented. In no case, so far as he is aware, has it been adverse.

With the exception of the proposed explanation of the origin of the lunar mountains, the views presented in the present volume are very much the same as those propounded nearly thirteen years ago.

December, 1870.

PREFACE TO THE SECOND EDITION.

THE First Edition (1500 copies) having been exhausted, and as the demand still continues, a Second Edition is now issued, in which the author has taken the opportunity of profiting by the criticisms and suggestions of his friends, as well as supplying additional matter for the further elucidation of his subject.

The Author's name was withheld in the First Edition, at the suggestion of a friend whose opinion he valued, and who feared that its publication might be supposed to compromise the Church with which both were connected. It was not long, however, before he was made aware that this was a very unnecessary precaution. Not only had no offence been taken, but the most flattering commendations which the work has received have come from his brethren in the ministry.

He must confess, however, that it was not altogether without a little trepidation that he ventured to publish views that were so entirely opposed to the traditions of all the Churches in all the ages; and being painfully aware that authors are not the best judges of their own productions; and that " He that is first in his own cause seemeth just; but his neighbour cometh and searcheth him," he was not unprepared to find that there were objections to his views which he had not anticipated, and difficulties which he had not removed; and he felt that he could not be altogether sure of his position, however impregnable it might appear to him, until it had been subjected to the searching examination of other minds.

To his pleased surprise the opinions of the press have been, he might say, almost unanimously, not only favourable, but laudatory, in some instances more so than he could even have hoped for. What to him, however, is most gratifying is that none of his positions has been assailed, nor one of his arguments controverted. In issuing this Second Edition, therefore, he does so with much more confidence than he did the First.

What is of more importance, pleasing testimony has been received in regard to the healthful influence it has exerted in restoring confidence in the Bible, where its teaching had been undermined by the rash speculations of scientific men. The case of one gentleman in particular was so remarkable, that it was judged expedient to make a reprint of several chapters in the form of a sixpenny tract, which may be put into the hands of those who are wavering. It is entitled "The Gospel of Christ and the Omnipotence of Prayer Consistent with Law" (Gall & Inglis, London and Edinburgh).

EDINBURGH, *October*, 1880.

CONTENTS.

———◆———

CHAPTER I.—The Scientific value of the Bible, *page* 9.

The Bible acknowledged to be the most extraordinary book in the world, 9—Presents to us the most extraordinary man the world has seen, 10—The Bible a collection of photographs, 11—Infinitely true, 12—Their difference and yet correspondence, 13—Avoids scientific revelations, 14—Its facts possessed of inductive value, 16.

CHAPTER II.—The Mosaic structure of Genesis, *page* 19.

Prophets since the world began, 20—Inspired legends incorporated by Moses, 21—Heber's genealogy, 22—Terah's genealogy, 23—Evidences of incorporation, 24—Adds to its value, 25—Apocalypse of creation, 26—Contemporaneous history best, 29—Influence on interpretation, 30.

CHAPTER III.—The Apocalypse of Creation, *page* 35.

Geology supposed to contradict Scripture, 35—Attempted reconciliations, 35—Gen. i. not a history but an apocalypse, 37—Its dramatic form, 38—Its double interpretation, 39.

CHAPTER IV.—Creation according to Law, *page* 43.

The operation of law God's style of working, 44—Evolution not contrary to Scripture, 46—Gen. i. refers to the creation of all worlds, 48—Pre-adamic remains, 49—Science and the Bible mutually helpful, 50.

CHAPTER V. OUR WORLD UNIQUE IN CREATION, *page* 51.

Our world the wonder of the universe, 51—Few stars capable of containing life, 53—Water necessary, 54—Testimony of geology, 56—Man scarce in the universe, 57—Fallen man only here, 58—The incarnation once only, 61—Divine love, 62.

CHAPTER VI.—THE COMING MAN, *page* 63.

Origin of our earth, 64—The Bible all about Christ, 65— Our world the products of combustion, 66—Vegetation an unburning, 67—Animal life re-burning, 68—Ascent of force, 69—Man the highest type of creation, 70—The image of God, 72.

CHAPTER VII.—HOLINESS MAN'S NORMAL STATE: SIN A DISEASE CONTAGIOUS AND HEREDITARY, *page* 75.

Speculations of anthropologists, 75—man naturally a savage or a brute, 76—Man normally holy, 77—Sin not an instinct but a disease, 78—Because suicidal, 79—Conscience, 82—Not uniform, 83—The religious faculty most diseased, 84.

CHAPTER VIII.—THE PHYSIOLOGY OF THE SPIRIT, *page* 88.

Gnosticism, 88—Dignity of matter recognised by Christianity,. 89—Spirit senses, 91—Elisha and Paul's spirit vision, 92— Spirit co-related to matter, 96—Science of force, 97—A substance though not matter, 98—Spirits organised substances, 103—Nature's economy, 104.

CHAPTER IX.—DEMONIACAL POSSESSION AND INSPIRATION, *page* 104.

The cerebro-spinal system, 105—Sensation and volition, 106—Alien spirits entering, 108—Difference of kind, 108— Legion in one body, 110—Appetite for possession, 111—Demoniacal inspiration, 112—No canonical period, 112—Paul and the pythoness, 113—Delphic oracle, 114—Heathen gods demons, 117—Ephesian converts, 120.

CHAPTER X.—Angels and Men one Species, *page* 121.

Angels, devils, and men, originally one species, 121—Adam's natural body, 121—Angels have spiritual bodies, 122—Called men, 125—Did eat, 126—Angels and devils once alike, 128—The devils lost their bodies, 128—Angels never enter into men, 129—Gadara, 129—The resurrection body angelic, 130.

CHAPTER XI.—The Disembodied State, *page* 131.

We incapable of understanding it, 131—Revealed by parable, 132—Death abnormal, 133—Not sleep, 133—Hades, 135—Paradise and Tartarus, 136—Gehenna, 137—Rich man, 138—Torment future, 139—Paradise enjoyments, 140—Our Lord in paradise, 142—Opened the prison doors, 144—Saints now go to heaven, 146—Ministering spirits, 147—Chariots, 149—Gabriel's flight, 150—Expectant friends, 151.

CHAPTER XII.—The Spiritual Body according to Law, *page* 152.

A real body, 152—Miracles not the suspension of law, 155—Different administrations co-ordinate, 156—Inorganic, 156—Vegetable, 157—Animal, 158—Ascent to man, 159—Each ascent inconceivable till seen, 159—A higher to be expected, the spiritual, 160—Darwin expects a higher man, 162—The supernatural according to law, 163.

CHAPTER XIII.—The Angels that Sinned, *page* 165.

Angels created on the sixth day, 166 — Man naturally immortal, 168—No provision for sin, 169—No created spirits, 169—Devils never assume a body, 170—Job and Micaiah, 170—Devils human-like spirits, 171—The abyss, 172—Sin of the angels, 173—Left their bodies, 174.

CHAPTER XIV.—The First Prince of this World, *page* 176.

Theories of the origin of man, 176—Pre-Adamic remains, 177—Indicated savage state, 178—Could not have been so originally, 180—Satan the first man, 181—A princely being, 182—His fall, 182—Immediate descendants, 185—Degradation, 186—No Messianic element, 186.

CHAPTER XV.—SATAN NEVER IN HEAVEN, *page* 187.

Christian mythology, 187—Milton, 188—Passages misinterpreted, 189—Satan only on earth, 191—His dignity recognised, 196—Not worse than many men, 198.

CHAPTER XVI.—ANTEDILUVIAN THEOLOGY, *page* 201.

Antediluvian prophets, 203—Prophecies written on the constellations, 204—Virgo, the promised seed, 207—Libra, the judgment, 209—Scorpio, the curse, 209—Sagittarius, the slayer of the scorpion, 210—Capricornus, the sacrifice, 210—Aquarius, pentecost, 211—Pisces, the "united" and the "upheld."

CHAPTER XVII.—THE RIVAL THRONES, *page* 213.

Satan's interest in the fall, 213—Christ came to undo the fall, 215—Son of man heir of Adam, 217—Primogeniture, 217—The younger preferred, 218—Christ's baptism, 218—Installed as Messiah, 218—Subjected to temptation, 219.

CHAPTER XVIII.—THE FIRST CONFLICT, *page* 221.

First temptation, 222—Satan's knowledge, 222—Subtlety of the temptation, 223—Wrong explanations, 224—Conformity to His Father's will, 226—Subjection to the Word, 230—Second temptation, 230—Third, 231—A compromise offered, 232—Why rejected, 233.

CHAPTER XIX.—SALVATION ACCORDING TO LAW, *page* 234.

Why must Christ die? 235—Co-ordinate administrations, 236—Law necessary, 236—Hume's argument, 237—God a judge, 238—Criminal justice different from mercantile, 239—No substitution without union, 240—Illustrations, 240—Christ and the sinner one, 242—Noah and the ark one, 244—Christ's person Divine, 245—General mercy of God, 246—The line between saved and unsaved, 247—Not unmerciful, 248—Man unmerciful, 249.

CHAPTER XX.—The Revelation of Anti-Christ, *page* 252.

Satan himself, 252—A possession, 253—Different from demons, 254—Has he already appeared? 255—The papal system, 256—Present in person, 257—The world's week, 258—Jerusalem the gnomon of prophecy, 259.

CHAPTER XXI.—The Resurrection according to Law, *page* 260.

The person of Christ fitted for His work, 261—Divine and human, 262—The resurrection a necessary part of salvation, 263—Sadducees silenced, 263—Resurrection of Christ, 265—Change at Christ's coming, 266—Resurrection of saints, 266—With what bodies? 267—Seed of a plant, 268—Soul reproduces body, 270—Different glories, 271—Soul-bodies and spirit-bodies, 272—Recovers development, 274—Life powers, 276—Species type, 277—Individual type, 277—Slow cascade, 278—An emaciated body, 279—Material lost never to be recovered, 279—Niagara dead, 279—Alive again, 280.

CHAPTER XXII.—The Conclusion, *page* 281.

Angels and devils different in constitution, 281—Angels have spiritual bodies, 282—Once had natural bodies, 282—Angels and devils once alike, 283—Satan sinned and died, 284—Satan's authority patriarchal, 284—Adam's fall a sequel to Satan's, 285—Human remains to be expected, 286—Satan's standing as an accuser, 287—Christ's death a victory over Satan, 287.

APPENDIX.

APPENDIX A.—Supposed Antediluvian Scriptures.

Contemporary history best—Genesis not an exception—
From Moses to Luke contemporary history, 289—Genesis
embraces twenty-three centuries, 290—Internal evidence of
compilation—Prophets before Moses—Their writings or legends
preserved—An attempted restoration offered, 290.

1. Apocalypse of creation by Noah,　　.　　.　　*page* 291
2. The Book of the prophet Adam, .　　.　　.　　,, 292
3. The Book of the prophet Seth,　.　　.　　.　　,, 293
4. The Book of the prophet Enoch,　　.　.　　,, 294
5. The First Book of the prophet Noah, .　　.　　,, 294
6. The Second Book of the prophet Noah,　　.　　,, 295
7. The Book of the prophet Shem, .　　.　　.　　,, 297

APPENDIX B.—The First Four Days of Creation,
page 298.

The supremacy of law—Scripture explained by nature—
Nature explained by Scripture—The unknown resembles the
known—The unity of nature, 298.

Darkness on the face of the Deep, *page* 299.

The fuel of the sun—The amount of its heat—Not electric
light—Products of combustion inside—The Zodiacal light—
Amount of meteoric fuel required, 300—The sun one of millions
of stars, 301—The astral kingdom of nature—their birth,
growth, and decay—Our own earth once a sun, 301—Its
interior molten lava, 302—Like trees in a forest the stars are of
different ages, 303—One-half of our world oxygen, 304—The
ether of the universe supplies the oxygen, 304—The moon has
no atmosphere outside, 305—Proofs of oxygen in the ether,
305—Once there were only meteorites and ether, 307—Dead
till the Spirit communicated power, 307.

The Creation of Light according to Law, *page* 308.

Once all elementary bodies, 308—Laws of nature teach how the elements would act, 309—Two kinds of meteoric matter, 310—The meteorites widely separated—Would begin to gravitate towards one another, 311—Corresponding attraction of ether, 312—Initiatory conflagrations, 312—Allotropic hydrogen, 315—Nebulæ changing their form.

The Creation of the Firmament according to Law, *page* 317.

The separation of star from star, 317—Deposition of water—the firmament not the atmosphere—reasons, 318—Second day's work the formation of stars, 319—Each star at first a sun, 320—Variable stars, 320—Aqueous atmosphere, 321—Deposition of water, 322.

The Creation of Dry Land according to Law, *page* 322.

Jupiter and Saturn's immense atmospheres, 323—Snow white, 324—Moon's crust unbroken, 325—Our Earth's crust always breaking, 326—Wrinkling of the crust raises the land, 328—Vegetation on the second day, 329—The future of the Earth, 330.

The Creation of the Sun according to Law, *page* 332.

Atmosphere of steam, universal twilight, 332—Condensation of the steam, 333—Sun like a flame of a candle, 334—The body of the sun small, 335—Proofs, 336—Meteoric masses, 337—Sun's heat due to friction chiefly, 339—Solar Spectrum, 340—Willow-leaf forms, 341—Eclipse, 342—Spots, 344—The nebular theory, 345.

The Creation of the Moon according to Law, *page* 346.

The moon once a star, 346—Fuel exhausted—last meteorites left their mark, 374—Great size of meteorites, 348—Great circular basins, 348—Copernicus, 351—Mare Crisium, 352—Moon not metallic, 353—Interior cavity, 354.

APPENDIX C, *page 355.*

THE EFFICACY OF PRAYER.—God eternal, 355—Prayer anticipated, 356—Death of Ahab, 356—Joshua's prayer, 357—
Planting a meteoric stratum at creation, 358—More wonderful than a miracle, 359.

APPENDIX D, *page 360.*

THE SOUL AND THE SPIRIT different, 360—Soul and animal
life, 361—Cerebro-spinal nerves, 362—Emotional nature, 363
—Ganglionic system of nerves, 364—Seat of the soul, 365.

APPENDIX E, *page 366.*

EMPLOYMENTS OF THE RESURRECTION.—Spiritual bodies, 364
—Ideal journey of Gabriel, 367—Passage through mid-heaven,
368—What he would see, 369—Arrival in Babylon, 372.

LIST OF PLATES.

		PAGE
ANTEDILUVIAN THEOLOGY—*Frontispiece.*		
THE ZODIACAL LIGHT,	...	63
VIRGO AND THE PROMISED SEED,	...	207
SAGITTARIUS, THE SLAYER OF THE SCORPION, ...	...	210
THE EARTH IN THREE STAGES OF DEVELOPMENT,	...	328
THE PLANETS AND THEIR ATMOSPHERES,	...	329
THE SUN AND PHOTOSPHERE,	...	341
THE MOON WITH ITS INTERIOR VAULT,	...	354

WOODCUTS.

	PAGE
SECTIONS OF THE FLAME OF A CANDLE,	334
THE SUN'S ATMOSPHERE, ...	336
FLAMES OF THE SUN'S PHOTOSPHERE,	341
PERPENDICULAR VIEW OF THE FLAMES,	342
TOTAL ECLIPSE OF THE SUN,	342
SPOTS OF THE SUN,	344
IDEAL SPECIMEN OF EARLY FORMATIONS ON THE MOON,...	350
COPERNICUS, A MOUNTAIN OF THE MOON,	351
THE CEREBRO-SPINAL SYSTEM OF NERVES,	362
THE GANGLIONIC SYSTEM OF NERVES,	364

PRIMEVAL MAN UNVEILED.

CHAPTER I.

THE SCIENTIFIC VALUE OF THE BIBLE.

THE BIBLE, that grand old Jewish compilation of Scriptures, which is admitted on all hands to be the most extraordinary book in the world, has for many centuries been the study of the most enlightened and gifted of the human race, who to this day have not been able either to fathom its mysteries or to let it alone. As there is but one sun in the firmament, so is there but one such book in the world. In its antiquity, in its grandeur, and in its commanding influence and power, it stands majestically alone ; and we might as well ask, which star is next in glory to the sun, as propose the question, which book is second to the Bible? It has never been without powerful and determined opponents, and yet it has never ceased to receive the profoundest homage of the profoundest thinkers of our race; and although both its character and its purpose require that no physical or philosophical dogmas should be revealed in its pages, yet, wherever philosophy and civilisation, morality and liberty predominate, there is the Bible enthroned as the book of books, and there is the homage most devoutly paid.

Its pretensions are as extraordinary as its history, because it professes to be DIVINE—divine in its origin, divine in its authority, and, what is still more startling, divine also in its power,—professing to produce an immediate and miraculous change on every one who really receives and submits to its teaching.

Its contents, too, are in keeping with its character, because it is a manifesto addressed to the whole human race, collectively and individually ; introducing, and presenting to them, as Ambassador and Plenipotentiary, the Lord Jesus Christ, confessedly the most extraordinary man that ever appeared upon the earth, and whom it declares to be the Prince Royal of heaven. It sets forth who and what we are, whence we came, and whither we are going. It tells us of the other members of the divine family to which we belong; and, after reciting the defections and rebellion of our race, it summons us to immediate personal and formal submission, with offers of amnesty and reconciliation, and entreaties and warnings in case of continued disloyalty and rebellion.

Without the slightest approach to self-advocacy or apology, it speaks not only with an authority which ignores criticism, but with an earnestness, and an artlessness, that seem never to have even thought of it. It is, indeed, a magnificent production; ample and yet condensed, it meets all the necessities and requirements of our nature, in every age and in every variety of human circumstances. Being addressed to universal man, it speaks to each individual as if he were alone in the universe ; and finds a response in the inner depths of his consciousness, so that it is felt to be a " discerner of the thoughts and intents of the heart." Although divine, there never was a book so thoroughly human, or so catholic in its affinities. All other books are more or less distorted and coloured, either by the times in which they were written, or the sources from which they came; the Bible alone is achromatically perfect, by reason of the different ages and the number and variety of the media through which its light has been transmitted.

One of the most remarkable peculiarities of the Bible is its wonderful and unfathomable depth. Other books, such as the Confession of Faith or the Thirty-nine Articles, have length and breadth, but, comparatively, they have no depth. They mean all that they say, and nothing more; they draw out their propositions in a logical and categorical form, and whatever is not on the surface is not there at all. It is not so with the Bible. It deals in centres, not circumferences, therefore it does not define, and because its symmetry is natural, not artificial, therefore it does not systematise. Other books evolve their meaning by being read along—the Bible may be read downward as well as onward, inward as well as outward; and, as it was intended for the study of children as well as philosophers, it differs from all human books of theology, as a flower differs from its scientific description, or as a botanic garden differs from a book of botany.

In style and structure it is altogether unique; being in fact a collection of pictures, or rather photographs, the general character of which can be understood by a child, although in their details, and their relations to each other, they afford inexhaustible subjects of study to the philosopher and the divine. In every one of them the central figure is the same, but his attitudes and his surroundings, as well as the point of view from which he is seen, are different in each. As photographs, they are possessed of a depth of meaning which is invaluable, because of their absolute truthfulness; for, although in consequence of their great antiquity they have been, as it were, worn at the edges, and in some cases patched and restored by officious and incompetent hands, yet we have no difficulty in distinguishing between their perfect inspiration and their imperfect preservation ; because they bear internal as well as external evidence that they are true sun-pictures, taken on the spot and at the time ; and are not, and could not be, the production of any merely human artist.   To continue the simile, it is the correspondence of these photographs with one another, and the identification of the same objects in the dim perspective of the different views, that afford occupation and delight to the Bible student ; and thus every successive recognition or rectification has added not only to the fulness and clearness of the views which they present, but to the proof of their wonderful and unquestionable veracity.

One of the most interesting circumstances connected with these long-continued and richly productive investigations has been the occasional discovery of errors, not in the photographs themselves, but in their previous interpretations.   Objects which in different photographs were supposed to be the same, have been found to be in reality different ; and objects which, in the distance, seemed to be contiguous, have been discovered to be widely separated from one another ; so that we need not wonder if these researches and discoveries should result in the gradual disentanglement of Scripture from old and mistaken theories, which our fathers in their simplicity believed to be equally Divine.   Science and monumental evidence are also photographs, and as such possess authority similar to that of the Bible.   It is *their* interpretation also which alone is fallible : they cannot be *really* inconsistent with the Bible or with one another, and their apparent disagreement in any one particular (as in the case of the two pictures of a stereograph), instead of being a contradiction, is only the parallax of the objects represented, and contains the elements from which we are to discover their distance, their dimensions, or their form.

But perhaps the most wonderful circumstance connected with this most wonderful book is, that it has not only survived the assaults of its enemies, but outlived the defences of its friends. Every succeeding conflict through which it has passed has issued not only in the overthrow of its assailants, but in the rectification of its defences, and the enlightenment of its defenders; so that every new difficulty has been the forerunner of some new revelation and discovery.

A principal cause of all these conflicts has been a misapprehension of the relation which the Scripture bears to scientific research. It seems to have been a fundamental principle that it should never reveal directly any philosophic truth, but should speak systematically in the language of current thought, and thus present its revelations, in the perspective, and in the proportions in which they appeared from the standpoint of the inspired writer; so that even in its most exalted revelations, it adapts itself to the habits of thought and expression of the age and country in which it was given forth.

A little consideration will show us that this was absolutely necessary. To have propounded one new doctrine in science, or to have anticipated one invention in art, would have been contrary to the very nature and intention of revelation. The Bible is a book for all men in all ages, whereas science and art are a progressive and never-ending career of discovery and invention. If the Bible, therefore, made any revelations whatever in such a field, it would have suggested a human origin, and a mind,

perhaps, in advance of the age which gave it birth, but
very soon to be left behind in the onward progress of
discovery.   In this respect, then, the Scriptures may be
said to stand on a level with other writings which are not
inspired; but even in this they exhibit the most wonderful evidence of their Divine inspiration; for, while they
carefully refrain from making any direct contribution to
the scientific knowledge of mankind, they have never
stumbled upon any statement which will not abide the
light of advancing science.   This feature is altogether
superhuman; they have preserved a thorough consistency
with all that science has yet discovered; so that, in the light
of the nineteenth century, we read the productions of the
world's infancy, and discover no fallacy and no weakness.
The writers of Scripture were never seduced into philosophic speculations or scientific blunders, which shows
that they were guided by One who, though He knew all
things, did not intend to reveal in this manner anything
except what was conducive to man's eternal well-being.

There is something very remarkable in the persistence
with which Scripture refuses to deal in scientific dogma.
Not only is there a marked and total absence of scientific
doctrine, there is, besides, a positive avoidance of it, a
studied phraseology which precludes the giving to the
statements of Scripture any scientific interpretation.
Even in the cosmogony of Moses, where, if anywhere, we
might expect a revelation of physical science, the work of
creation is shrouded in the form of a sacred drama, which
exhibits all that is Divine, and reveals only as much of the
physical as would enable future philosophers to recognise,
but never to discover.   One of the writers of the Bible,
whose scientific investigations astonished the world during
his lifetime, and stocked the philosophy of surrounding

nations, was not permitted to insert one sentence of natural science in the sacred volume. So important were his scientific discoveries, and so rich his prelections, that pilgrimages were undertaken from the most distant countries, that men might sit at his feet and hear the wisdom that was continually flowing from his lips; and, to this day, in the land which was the cradle of the world's sciences, his name has survived as the greatest and wisest of men, where almost everything else has been forgotten. It is only through the writings of Aristotle, and the teaching of such men as Pythagoras, Euclid, and Aristarchus, that we get a glimpse of the sciences of which we have reason to believe Solomon was the father. Had it not been for these, and such as these, who, during the succeeding centuries, gathered up the fragments that remained, in Syria, and Egypt, and Babylonia, where they had been scattered broadcast by the royal lecturer, it is probable that his scientific discoveries would have been irrecoverably lost; and it is questionable whether we do not owe more to the power and influence of Alexander in gathering the manuscripts, than to the genius of Aristotle and others in digesting them.

How interesting also to meditate on this aspect of our Saviour's sojourning upon earth. The human mind of Jesus, so pure, so calm, so cultivated, could not for thirty years have conversed with nature and with God, without making large discoveries in science, and anticipating mighty achievements in invention; and yet not one word was allowed to escape his lips that would betray even the consciousness of such a knowledge. That which would have raised him higher than Aristotle, because a greater than Solomon was there, was equally suppressed with that which would have made him mightier than

Cæsar. So far was He in advance of all the world's wisdom and genius, that the highest and the boldest learned to be silent in his presence. The testimony of those who knew him best was, "Now are we sure that thou knowest all things," and the universal verdict was, "Never man spake like this man." Even now, after nearly two thousand years, He still stands altogether unapproached and alone; so that even the world's philosophers, although they deny his mission, cannot conceal their amazement at the acknowledged grandeur of what they are pleased to call his ethical discoveries. How was it that He did not teach his disciples one truth either in art or science? Not because He did not know it, but because it was not consistent with his mission to make such revelations.

And yet the Bible has a scientific value, and that of the very highest kind, and in the department in which it alone is capable of giving its testimony; but it must be studied, not deductively, but inductively. So long as we attempt to extract natural science from Scripture sentences, the result is so manifestly absurd as to leave us nothing for our pains. But when we collect and arrange the accredited FACTS that are guaranteed in Scripture *history*, we may safely build upon them any superstructure that they can legitimately bear. It is the *facts* of Scripture that are the true subjects of scientific inquiry; and it is one purpose of the following chapters to show that they are most valuable contributions to anthropology, the more valuable, because they are gleanings in a field not accessible to us in the present day. The soldier who had part of his body shot away, and yet survived the accident, enabled the physicians of his day to know, by actual and visible experiment, what changes took place upon different kinds of food introduced into his stomach;

and his case was regarded by the medical profession as a most valuable opportunity of ascertaining facts which might otherwise never have been known. A traveller, in like manner, who, by some rare accident, is enabled to examine some locality or witness some event which was never before, and may never again be seen, would be an extremely valuable contributor to any science dependent on such phenomena as those which he had witnessed. It is upon this principle that the facts and phenomena of Scripture ought to be valuable to the scientific inquirer, because they are, many of them, disclosures of things not now seen, and yet intimately connected with things that are. It was impossible, in a narrative which describes events and phenomena connected with heaven and earth, God and man, angels and devils, that there should not be many facts related, which, when viewed in connection with modern science and with each other, are possessed of the highest scientific value. Any objection to receive them as legitimate contributions to natural science, cannot be justified on any grounds consistent with the acknowledgment of the honesty of the witnesses whose testimony they are; and, although many of them may appear as if they were incapable of being incorporated with the ascertained results of modern observation and experiment, a more mature philosophy will find in them, not isolated and heterogeneous elements, but connecting links and consistent phenomena. There is no reason why Scripture testimony upon scientific subjects should be excluded, where that testimony is possessed of an inductive character.

There is good reason why such a book as the " Arabian Nights' Entertainments " should be read apart from all our studies of geography, history, and natural philosophy; but it is not so with the Bible. Its scenes are not laid in fictitious localities, nor are its events unconnected with the world as we find it. On the contrary, it is linking itself with every known fact more strongly and more distinctly every day; and history, geography, and even other sciences, are continually bringing up fresh evidences of its entire truthfulness. The Palestine of the traveller is the same holy land that was trodden by the Son of God; the earth of the geologist is the same as that of which Moses wrote in Genesis; and in like manner the heaven of the astronomer, is no other than that into which Christ ascended, when he parted from his wondering disciples on the Mount of Olives. All truth is one; and if we by a kind of stereoscopic vision can see the same objects with the scientific, and at the same time with the historic eye, and find both representations to agree, they will stand out before us with a distinctness and a visible reality such as they could not otherwise assume. The scientific Christian may know and understand things connected with the Bible which the unscientific Christian cannot know; and the Christian philosopher may know and understand things connected with science which are unintelligible to the man who has not studied the Bible.

CHAPTER II.

THE MOSAIC STRUCTURE OF GENESIS.

THE reader has probably seen a photograph of the Royal family, in which the Queen appears as a widow, and Prince Albert is represented by a marble bust. There is in that photograph a combination of nature and art, which is very intelligible, and which may help to illustrate the subject of the present chapter. The sculpture is art; the representation of the living persons is not art, but nature. The bust may be a very inadequate representation of the Prince; but the position which it occupies in the group, the loving looks which they give to the marble likeness, and the representation of the bust itself are all perfect, so that there can be no mistake about them. We have in this photograph an illustration of the inspiration and non-inspiration of Scripture. The whole scene is there as it actually was in nature—it is absolutely accurate even in the most minute details. In regard to the bust we may have no certainty of its likeness to the Prince; but this we do know, that we have an accurate representation of itself as it existed at the time, and that it was regarded with favour by the Royal family; inasmuch as its being there is a certificate of the likeness. But let us suppose that, instead of a marble bust, there had been a photographic picture of the Prince, we should then have all nature and no art, because, the portrait being itself a photograph, there could be no error in the likeness.

In the Bible, we have literary photographs analogous

to these. That which is inspired is the narrative; but in some cases the words which are recorded are not inspired, because they are spoken by uninspired and sometimes wicked men ; and, therefore, although we may be certain that the words were really spoken, just as we are sure that the marble bust of Prince Albert was really in existence when the photograph was taken, the words themselves may not be inspired, and may be altogether wrong. We must distinguish between the inspiration of the narrative as a narrative, and the inspiration of the words which are recorded in the narrative.

In the first chapter of Luke we have some interesting specimens of this kind of reflected photography. Luke, the inspired historian, records the inspired words of the angel and Mary, of Zacharias and Elizabeth, and of Simeon and Anna; not fewer than six distinct subjects being photographed in one picture. Not only is Luke inspired, so that we may be sure that all the prophecies are correctly reported, but the prophecies themselves are inspired, and thus we know that what they said was true. But this is not all ; in one of these reflected photographs we have still another reflection, because Zacharias by the Holy Ghost informs us that the coming of the promised Messiah had been predicted "by all the holy prophets which had been since the world began." And does not this throw some light on the composition of Genesis? We naturally ask, who were those holy prophets who spake of the coming Messiah during the two thousand years that passed between the time of Adam and the time of Moses? Where are their writings? Have none of them survived? Did Adam and Seth, and Enoch and Noah live for centuries, and leave no family records behind them? or, if at that time the art of writing was

not yet invented, did they not leave traditions or legends,
which might be handed down from father to son, " so
that they might show to the generations to come the
praises of the Lord, and His strength, and His wonderful
works that He hath done ? " (Ps. lxxviii. 4.)   "That
the children which should be born should arise and
declare them to their children, that they might set their
hope in God, and not forget the works of God " (v. 6).
We have every reason to believe that these legends were
numerous ; and, being stereotyped into set forms, became
well-known formulas, sacred and unalterable.   The language might change, and the dialect in which they were
composed might become old-fashioned ; but the legends
themselves would remain unaltered, even when they had
become almost unintelligible.   Such legends would be
carefully preserved, and not the less so because of their
obscurity.   " I will open my mouth in a parable.   I will
utter dark sayings of old which we have heard and known,
and our fathers have told us."

Supposing, then, that such traditions or legends really
existed, and that they were carefully preserved and handed
down from generation to generation, we have abundant
indications in the Book of Genesis that Moses received
them, and that they were faithfully incorporated in the
inspired narrative.   It may have been that he made such
necessary alterations as the change of language required,
and that he condensed and made interpolations in them
so as to form a continuous narrative ; and yet we observe
that, in inserting these ancient records, Moses most carefully preserves these sacred texts, showing the reverence
which inspiration has for inspiration.   So evident is this
Mosaic style of composition, inlaying without blending,
and incorporating without changing, that it appears to

have been noticed even in early ages, and to have given its name to a branch of art to which it bears a close resemblance—viz., mosaic work.

For the sake of easy illustration, let us examine and compare two of these family records tesselated in the Mosaic history; one of them is in the tenth, and the other in the eleventh chapter of Genesis. That they are both of them monographs is evident not only from their contents, but from their titles. One of them commences thus: "These are the generations of the sons of Noah;" the other thus: "These are the generations of Shem." Now, had Moses been the original author of both, the one would no doubt have corresponded with the other, and we should have had a symmetrical statement of the genealogy, not as it came down to him in two fragmentary documents, but in one continuous narrative digested from both.

The former of these genealogies is deeply interesting, as it bears internal evidence, amounting almost to certainty, that it was composed by Heber, from his own personal knowledge, at a time when he was living with his younger son, Joktan, and surrounded by his family, in the neighbourhood of Mesha. Being the last of all the long-lived patriarchs, and surviving his children to the fifth generation, he would descend among his posterity like an ancient piece of family property; father bequeathing him to son, and son bequeathing him to grandson, until the death of Abraham, when the last flickerings of his long tenacious life were just about to expire. We can scarcely doubt that "all the sons of Heber" were no other than the Hebrews, and from him this genealogy would be received and preserved among the Hebrews. That it was written before the destruction of Sodom is proved by the 19th verse, "And the border of the Canaanites was from Sidon as thou comest to Gerar, unto Gaza, *as thou goest unto Sodom and Gomorrah, and Admah and Zeboim,* even unto Lasha." At the time of Moses, people did not "go unto Sodom and Gomorrah, Admah and Zeboim;" but before the time of Lot they did: the date of the legend, therefore, must be *at least* as old as Abraham. At the time of Moses, these cities of the plain were not in existence, and no historian would describe a country by referring to cities the site of which was unknown. But Moses, having found it so, would not alter the words, any more than the title; because, if he had, he would to that extent have destroyed its authenticity as part of the book of "The generations of the sons of Noah." The document, though very imperfect and fragmentary in itself, must have been precious in the estimation of Moses on account of its antiquity and authenticity; and because, in addition to the information which it supplied regarding the family of Joktan, Peleg's younger brother, it seems to have contained all that Moses was able to collect regarding the descendants of Japhet and Ham, who, like Joktan, were not in the line of the Messianic genealogy. It is not unlikely that it came into Moses' hands, not through his father Amram, but through his father-in-law Jethro, with other documents, when he was married to his daughter in Midian.

The genealogy of the eleventh chapter is evidently more orderly in its style, and was apparently compiled by Terah from information handed down from father to son in the family from which he was himself descended —that is to say, not through the line of Joktan, as in the tenth chapter, but through the line of Peleg.

It is strange that this view of the origin of these
writings should have been supposed to detract from their
value, as if it were inconsistent with their inspiration.
It ought rather to increase our sense of their value, as it
exhibits in a very impressive manner their extreme antiquity and truthfulness. Of course, there was nothing
impossible in the idea of Moses writing out the genealogies which he has preserved, without any aid from public
or family registers ; the names may have been revealed
to him miraculously, and he may then and there have
written them as they were revealed; but we do not
account for Matthew's genealogies in that way : why then
should we, with less reason, so account for that of Moses?
It is a rule in history, that the nearer the historian lived
to the events which he relates, the more trustworthy and
satisfactory is his history ; and if there be in Genesis an
appearance of the inserting of documents which were
written by the parties who witnessed the events that are
related, their value must be greatly enhanced; while we
have the additional security afforded by the prophetic
authority of Moses, to guarantee not only their genuine-
ness, but their inspiration. Every one must acknowledge,
that whatever be the facts of the case, there is, in the
book of Genesis, at least the *appearance* of the incorporation of different documents in the general narrative ;
and we are no more entitled to suppose that Moses composed them in that form at first, than geologists are
entitled to account for fossil bones, by supposing (as some
have ventured to do) that they were created in a fossil
state. Nowhere does Moses claim to be the original
author of these records, neither does Scripture assert that
they were written by him; on the contrary the document-
ary character of the history is distinctly avowed, and as

we are informed in Scripture (Luke i. 70 ; Acts iii. 21), that there was a succession of inspired men from the time of Adam, we have no inducement, in the interests of either the authenticity or the inspiration of Scripture, to attempt, by unnatural and improbable theories to evade the conclusion to which the structure of the book of Genesis so obviously leads us.

Supposing, then, that we had satisfactory evidence that these early chapters of Genesis were written at the times and under the circumstances which an examination of their internal structure would indicate; supposing, also, that we had reason to believe that the second and third chapters of Genesis were written or composed by Adam himself, and that the story of Eden has come down to us in the very words of the man who ate the forbidden fruit, as he rehearsed it to generation after generation of his descendants—and in which it descended unaltered, even after he died, until it reached the hands of Moses, to be incorporated finally in the canon of Scripture—what would there be in all this that should shake our confidence in the truthfulness of the story ? Would not this view add more to the value and the interest of the narrative, if not to our faith in its credibility, than if, with an interval of two thousand years, and without any intermediate tradition or history, we supposed that Moses received it by immediate inspiration, as a discovery of facts which neither he nor his fathers previously knew?

It may seem an exception or a contradiction to this explanation of the record, that in the first chapter of Genesis we have not a history, but a revelation. We have there a record of events, which no human eye could have seen, and no human tongue could describe; and, it may be said, if it was so in regard to the first chapter of

Genesis, why might it not be so also in regard to those that follow? But this, so far from being an objection, will be found on examination to be rather a confirmation of these views. The first chapter of Genesis is really no part of Old Testament history; and upon that account it can never be rightly understood so long as it is interpreted in that connection. The Old Testament history, which is the history of the ancestry of Christ, commences at the fourth verse of the second chapter, giving an account of the creation of Adam, who was the first of the Messianic race, with the history of his fall, and the promise of his restoration by means of a future deliverer. Downwards, from the garden of Eden, we have the human history recorded by human hands and human witnesses, until, arriving at the period when the canon of Scripture is to be closed, the Spirit of God takes up the theme where there could be no witnesses, and we behold the boundless future, not in a history, but in an Apocalypse. It is not so obvious, but it is equally true, that, as the Bible ends, so does it begin. It ends with an apocalyptic vision of the future, and it begins with an apocalyptic vision of the past. The genealogy of Christ begins, not with the story of creation, but with the story of Eden. Jesus was the son of Joseph, who was the son of David, who was the son of Abraham, who was the son of Noah, who was the son of Adam, who was the son of God. But long before the time of Adam there were events replete with incident, not only in the distant orbs of heaven, but upon this little planet itself, which have no corresponding chapters in the Bible. The Bible does not profess to be a history even of the Adamic race, far less does it profess to provide a record of the pre-Adamic. It is only of the branch from which the Christ was to be descended, that the history is found in the book of God.   China and India, Assyria and. Egypt, supplied far more striking features of our world's history than the tribe of Judah, and yet in comparison with it they only appear in the background, if they appear at all.   We can but guess at their antiquities, and are left to grope our way among the world's archives to discover their existence, alongside of Abraham and Isaac and Jacob, the children of the promise.   Even before the story of Eden, there was a tragic story of a still earlier fall, the records of which must now be sought for in the Danish shell-heaps, the Brixton caverns, and the mud of the Nile.   In regard to all this, Scripture is as silent as it is upon the civilisation of Egypt and the splendour of Nineveh; that is to say, it is silent except in so far as they touched the Messianic story in some part of its circumference.

Who, then, was the author of the first chapter of Genesis?   To whom was that great vision revealed?   We cannot positively tell, nor is it important that we should; because, unlike all the succeeding chapters, it might as well have been the writing of a later as of an earlier prophet.   So far as the present Essay is concerned, it is of no importance who was the author; and therefore we transfer to the Appendix the few thoughts that have suggested themselves on the subject; showing that, in all probability, it was to Noah that this revelation was made, and that it was written at least a thousand years later than the chapter which immediately follows.

It cannot be objected to this conjecture that we should expect the earliest history to come through the earliest prophet; because, as has been already stated, this first chapter of Genesis is not a history but an apocalypse. As regards human history, that expectation is a reasonable one, and therefore we discover in the succeeding

chapters traces of the hands of Adam, Seth, and Noah;
but as regards the first chapter, it might as well have
been revealed to any one prophet as to another. Human
memory and human testimony were not called into exercise in its production, and therefore there was no need of
its being early committed to memory or writing. All the
other prophets recorded that which they had seen and
heard, and that which had taken place in their own experience, or at least in their own lifetime; and there is a
satisfaction in the thought that we receive the narratives
at firsthand—Adam telling the story of his fall, and Noah
telling the story of the flood. Bishop Colenso would have
us to believe that the history of the Exodus was written
three hundred years after the time of Moses. Now, let us
suppose for a moment that this conjecture were true, and
that the book of Exodus was written, not by Moses, but
by Samuel, or some other of the prophets, without the
help of any national documents; we ask, Would that
increase our admiration of the book or our confidence in
the truth of the history which it records? Certainly not.
We want the history of Moses, not from Samuel, but from
Moses himself, if we can get it, leaving the question of
inspiration aside altogether. An interval of three hundred years is quite too much for traditional accuracy;
and as for inspired history without tradition or document-
ary materials, all that we can say is, that it is a most
unnecessary and unlikely possibility. And if that be our
feeling in regard to Exodus and the three hundred years
between Moses and Samuel, what shall we say of the still
greater improbability, that in recording the story of the
fall, there should be an interval, not of three hundred,
but of two thousand years, with details as if they had
been of yesterday. How differently then must we feel,

in surrendering ourselves to the natural interpretation of the record as Moses has given it to us, as a compilation of narratives which had been carefully preserved and finally incorporated in the book of Genesis. The ninetieth psalm which was written by Moses, was an inspired scripture, yet it floated loose for four or five hundred years before being incorporated in the canon. The story of Eden reaches us authentic and fresh from the lips of the man who once wandered in its sunny glades. The story of the flood comes with tenfold more interest when told by the man who floated on its waters, and the history of the patriarchs acquires an additional charm when we read it as the autobiography of the men themselves.

Inspiration has much more method and reason in it than is sometimes supposed. It does not communicate omniscience, and it must not be understood as if it did. Although plenarily inspired, the Bible is still human testimony, and all that is necessarily guaranteed is its entire truthfulness. They spake that which they knew, and testified that which they had seen; this is the formula provided by the great Master Himself as the ground upon which He demands implicit faith in his testimony. It is a reasonable principle, and it is precious, because it solves many difficulties. What could be more satisfactory, for example, if Adam was a prophet, than that he should be the historian of the fall; if Noah was a prophet, than that he should be the historian of the flood; and if Moses was a prophet, than that he should be the historian of the Exodus? And if Adam was the historian of the fall, and if the second chapter of Genesis was written two thousand years before the time of Moses, would not this open up a most interesting inquiry in regard to its *interpretation?* Many of the difficulties experienced in interpreting Scripture arise from overlooking this great principle, which is the only canon of interpretation that does not involve us in scientific difficulties. We are addressed by human witnesses, not by divine; and no error can arise in consequence, unless we mistake the one for the other, and forget that the language which they use is in every respect their own. Inspiration guarantees the competency and truthfulness of the witnesses, not the elegance or philosophical accuracy of the expressions. Viewed in this light, it was of immense importance that Moses should preserve the evidences of his having incorporated writings which were not his own. The testimony of an eye-witness *must* be different from that of a historian. The eye-witness uses language which describes the scene *from his point of view,* introducing details which he saw, and leaving out important facts which he did not see, although this would be inexcusable in a historian. The question, therefore, whether Adam or Moses wrote the history of the fall, or whether Noah or Moses wrote the history of the flood, would make a very important difference as regards the interpretation. If it was Moses that wrote both, then it was pure revelation, and a statement of absolute facts; if it was Adam and Noah who were the historians, the narrative must be interpreted accordingly as the testimony of eye-witnesses, and a statement, not of absolute facts, but of that which they saw and bore witness to as they appeared to them.

If the account of the Deluge was written by Noah, it is by no means certain that it was universal, because, on the supposition that it was the testimony of an eye-witness describing the events as they came under his notice, there are none of the statements in that history which might not be interpreted like many other passages, in a sense much more limited than a rigid and literal understanding of them would imply. The flood was no doubt very extensive, because it was the very last of those great cataclysms to which the earth was subjected during those cosmical changes which were inevitable in the early periods of its history; but the high hills of which Noah speaks as having been covered by the waters may have been only those which were within his view. This is the more likely, as he mentions how far these mountains were submerged; and as he tells us that they were covered to the depth of fifteen cubits, it is evident that his measurement was obtained by calculation from careful observations and reckonings made at the time. Astronomers have discovered ample evidence to show that the antediluvian patriarchs were profound mathematicians ; and if Noah was competent as an engineer to be the builder of the ark, he may also have been competent to work out the problem which he has recorded. If, on the other hand, Moses, and not Noah, was the historian, we cannot escape from the conclusion that the Deluge was universal, and that the water rose fifteen cubits above the top of the highest peak of the Himalayas.

If Adam, and not Moses, was the writer of the second and third chapters of Genesis, we have a most effective key to the geographical difficulty which has puzzled commentators not a little in the topography of Eden. A difference of two thousand years, in the compilation of a Gazetteer, is not a trifle to be overlooked in consulting it. The names of places might undergo a complete revolution in much less time than that, so that the same names might be applied to very different countries and rivers in the time of Adam from those which are called by those names now; so that the argument drawn from the description of Eden to prove that the flood did not alter the geographical features of the earth is not a very conclusive one. Mont Blanc means the white mountan, Ben More means the big mountain; but there might be other white mountains, and other big mountains besides those in Switzerland and Scotland. Boston and Halifax may be found either in England or America; and the question which of them was meant might depend upon the century in which the author lived who referred to them; and so Cush and Phrath and Hiddekel might mean very different places, and would be spoken of in very different ways, according as Adam or Moses was the historian. A remark made by Adam, in regard to these places, might be most natural and appropriate as coming from him, but most inappropriate and misleading, if we understand it to have come originally from Moses. For example, the statement in Gen. ii. 12, "And the gold of that land is good: there is bdellium and the onyx stone," is not only intelligible but interesting, coming from the lips of Adam, in the early infancy of the world, while Ophir and Sheba were yet unknown; whereas, if it had come from the pen of Moses, two thousand years after, we should not know what to make of it; because, at a time when physical geography had made some respectable progress, it would seem to communicate either too much or too little.

Again, the narrative of the temptation in Eden is much more intelligible, as well as more interesting, if it be Adam and not Moses who is the historian. In the mouth of Moses, the statement in regard to the serpent is provokingly perplexing, because it seems to be a con-

tribution offered to the science of zoology. It is not
easy to see either the pertinence or the intention of the
remark, that it was "more subtle than any beast of the
field;" and, if it had been made by Moses, we should
wonder what made him think so; but when we regard
the narrative as coming from an eye and ear-witness of
the scene, it is no longer understood as a zoological
dogma, but as a most natural remark, coming from Adam
himself, in reference to the incident which he was about
to relate.   Had it been St. John that was the historian,
he would no doubt have informed us, that although it
was the serpent that spoke, it was the devil, that "old
serpent," who was the tempter; but as we have no reason
to suppose that Adam knew anything about Satan, the
narrative is nothing more than what might have been
expected from him as an honest witness, confining himself
to the facts which had come under his own observation,
and giving his own impressions regarding them.   Never,
in all his experience, had he known any of the lower
animals possessed of so much intelligence and cunning;
and, therefore, without presuming to decide how far the
incident was ordinary or extraordinary, he merely re-
marks, as the result of his experience, that the serpent
was more subtle than any beast of the field.   We might
apply the same rule of interpretation to other passages of
Scripture which commentators find great difficulty in re-
conciling with absolute facts; but it is not necessary to
pursue the subject further, if we have succeeded in showing that the first chapter of Genesis is a separate and
independent monograph; and that the narrative which
follows is the real commencement of the Messianic story.
To those who feel an interest in the inquiry, and would
wish to prosecute it, we may remark that it was long ago

observed that there are portions of the book of Genesis distinguished by the different names given to God in the narrative. In some He is called "The Lord" (Jehovah); in others, "The Lord God;" in others, simply "God," indicating, as was thought, a difference of authorship. This of itself, and if it had stood alone, would, perhaps, have been a very weak speculation, but it is not alone. We have other far more decisive indications of the same fact, to some of which we have already alluded : we have also the very titles of the different monographs preserved and inserted in their places, as "This is the book of the generations of Adam :" "These are the generations of the heavens and the earth :" "These are the generations of Noah," and so on. (A remarkable confirmation of this view will be found in Ezra ii. 1 : "These are the children of the province that went up," &c. That this was a separate document is proved by Neh. vii. 5, 6.) There is, besides, what might be called the literary perspective of each document, which enables us to discover the standpoint of the writer, and which is most observable in the close of each history; because there we see the period at which the historian had arrived, and are thus guided not only to the authorship, but even to the date of the composition.

The present Essay, however, has no special interest in these details, and, therefore, we do no more than offer in the Appendix (A.) what appears to be a very natural, though we are far from saying a certain, solution of the inquiry.

CHAPTER III.

THE APOCALYPSE OF CREATION.

WHEN geology was first becoming a science, men were startled at its revelations and many thought that at length Scripture had been proved to be untrue. The Mosaic account of creation seemed not only superseded, but to have actually met with a complete contradiction in its most important feature, that the " heavens and the earth, and all that in them is," were created in six days; inasmuch as the new science of geology gave an equally decided testimony that the time occupied could only be measured by thousands of years.

So complete and so decided seemed the contradiction, that many Christian men at once abandoned all hope of reconciliation; and, choosing their side, did not hesitate to affirm that geology was a fallacy, and its conclusions false. This class of theologians was never very large, and at the present day it is very nearly extinct. It was perceived that such a defence was nothing less than an unconditional surrender of the Divine authority of Scripture : and, therefore, various explanations were offered to account for the apparent contradiction.

The first and most successful was the interpretation given to the word "day" in the Mosaic narrative, by which it was held to mean, not a period of twenty-four hours, but a period of indefinite extent, stretching, it might be, to a thousand, or even many thousands of years; and then it was supposed that all the incidents of the Mosaic nar-

rative would be found to correspond with the discoveries
of geology. In a Biblical point of view, there could be
no insuperable objection to such an interpretation; and
at first sight it did appear as if it would be found to harmonise also with the teaching of geology; and as if the
time would come when we should be able to mark off
upon our maps the various formations of the different
days. More accurate investigation, however, proved this
theory to be false; and although there was a wonderful
correspondence in the general features of the organic progression in the order of creation, in the Mosaic and the
geologic cosmogony, still it was found that they did not
coincide. Instead of finding first a creation of plants,
then of fishes and birds, and then of quadrupeds, it was
observed, that although there was a progression in that
direction, every geologic era had its own plants, its own
fishes, and its own land animals.

Another and more cautious theory was adopted by
another class of interpreters. Conceding to the geologist
all that he does, or may yet demand, in regard to the
creation, or creations of the world before Adam, but fixing
on the present condition of the earth as the creation of
which Moses wrote, they affirmed that all that is written
in Genesis is literally true, but that the six days of creation found the earth in a state of ruin consequent on
some great natural catastrophe, which had extinguished
all vegetable and animal life of previous creations, and
that in a hundred and forty and four hours it was again
restored to order, life, and beauty.

This explanation can scarcely be said to be satisfactory; because, apart from many other difficulties, it has
this fatal objection, that in order to secure a literal
interpretation in one particular, it sacrifices the grand

and primary meaning of the whole; so that the petty gain could never be compensated by such a loss.

The fundamental error appears to lie in ever expecting a scientific, or even a historic, exposition of geological truth in any inspired revelation. They who require or expect in Genesis a treatise on geology, will be equally disappointed with those who look for a book of history in the Revelation of St. John. We have already shown that Scripture purposely avoids giving any assistance either in art or science; and that this is one of those grand distinctive features which give evidence of the divinity of its origin. In prospect of future discoveries in science, it was important that the Divine author should so guide the sacred penman as to show that He was intimately acquainted with the whole subject, though He made him write in a cipher, which could only be understood gradually as discovery advanced. In a word, it was necessary to adopt the same plan of revelation as that which guided the pen of prophecy; the strictly prophetic writings being so worded, that they could never be mistaken for history.

The same principle was necessary, though for a different reason, in writing an account of creation. Future discovery must not be anticipated, any more than future history; and yet there must be sufficient evidence to show that the author could have anticipated both if he had been so inclined. Let us examine, then, whether this be the true character of the first chapter of Genesis; and if so, to what conclusions it would lead us. For this purpose we must inquire what are the characteristic features of the prophetic, or rather of the apocalyptic style.

First of all, we find that it assumes the *dramatic* form,

dividing the history into different acts or scenes, which will on that account be more easily remembered, and representing the incidents thus isolated, in a pictorial, and, at the same time, allegoric form, so as to give strong impressions regarding their *general* character, rather than an accurate knowledge of their *details*. Such is invariably the style, not only of prophecy, but of every description of things which we are for the time incapable of understanding. Take, for example, the description of Christ's glory and the saints' inheritance in heaven. He leads them like a shepherd, and they drink of the water of life that flows from the throne of God; and God wipes away the tears from their eyes.

In the same style, but more completely in the dramatic form, is Daniel's prophecy regarding the four great monarchies of the world. Each of them is represented by a single beast, whose nature and appearance symbolise the characters of their respective governments. By this means the history of the world is sketched off in a few sentences, brilliantly coloured, and full of meaning.

Look next at the book of Revelation, in which the subsequent history of the world is represented. So completely has the dramatic form been assumed, that a mingled narrative of political and ecclesiastical events is crowded into three acts, each having only six or seven scenic representations.

The similarity of the opening chapter of Genesis to the closing scene of the world's history in Revelation is very marked. The septenary arrangement is conspicuous in both, and the dramatic form is the same. The seven seals, trumpets, and vials correspond with the seven days of creation. We find also a symbolic character given to each; in the first trumpet and vial, the earth is introduced; in the second, the sea; in the third, the rivers and fountains of water; in the fourth, the sun; and so on. And so in Genesis we find a single object chosen to represent the work of each day; in the first, the light; in the second, the firmament; in the third, the dry land; in the fourth, the sun and moon; and so on. The dramatic form is still further conspicuous in both narratives, in the words as well as the actions of this septenary arrangement. Repeatedly do we find the voice supplementing the vision when that which is spoken could not be represented by action and scenery alone. Thus, in St. John's Revelation we find the vision of the balances held by the rider on the black horse supplemented by the voice which said—*" A measure of wheat for a penny, and three measures of barley for a penny, and see thou hurt not the oil and the wine"* (Rev. vi. 6); and so also in the 10th, 11th, and 16th verses. In the Apocalypse of creation the very same structure may be observed in the words spoken by the Creator— *" Let there be light;"* *" Let there be a firmament in the midst of the waters, and let it divide the waters from the waters,"* &c. These words, of course, were not *spoken* at creation, but they are a dramatic representation of a fact which then took place; upon the same principle that the voice in Revelation does not predict words which were afterwards to be spoken, but realities which were afterwards to come to pass.

Another occasional characteristic in the style of prophecy is its double signification or application to different circumstances and events. For example, the country promised to Abraham and his seed was not only the land of Palestine, which was entailed on his posterity after the flesh, but that heavenly inheritance which is given to those who, by faith, are Abraham's seed and heirs according to the promise. The seventy years prophesied of by Jeremiah applied to three distinct periods of captivity, each of which extended over seventy years. David, in many allusions to himself and Solomon, used by inspiration expressions which could legitimately apply only to David's Lord; and Christ Himself, in foretelling the destruction of Jerusalem, spoke in sentences which at the same time described the last judgment; inasmuch as his references to both are conceived in language so constructed, that it is impossible to apply them all literally to either separately; and yet the general features of both are most accurately and, at the same time, most graphically represented. This feature also, is distinctly observable in the account of Creation, the very words in which it is recorded being also in numerous passages appropriated and applied to the work of Redemption.

We cannot but be struck with the singular fact that the six thousand years of the world's travail are to issue in a millennium of Sabbatic rest; and being now far advanced in the sixth thousand years of the world's labours and unrest, we have reason to believe that probably it is the last.

If these views be correct, the seven days of creation are neither seven literal days of twenty-four hours each, nor yet seven definite historical periods, the events of which are literally recorded; but, as the seven seals, trumpets, and vials of St. John's Revelation represented the history of the future by a typical representation of each of its grand divisions, *without any of them being chronologically defined,* so do the seven days of the Mosaic cosmogony represent, in a dramatic and typical form, the successive changes which took place at creation, each grand feature being boldly sketched out in one scenic representation *characteristic* of that particular epoch.

The present state of physical science is not by any means so far advanced as to enable us to pronounce a final judgment on the literality of the narrative in the first chapter of Genesis.   It may be a far more literal account of creation than we at present suppose; and we may find it so, when coming to know more about it, we shall be able to appreciate more accurately the full scientific value of each of the elements of this wonderful narrative. He who revealed it knew more than we do; and even now although it was written three thousand years ago, we are able to see reflected in it deep scientific truths, as well as the great general features of organic development and geological discovery.   So much is this the case, that we might safely challenge the best geologist in the world to write, even upon his own theory, in as few sentences as Moses (or Noah) has done, an account of creation which would be equally intelligible to an uneducated mind. Let any man try it, and we will venture to predict that, fifty years after this, it would be found that he had written it wrong, while the sacred narrative would still be found to be divinely true.

One purpose of the present Essay is to show that the want of harmony between the statements of the Bible and the teaching of modern science is apparent only, and not real, and that truth has suffered not more from a rash and hasty spirit of speculation on the part of naturalists, in some of whom the wish was father to the thought, than from the timorous tenacity with which earnest Christians are apt to cling to old beliefs and interpretations for which the Bible is not responsible.   It has been said that it is much easier to recognise than to discover,

D

and that a much lower power of the telescope is sufficient
to enable us to see that which we know, than to discover
that which we do not know or understand; not because
imagination takes the place of sight, but because sight is
really aided in its anticipations. For the same reason,
every advance in physical science as well as in philology
is a power added to Bible interpretation, not because it
enables us to distort, but because it enables us to dispense
with distortion. The old beliefs took their rise when
nature was not understood, or rather, when it was misunderstood; and therefore, to produce harmony, the Bible
at that time required to be misinterpreted. Had the
Bible been false, there would have been little damage
done; but because it was true, violence had to be done
to it in order to make it conformable to the false ideas
then prevalent regarding nature. The correction of these
scientific errors, therefore, must always be accompanied
with a corresponding relief to the Bible interpreter, and
a corresponding change in the interpretation.

The discoveries of the present century have already
done much in this direction, but not so much as they
were really capable of doing. A large amount of fictitious
interpretation, partly of heathen, and partly of mediæval
origin, still remains and encumbers our Christian-faith,
very much to its disadvantage. The truth is, that our
modern mythology, which has not the slightest warrant
in the Word of God, is quite unable to stand the test of
either astronomy or geology, and must be looked at by
scientific men very much in the light of a superstition,
unless they religiously take care never to allow it to come
into the field of view at the same time. But this is
always precarious, and therefore, it is of not a little
importance from time to time, to review our interpreta-

tions, and to give them the benefit of all the light which modern science is capable of shedding upon them.

Our subject naturally divides itself into astronomical and biological investigations; but although recent discoveries have very much affected both departments, they are not sufficiently homogeneous to be conveniently brought together.   We pursue here the more interesting and important topics which also more immediately affect the Christian faith, transferring to the Appendix those which are connected with astronomical researches.

CHAPTER IV.

CREATION ACCORDING TO LAW.

THE light of modern science, as it advances, is continually clearing away mystery, and its discoveries are every day linking into one grand and continuous whole, things that we were accustomed to regard as incongruous and antagonistic.   But above all, it is subjecting the phenomena of nature to the dominion of law; and, while narrowing the sphere of miracle, it is extending tenfold the proofs of the infinite wisdom and goodness of God in his normal administrations.

The continual retreat of Bible interpreters before the onward march of science is due to the false position which they originally occupied; and the defensive attitude, which the Bible is constantly made to assume in presence of scientific discovery, can never be changed until that position is altogether abandoned.   The idea that the operation of what are called the laws of nature is less immediately the act of God than what is called miracle, has been too hastily admitted by theologians; and they have thus been led to view with suspicion, or even alarm, any attempt to account for the phenomena of creation by the action of the natural laws; as if miraculous inter- ferences were the grand argument upon which natural theology must be made to rest. The consequence has been that, under such advocacy, the argument for the being of a God has been growing weaker, instead of stronger, by every new discovery which ascribes to the action of law the glories of creation.

In our old schools of natural theology we were taught to look upon the universe around us as the miraculous production of creative power; as if the mountains and the valleys, the atmosphere and the ocean, were all created in the state in which we find them. We were led to understand that the solar system was a piece of divine mechanism, the sun created as the source of light, and planted in the centre by the hand of God, endowed with all its prodigious powers; while the planets at regular intervals were formed as we see them, and then launched into space with a projectile force that exactly corresponded with their intended orbit; and if any one had suggested that the universe was not formed at first as we see it, but had grown into its present state by the operation of the natural laws, he would have been regarded as an atheist who wanted to rob God of His glory, and hand over the universe to the fatherhood of impersonal laws.

But why should such an idea be entertained? The existence of a law presupposes the existence of a legislator, and the operation of a law presupposes the existence of an executive. In the one we have a constant testimony to the infinite wisdom and goodness of God, who could make such wonder-working laws; and, in the other, we have a -perpetual and visible exhibition of His presence and His power in their administration. A miracle (in the sense in which it is generally understood as an interference on the part of God without the operation of law) might be resorted to in order to avert evil or accomplish good; but to produce the same end by the operation of law is the style of God's working, and of God's only. It is possible at least to conceive that a creature could make a flower, but it is impossible to conceive that he could make a law that would make a flower; because that would imply the possession of powers peculiar to God. The more wonderful the law, the more wonderful is the God who made the law, and all the more wonderful, because the law seems to intervene between God and His workmanship.

But *does* the law intervene? We deny that it really does, because what we call the laws of nature are nothing more than the modes of God's acting in each of His administrations, whether it be the organic or the inorganic, the social or the intellectual, the moral or the personal: and it is only because of its infinite perfection and utter unlikeness to the operations of created intelligences that we take refuge from our ignorance and inappreciation, in the fiction of a law as distinct from a personal God. If we had ever been able to detect caprice, or inaccuracy, or changeableness—if at any time we had observed in nature an abnormal righting of a normal wrong, we would at once have recognised a personal and intelligent Deity as the agent; but when throughout nature we can see no imperfection and no caprice, but only the never-ending, never-bending action of an infinitely perfect administration, we exclaim, "It is a law, and not a person;" and thus the very perfection of divinity veils from our eyes the presence of a God.

Why should Christians be so much alarmed about the speculations of Mr. Darwin and his school, as if the miraculous production of new species would be a better argument for the being of a God than the development of new species according to law ? With the exception of the creation of man, there is really nothing in Scripture to contradict the doctrine of development; and the gulf between man and the brute is too wide to allow Mr. Darwin to step across, even though he should succeed in establishing his theory. His opponents, in his own field of inquiry, are sufficiently formidable to serve all the purposes of orthodoxy, without theologians having to compromise their own position by mingling in the strife. The interests of Christianity are not, in the remotest degree, affected by whatever conclusion these philosophers may come to; because the arguments of natural theology rest not on the means by which beneficent design is carried into effect, but on the wisdom and the goodness that are displayed in the result.

This hankering after the miraculous in creation is a blunder in its very principle; because it proceeds upon the assumption that the production of a plant, or an animal, by a miracle would be a better display of the wisdom and power of God than its production according to law. The very opposite of this is the case, as might easily be shown by an illustration. Let us suppose that two clockmakers were to exhibit specimens of their handicraft, in order to prove their skill. One of them makes a clock which sways the pendulum and moves the hands by springs and wheels contrived for the purpose; but, as he has provided no machinery for striking the hours, he attends in person and strikes the hours himself. The other clockmaker constructs a clock having two distinct systems of wheels, one of which is continually in action moving the hands and swaying the pendulum; while the other, which is only occasionally called into operation, strikes the hours by machinery at distant and regular intervals. We ask which of these two mechanicians would be regarded as having given evidence of the highest degree of inventive genius and skill? There can be no doubt that it would be the latter; and, therefore, unless we are prepared to give up the evidence for the existence of God in the operation of the natural laws, the production of new species by the operation of some natural law, with which we are as yet unacquainted, but which comes into operation under certain circumstances, and, it may be, at distant intervals of time, so far from detracting from the evidences of natural theology, would be an addition to the demonstration of the being of a God.

We have already shown that the first chapter of Genesis is not a part of the Old Testament history, but an Apocalypse of the past, corresponding with the Revelation of St. John, which closes the canon of Scripture, and which reveals by inspiration the coming future. The more thoroughly we make this distinction, the better will we be prepared to understand its true meaning. In this sublime vision we behold, not the creation of this planet only, but the process and order that rule throughout the universe in the formation and furnishing of all the worlds. There is first the separation of the waters from the waters; then the uprising of the land from beneath the shoreless ocean; then the creation of organic life in the vegetable and animal kingdoms; and last of all, the tenancy of man. This is the order in which universal

creation proceeds; and although we have reason to believe
that only in a few favoured instances the work is crowned
by the introduction of the human species, we have in this
vision a type and summary of all creation; so that,
although the human history of other worlds will be wonderfully different, the first chapter of their Genesis will be
the same in all.

If this view be correct, the narrative of the creation
of Adam in the *second* chapter of Genesis differs from
the corresponding record of the creation of man in the
first in being not general, but specific.   In the first chapter, to which belong also the first three verses of the
second chapter, the creation of man after the image of
God has reference to the place which the human species
occupies in the order of being, and describes every such
creation, wherever it takes place.   The narrative in the
second chapter, on the contrary, beginning at the fourth
verse, has exclusive reference to the Messianic race in the
person of Adam, whose origin, along with that of Eve, is
there described.

We have also shown that the story of creation, being
the natural history of the universe, must needs be told
in an apocalyptic form, as the Scripture systematically
avoids anticipating or superseding scientific discovery.
So long, therefore, as we confound the Apocalypse of
creation in the first chapter with the Messianic narrative
which follows, we do double damage to the credibility of
Scripture, because we not only err thereby in attaching a
literal meaning to that which should be interpreted
apocalyptically, but by doing so we endanger the credibility of the history itself; since, unless we distinguish
between the two, seeing there is evidently a symbolic
element in the first chapter, we lead the unwary reader

to attach also a symbolic interpretation to the second; and he is thus tempted to pronounce the whole a myth. We should never make such a mistake in regard to the Apocalypse of St. John, partly because it speaks of the future and not of the past, but chiefly because it is a book separate from the four Evangelists and the Acts of the Apostles.

Of late years we have been startled by repeated announcements that human remains had been discovered in situations which indicate an antiquity many thousands of years prior to the time of Adam. From Denmark, from the Continent, from Egypt, from America, and even from districts in our own country, these have been crowding upon us; and although it cannot be said that in any one case the evidence has amounted to demonstration, it cannot be denied that their cumulative value has now become very formidable.

It would be unfortunate if the defenders of the Bible should be driven into the position of either surrendering the inspiration of Scripture, or denying the conclusions of geologists; so that we should have not only to fight the battle of inspiration on geological ground, but to suspend the credibility of the Bible and the truth of Christianity on the issue of a scientific controversy. No wonder that geologists have viewed with contempt the intrusion of polemical theology among the inductive sciences, and have shown but scant courtesy to the intruder. For all this we have ourselves to blame, in mistaking an apocalyptic vision for a scientific narrative, and handing it over to the geologists for acceptance as their geological primer.

The moment we make the distinction which we have indicated, we discover the mistake, and are enabled to leave scientific men to pursue their studies without attempting to coerce them by the fear of heresy. The Bible narrative does not commence with creation, as is commonly supposed, but with the formation of Adam and Eve, millions of years after our planet had been created. Its previous history, so far as Scripture is concerned, is yet unwritten. There may have been not one, but twenty different races upon the earth before the time of Adam, just as there may be twenty different races of men on other worlds; and if so, the first chapter of Genesis, being a vision of universal creation, typically describes them all.

But even the Bible is not altogether silent in regard to a previous population of our globe, although it makes no dogmatic statement upon the subject. If geologists have discovered the *mortal* remains of this primeval race, we shall endeavour to show in succeeding chapters that Scripture supplies us with abundant evidence of the continued existence of their *immortal* remains still to be found in the midst of us, and possessed of a character which could not be accounted for in any other way. Scripture and science thus walk hand in hand together, and mutually throw light upon each other's teaching. That which Scripture does not tell is revealed by science, and that which science cannot tell is revealed by Scripture.

CHAPTER V.

OUR WORLD UNIQUE IN CREATION.

ACCORDING to the Bible, this little planet upon which we dwell, although in the eyes of the astronomer it appears only as a grain of sand on the sea-shore, or the leaf of a tree in an extensive forest, is not only the most important member of the system of which it forms a part, but is the most distinguished world in the whole universe of stars. So grand and so distinctive have been the events which have transpired upon its surface, and so incapable are they of suppression or repetition, that there cannot be an intelligent being in the universe, extending even to the most distant nebulæ, who either has not already heard, or will not yet hear of it. An astronomy which does not recognise this, leaves out its grandest and most distinguishing feature. It would be like a history which left out all mention of the birth at Bethlehem, or a book of geography written in the Capitol, which knew nothing of Rome, except as a few square miles of masonry and rubbish, which had been discovered on the banks of the Tiber.

The pre-eminence which the Bible ascribes to our world in the history of the universe, as the place where the Son of God became incarnate, and suffered and died for sin, seems at first sight to be altogether inconsistent with the position which it occupies in the material creation; and yet the more we examine the facts of the case, and the discoveries of science, the less apparent does the inconsistency appear.

It is true that the first impressions produced by the discoveries of astronomy would lead us to suppose that, as our world is only one among many millions, it must be a specimen of all the rest, and that vegetables, animals, and man, must be the programme of every other. By-and-by, however, we begin to discover that this is not actually the case; and every fresh discovery, instead of leading us towards our foregone conclusion, tends in the very opposite direction. Romantic and transcendental speculations, which are indulged in to refute and counter-balance the testimony of science become ridiculous when the light of science and common sense is allowed to shine upon them; because they are found to be inconsistent with sober facts, and are unsupported by anything except prejudice and undaunted imagination. Instead of the Bible being inconsistent with the sublimities of astronomy, in what it says in regard to the singularity of this world and its destiny, science has been obliged to confess that the further it goes, the more consistent are its findings with this very testimony. Even although Scripture had been silent on the subject, we should still have been discovering more and more clearly every day that our planet is not one of a thousand only, but one of a million, if not altogether unique in creation; and that the absurd speculations which have peopled every star with moral and intelligent beings, and supposed that every planet is the abode of vegetable and animal life, will have to take their place among the abandoned delusions of earlier times.

What have we to teach us but the things which we see or the things which we have been told? and where do we see, or when have we been told, anything which would lead us to believe that there is any other world inhabited by creatures like ourselves? With the exception of the

Bible, everything that we see and know proclaims that
we are alone in creation, and that there is not likely to
be another world which contains moral and intelligent
beings besides our own.   Astronomy teaches us that the
millions of stars with which we are surrounded are no
more capable of affording habitations for plants and animals than the fiery bowels of the volcano.   They are, in
fact, suns like our own, whose heat and light may warm
and cheer the planetary systems around them, if there be
any such, but which themselves are nothing but consuming fires.   Analogy, indeed, would lead us to suppose
that there may be planets revolving around these distant
suns, and the supposition is quite legitimate; but when
we examine the planets of our own system, to enable us
to form an estimate of the qualities and capabilities of
these supposititious systems, we are forced to acknowledge
that, if (with the exception of our own world) the planets
of our solar system are a fair specimen of the systems
which exist elsewhere, there is little likelihood of either
plants or animals living upon their surface.   A wild
spirit of hungry speculation has conjectured that, as this
world is inhabited by plants and animals, every other
world must be the same; and when it is met by the
obvious fact that this world is naturally fitted to be the
abode of plants and animals, whereas no other, so far as
we are able to judge, is possessed of the same kind of
fitness, still the speculation survives, and is fed upon the
fancy that God *could* make plants and animals which
might exist upon other globes under conditions which
experience has shown to be incompatible with their existence upon ours.   Nothing could be more self-contradict-
ory than such reasoning, because it ends by denying the
premises upon which it is built.   It first assumes a fact

for which there is not the vestige of a proof, that our planet is a fair specimen of all other planets ; and when it is found that facts point to the very opposite conclusion, the force of this is evaded by a second assumption, still more absurd, that the laws of nature in this planet are different from the laws of nature in the others. If we are to be guided by analogy at all in the matter, common sense would reverse the assertions, and lead us to expect that the laws would be the same in all, but that the circumstances would be different.

If there be one thing more than another which we may say has been ascertained in regard to organic life it is this, that the supply of water is an absolute necessity. We do observe a most wonderful variety in the circumstances under which organic life is capable of existing ; so that many have been inclined to suppose that it may exist under *any* circumstances ; but, besides the fact that there is a central range of favourable circumstances in which vegetable and animal life is most exuberant and exalted, and that as circumstances decline from that range on either side, organic life diminishes and degenerates, there is another fact which is absolute and knows no modification ; and it is this, that where there is not warmth sufficient to melt ice, or where there is not sufficient atmospheric pressure to prevent boiling, there organic life, without a miracle, is an absolute impossibility. To say that God *could* do so and so, is simply to utter a truism, whose real meaning is, that God could work according to *our* plan as well as His own.

So far from analogy teaching us that there is animal and vegetable life in the moon and the other planets of our system, it rather indicates that there is little or none. We have abundance of analogies within our reach, and upon our own planet, that are perfectly decisive of the question. If we had found that animal and vegetable life is as plentiful and exuberant in the burning deserts of Africa, or the silent solitudes of the arctic and antarctic regions, as in the sunny plains of Italy or France, we might have inferred that on the burning surface of Venus and Mercury, or on the bare lava mountains of the rainless moon, there would be the same universal adaptation of organic life to every variety of circumstances; but it is not so.   We find that there is a law which depends not on astronomical but on chemical and physiological necessities, that recognises the power of heat to boil, and the power of cold to freeze, as well as the power of oxygen, phosphorus, nitrogen, carbon, and other substances, to form compounds under certain circumstances favourable to organic life.   Wherever these circumstances unite to favour their action, there organic life is most abundant and exuberant; but wherever these are more or less awanting, there organic life becomes more or less feeble, and at length altogether disappears; teaching us that, according as these other planets approach in their circumstances to the genial climates of our earth, so is it likely that organic life will prevail upon their surface; whereas in regard to those whose condition makes them resemble the portions of our world where desolation and death prevail, either through excessive heat or excessive cold, or in consequence of a want of atmosphere or water, we must come to the conclusion that the same law prevails in them, and that they too are devoid of life.   Nothing but a wild and wayward fancy which disowns facts while it professes to follow analogies could come to any other conclusion. There is a unity in all God's works that is perfectly surprising, even in the endless variety of its types and

developments. Look at the vertebrate system, with its
wonderful variety of analogies, but still the same style of
mechanism in man and beasts, and birds and fishes. Look
at the varied senses, dealing with the same optical laws
for sight, the same acoustical laws for hearing, the same
chemical laws for taste and smell. See how the animal
senses all depend on the same kind of nervous tissue, and
are all based upon the same plan. See how wonderfully
the chemical properties of the oxides, the phosphates, and
the carbonates of different substances are found to be
suited to the almost miraculous uses that are made of
them in organic life, and how inexorably nature refuses
to adopt any other for either beast, or bird, or reptile.
Looking at these undoubted facts, it remains for us to
ask what possible ground we can have for supposing that
a principle which is so determinedly adhered to on our
own planet has been abandoned in every other, more
especially as recent discoveries by the spectrum analysis
point to the probability that the materials are almost
precisely the same.

But the testimony of geology is still more remarkable
and decisive, because, even supposing that there were
thousands of planets whose atmosphere and climate are as
favourable to organic life as our own, we have no certain
grounds for believing that any one of them is inhabited by
a creature such as man. Geology proclaims that our world
is altogether exceptional in this respect, and that the
presence of man upon its surface is a circumstance which
is not likely to be repeated in one of a thousand such
worlds. This is most clearly indicated by an examination of the records of our planet, the past history of which,
for millions of ages, is found written in no uncertain
characters on the strata of which its outer crust is com-

posed. These, lying one above the other, and each requiring thousands of years to accumulate, enable us to read its past history; because, as each stratum contains embedded in it the remains of the plants and the animals which were existing at the period of its deposition, we can in imagination restore the landscapes and living creatures of each age, beginning with the earliest appearance of vegetation and animal life. These succeed each other in the history of our planet, presenting us with species which appear at one period for the first time, and after continuing for perhaps thousands of years, disappear, never again to be seen, except in the stony sepulchres which receive and preserve their remains. In this manner we have records of entire creations, rising and falling—rising over the ruins of former organisms, and falling to give place to new occupants of their habitations. During all these hundreds of thousands of years we have successive groups of fishes, saurians, birds, beasts, and insects; but in all their history there is not a vestige of human remains to be found among them. Even in regard to those remains which have been discovered, and which have led geologists to suppose that, thousands of years before Adam, the earth was inhabited by a race of human beings, the date which is assigned to them is perfectly modern; and the only question to which they give rise is, whether they are inscribed on the *last* or only the *second last* page of the last volume of a work whose volumes have never yet been counted. It is only at the very close of the geologic era that man appears.

His entrance, too, is abrupt. All other creatures come in groups, preceded and succeeded by kindred races, and side by side with relatives; but man appears alone, as if, in regard to all that preceded him, the earth had "brought

E

forth grass and herbs yielding seed, and trees yielding
fruit," and as if the waters and the earth, at God's bidding,
had brought forth their motley races in successive eras of
geologic time ; each creation in its order varying in
beauty, and, though changing in form, yet always oscil-
lating within certain limits, till, on one peculiar and
unprecedented day, God said, "Let us make man in our
image, after our likeness, and let them have dominion
over all the earth.   So God created man in his own
image, and breathed into his nostrils the breath of life ;
and man became a living soul."   Such is the testimony
which geology provides when questioned in the name of
simple truth and unprejudiced philosophy, even though
the statements of the Bible had never been heard of ;
and whatever else it may affirm, geology can never swerve
from a clear and distinct annunciation of the fact, that
man is a miracle in the universe, whose advent is sufficiently important to become an era in universal history.
According to geology, not once in hundreds of thousands
of years will there blossom on any planet so wonderful a
flower as MAN.   The last six thousand years—or if the
geologist prefers it, the last fifty thousand years—are but as
yesterday in geologic reckoning, when compared with the
eras which preceded them ; and if we were to look back on
the far-stretching ages of the previous history, all that
would present itself would be a countless succession of the
lower animals ; creation on creation rising, culminating,
and departing, each leaving for its record nothing but its
petrified remains.   If, during those long ages, some wandering intelligence had flitted about creation to see what
each world contained, the same hasty philosophy which
peoples every star would, from the same premises, and
judging of other worlds by what he found in this, conclude

that there was not a single planet in creation which contained a moral and intelligent race of beings. It is only when we discover the miraculous creation of these latter days that we admit the possibility of such an event also in other worlds. If, in each geological deposit, we had uniformly, or even occasionally, discovered traces of intelligent beings mingled with those of the lower creations, we might have been justified in regarding the present dynasty of man as an ordinary representation of what might be expected in other worlds. But when we find, throughout the eras that have rolled onward and onwards through the past, not one trace of an intelligent being, or anything that would even hold out the prospect of a coming man, we are shut up to the conclusion, that though this little spot of earth may, to the astronomer, appear lost in the magnificence of the stellar universe, geology unites with revelation in representing it as a very gem of creation, one out of a million, if not altogether unique. There may be, and Scripture assures us that there are, other worlds as fair as, and perhaps fairer and more luxuriant in every respect than our own. Their number, however, cannot be very great; and in regard to them it is very evident that upon none of them would it be possible that the Son of God should become incarnate and die, unless it were upon some world, like our own, ruined by sin and inhabited by a fallen race. Upon this point science is altogether silent, except in asserting, as will be shown in a succeeding chapter (chap. vii.), that sin is a disease, and that the normal state of man *must be* one of stainless purity. But although neither astronomy nor geology can inform us whether there are other worlds inhabited by human beings, Scripture does give us information on the subject; and that information is altogether in the direction of there being no other fallen race but Satan's and our own; and if there be one thing more than another by which the Satanic and the Adamic families are characterised, it is this, that they *both* belong to this world, and that the will of God is *not* done on earth as it is done in heaven; for in connection with this part of the Lord's Prayer, we must remember that in Scripture "heaven" and "the heavens" always mean the sky.

If it could be proved that man is normally a savage, and genealogically a brute, the burden would of course lie with us to prove the exceptional holiness of the families in the heavens; but we deny the assumption, and call upon the anthropologists for their proof. That there are other moral and intelligent beings in the stellar universe, we admit, because the Bible tells us that there are. They are God's great family in the heavens, from which we had been alienated and separated by sin; and it was the very purpose of Christ's mission to our planet to bring about a reconciliation of those who had been thus estranged, " that in the dispensation of the fulness of times he might gather together in one all things in Christ, both which are in heaven, and which are on earth " (Eph. i. 10); so that of Him " the *whole* family in heaven and earth might be named " (Eph. iii. 15). Not that we assert that there are no fallen races in the heavens; all that we affirm is, that there is an utter and total want of any indications that there are. There is but one hell, and that was prepared for Satan and his angels; and there is but one judgment-seat, and that judgment-seat is to be erected on earth, before which devils and men shall stand, but no other; and the very fact that it was to this world, and to this world only, that the Son of God was sent on His errand of mercy, indicates the probability, although not the certainty, that this is the only world which needed Him. The parable of The Lost Sheep seems to supply a key to the whole. Out of a hundred sheep, there was but one that went astray, and it was towards that one, out of the whole hundred, that the shepherd's heart went forth, and to the recovery of that one, out of the whole hundred, that he gave his earnest and self-sacrificing labours. It may be that our world is only one of a multitude; but being the only one that went astray, the Great Shepherd took not on Him the nature of angels, but came down to this sin-blighted world, leaving, as it were, the ninety-nine in the wilderness that needed no repentance, in order to win back this one and only wanderer to the fold. The testimony of Scripture is all in the same direction; and there is nothing to be found, either in astronomy or geology, which is in the smallest degree inconsistent with its teaching. But whether this be the only world which contains a fallen race or no, of this we are at least certain, that it is to this third planet, circling round an undistinguished star, that every eye in the universe will yet be turned, as the spot upon which the greatest wonder in the universe transpired, the incarnation and crucifixion of the Son of Man—the very world that God so loved that He gave His only-begotten Son, that whosoever believeth on Him should not perish, but have everlasting life.

The anthropologist repudiates the idea that the God of such a universe should demean Himself to this; but he is wrong. The God of his theology is only half a God, because the moral hemisphere of his divinity is awanting. The anthropologist delights to revel in the physical glory of the Creator, and acknowledges that it transcends all human imagination in the inexhaustible profusion of His wisdom and power; but that is all :—he refuses Him a field on which to exhibit His *moral* grandeur. Our very novelists can create a character more lovely and more divine than the God of the anthropologists; so that, if those developments of the Divine character, which Christianity, above every other system, exhibits with surpassing lustre, be not true, there is a want in the Godhead, and a vacuum in the universe. It is only lately that men have discovered the beauty and moral grandeur of SELF-SACRIFICING LOVE; and writers of fiction have only recently come to know that this is the very brightest tint which they can put upon their palette, when they wish to paint a beauty which will take the human heart by storm. Would it not be strange if the Creator implanted in our breast such an admiration of a virtue which He did not himself possess? And if He does possess it, where shall we find it exemplified in its divine perfection if it be not in the CROSS OF CHRIST? The cross of Christ dazzles the eyes even of angels in the estimate which it presents of God's infinite holiness and justice; while, at the same time, it astonishes them by its power, in breaking hearts that would have resisted and resented the very sufferings of hell; and melting the sinner by love, who never would have been conquered by anger. But their greatest wonder of all is excited by the infinity of the love and condescension of Christ in dying, not for His friends, but for His enemies, and bearing the curse of a world's guilt naked upon a bloody cross, who never needed to have left His throne. The very idea of such moral grandeur as that could no more have been conceived without being revealed, than any of the sublimities of creation.

The great reservoir of the Sun's fuel.

CHAPTER VI.

THE COMING MAN.

MODERN science has lately made great advances towards the solution of the mysteries of the solar system, and the past history of our own planet in particular. It is now nearly certain that the sun is nothing more than a gigantic conflagration going on in the heavens, and that it would long ago have been exhausted had it not been for a vast reservoir of fuel which has been discovered circling round it, and which is sufficient to maintain it in action for many thousands of years yet to come. This reservoir of fuel consists of meteoric iron and other cosmical matter, all combustible, scattered over an immense field of space, extending from the sun outwards, and covering a circular region upwards of a hundred and fifty millions of miles in diameter. We can actually see it; for although it is but celestial dust, and the particles are floating at immense distances from one another, yet when the sun shines upon it, as it shines upon floating dust in a room, it becomes distinctly visible, and in tropical countries is known by the name of the Zodiacal Light. This great meteoric system extends to within a short distance of our own orbit, and may probably be connected with those meteoric showers with which we are familiar, although this is by no means certain. When that great storehouse of fuel is exhausted however, as sooner or later it must be, the sun will have completed the period of its existence as a sun; and the incandescent lava, which is the product of combustion, will then begin to cool down into a solid ball, resembling not a sun or a star, but a planet, of the same composition as our own world.

In regard to the origin of our own earth, it may also be said that we have very nearly arrived at a solution. It too seems to have been at one time a miniature sun; but its meteoric fuel having been long ago exhausted, its outer crust has been hardened to such an extent that we can walk in safety over its glowing interior, and only now and again in the earthquake, and here and there in the volcano, are reminded of its fiery contents. No theory which has yet been broached can account for earthquakes and volcanoes according to any known laws, except the supposition that the earth was once a sun. It cannot be said, however, that all this has been fully and scientifically proved; but as every step in advance unequivocally points in this direction, there can be little doubt that it is the conclusion to which we are practically tending. And if so, it is clearly of some importance to re-examine the first chapter of Genesis under this new light, and to ascertain how far the apocalyptic drama corresponds with the scientific reality.

We cannot afford, however, to encumber our present subject with astronomical speculations (though one of our objects is to bring all the phenomena of Creation and Providence under the reign of law); and therefore we have relegated to the Appendix the astronomical department, which comprehends the work of the first four days of creation, and confine our attention at present to the anthropology of science and of the Bible.

In order fully to understand the Bible, we must ever keep in mind that from beginning to end it is all about the Lord Jesus Christ, and that nothing has been admitted into its pages which has not a reference to him or his Church. Its history is a history of the ancestry of Christ, which commences in the second chapter of Genesis (not the first); and if it shall hereafter be *proved* that there were, or even that there are, other races upon the earth which are not descended from Adam, the credibility of the Bible would not in the slightest degree be impaired. That is a question for naturalists, not for theologians; and it may be safely left in their hands, without allowing Christianity to be deposited as part of the stakes for which they are to contend. The only difference which an answer in the affirmative would make to the Bible student is, that he should have to surrender the interpretation usually assigned to certain passages of Scripture, and allow them a latitude not greater than that which is freely accorded to many others.

But not only the *Word*, but also the *works* of God, have reference to Christ, the brightness of the Father's glory, and the express image of His person. He was the final end of all creation, for " of Him, and through Him, and to Him are all things, world without end." When the meteorites and the ether were called into existence, God had the incarnation of Christ in view. In the very selection and collocation of the materials of which our world is composed, scattered as they were in space, God had in view the incarnation of Christ. The carbon, the phosphorus, the calcium, the hydrogen, the nitrogen,—whatever elements were needed for the production of the body of the Son of Man, were all purposely provided from the foundation of the world millions of millions of years before they were needed, so that, throughout all their revolutions, they were never lost sight of, and by the operation of natural laws at length found their destined place. Well might He, in prophetic language, sing the song of creation, " Thine eyes did see my substance, yet being unperfect; and in thy book all my members were written which in continuance were fashioned when as yet there was none of them." From the first day of creation, when God said, Let there be light and there was light, the train was set in motion which was to terminate in the resurrection glory of the Son of Man.

Animal life, from its lowest rudiments, is based upon the principle of *power derived from combustion* (so that a steam engine is really an artificial animal, the coal being as it were its food), the heat and power of the body being produced by the oxidation—that is the combustion of the carbon in the blood, for which purpose it is brought into contact with the air in the lungs. Like a candle or a fire, the sun could not continue to give out that enormous amount of light and heat upon which we continually depend, without its meteoric fuel; and the horse, like the steam-engine, could not exert any power unless it received its daily food, which is its anthracite.

But if our planet, with its earths and its ocean—which, be it observed, are all oxides—be nothing more than the ashes, or rather the products, of a former combustion, how is animal life to be supported by oxidation in a world where all has already been oxidised? in other words, how can there be combustion where all has been already burned? The answer is simple. An intermediate system was necessary to prepare for its advent, whose grand function should be deoxidation, or unburning that which had already been burned, and presenting it in a form in which it could be re-oxidised or burned a second time in the animal economy. THAT INTERMEDIATE SYSTEM IS THE VEGETABLE KINGDOM.

Vegetable life is dependent on the exuberance of inorganic power. Combustion, especially when it is violent, has a power of rebound by which it analyses chemical compositions, and divorces the substances which had been previously combined. This is called the deoxidising power, possessed by the sun's rays, which, when brought to bear upon any chemical compound, tends to separate the one part from the other; and when they do so, the force thus employed becomes lodged in the substances so separated. The substances which produced power by being oxidised expended their power in the oxidation; but when they are deoxidised by the sun's rays, they recover the power which they had lost, and become again combustible. That is to say, they again become capable of producing power by their oxidation;—the process of burning being reversed, the substances may, at any time, be burned a second time. Now, the vegetable kingdom was God's purpose for utilising this principle, so that it might afterwards be placed at the service of the animal kingdom, which was to live, and work, and reign, by again oxidising that which had thus been deoxidised. With such a thought, so simple in its grandeur and power, God has developed a whole kingdom of luxuriant magnificence and beauty; exhibiting, not the action of a principle in its one most perfect form, but an inexhaustible exuberance of creative fancy, ringing the changes upon this one thought in a thousand melodies, each of which again rings its changes in a thousand variations. Not only is the object attained, and deoxidation secured, but, during the process, nature is spangled over with creations of beauty and grandeur, as if its music and its beauty were its only toil.

Here, too, we find the first ascent of that grand duality, the material and the immaterial, imported from inorganic nature into organic life, sharing one another's secrets, and carrying on their united reign. The soul of the plant! how strange the expression! and yet where is the vocabulary in which to find its substitute? May we not say that this is the first type of material and immaterial man?

Such was the work of the third day, which required the intermediate sunning of the fourth before it was sufficiently mature to afford comfort and enjoyment to the sentient creation; and now begins the second ascent of matter, with its co-ordinate accompaniment of animal life, with oxidation again in the ascendant. The substances which were unburned in the vegetable, are again burned in the animal economy; and the immaterial forces which had entered a new sphere in their ascent into vegetable life, and exhibited something approaching to individuality, again mount up into a still higher region, where they become possessed of still higher powers, and exhibit an individuality more pronounced than before.

No doubt this correlation of organic force to organic matter finds its analogue in the correlation of inorganic force to inorganic matter; but here especially, in the animal kingdom, there is something more—a new thing, a substance and yet not matter, more highly organised than the organism which it dominates, rectifying its processes, and retaining in its mysterious keeping, the sacred ark of its type. Again we behold, but in rapidly-advancing grades, the prototypes of their ultimate development, Man. First, we behold in the tiny thread of nervous matter in the mollusc, and, still more, in the vertebrate system of the fish, the first approaches to the human body, with its mysterious chamber of conference the brain. Onwards and upwards the march of organism still advances towards its further development; and the fish, the lizard, the gorilla, and the dog carry us to the very frontier of the last creation, Man.

Scripture will be found to teach that human nature is the very highest type of created being, and that everywhere throughout the universe, though there may be some little variety, the type is one. The great characteristic feature in God's work in creation appears to be unity of type, with variety of development. Mankind, in speculating on what is unknown, have always been inclined to reverse the principle by imagining a variety of types with a unity of development. We can look back on the time when the unknown regions of the earth were peopled with imaginary beings—mermaids and centaurs, giants and fairies; but geographical discovery and advancing knowledge have proved the fictitious character of these abnormal creatures; and, as we are surprised to find in the sun and in the distant stars the very same familiar substances that are round about us on earth, so may we expect, when the veil shall be drawn aside which at present hides celestial objects from our view, that a wonderful and beautiful unity reigns throughout all God's works, and that the endless varieties both of animal and vegetable structure which have their dwellings in other worlds, circle round the same types of organisation, many, if not most of which we see around us every day.

The more enlarged our knowledge of God's works, the more do we gravitate towards this conclusion; and, although Scripture may appear at first sight to introduce us to a system or systems of existence whose peculiarity is innovation and unsteadiness—innovation upon types, and un-

steadiness of law—nothing can be more false than such
an impression. In ages past, it has been the atmosphere
in which all sober thinkers have delighted to breathe; and
although it presents to our view a series of phenomena
beyond the range of our present experience, and although
these phenomena have been distorted by the wild fancies
of bold but wayward imaginations, it will be found, when
they are studied with a child-like and unprejudiced simplicity, that they will startle the philosopher not so much
by their discords as by their harmonies with science.

Whenever the reins are given to the imagination, there
is no absurdity too great for acceptance. The inhabitants
of Sirius, according to one author, are nine miles in height;
another hazards the opinion, that in other worlds, instead
of the souls being lodged in bodies, the bodies are lodged
in external souls. One popular writer propounds the idea
that two or three universes may exist in the same space
without being cognisant of each other's existence. A
second indulges the thought, that within a point so small
as to elude all the powers of the microscope, there may
be another universe, the mechanism of whose worlds is
filled with the evidences of a Creator's glory; while a
third is inspired with the imagination, that there may be
beings so immeasurably superior to man, that all the
visible universe that presents itself to our gaze may be a
microscopic object altogether invisible to their eyes, and
that the spaces between sun and sun, and between system
and system, may be no greater to them than the distances between the pores in a grain of sand.

How different is the language of Scripture ! how sober
its revelations, and yet how much more truly grand !
In contrast with all this imaginative dissipation, it presents to us the human nature of Jesus as the connecting

link by which we are related to all the intelligent inhabitants of the universe. The heathen mythologies, and
the superstitions of the different nations, tell us of
gigantic creatures and diminutive elves; but the Bible
speaks of the whole family of God, both in heaven and
in earth as one; and when any, even the highest and
brightest of those that stand before His throne, is introduced to our notice in Bible history, he is uniformly presented to us a brother MAN.

Scripture, interpreted by science, will be found to teach
that human nature is the very highest type of created
intelligence; and the question naturally presents itself,
whether all the moral and intelligent creatures that people
the universe do not belong exclusively to the .human
species? A careful examination will show us that it is
so, and that the physical constitution of men, angels, and
devils is in every respect identical, their apparently different natures being nothing more than the different
states of being of which that nature is susceptible.

When we are informed that man was made after the
image of God, this almost amounts to a declaration that
his was the highest style of created being, and that no
loftier type or pattern could ever appear. The image of
God must be a perfect image—as perfect as a mere image
can be. The original of which he is a copy is the highest
possible, and the artist being God himself, we may be
sure that it was executed in the very highest style.

Not that there was no advance possible for Adam, or
that he alone, in his own person, illustrated all the features which were copied from the Divine Original; still
less that if he had been left in his fallen state, he would
ever have developed that image in all its constitutional
completeness. It will be shown in the succeeding pages,

that we must look to the resurrection state of the redeemed, and to the fully developed state of the angels, as that which was in the mind of the Creator when he said, "Let us make man in our image." We must also observe that in the record of Creation the progress is always upwards, the highest being last, and that last was Man. All things not only on earth, but in heaven, were created within the six days; and if the angels are not included in the creation of "man," where shall we find a place in the first chapter of Genesis for their creation.

It is true that it is the spirit, or rather the mind, that is created in God's image, and not the body; but this does not affect the conclusion, for it is the result and not the means that constitutes the likeness. We think, and God thinks—we observe, and God observes—we feel and God feels ; but in all this there is an infinite difference, for God thinks, and observes, and feels absolutely and essentially, and in a manner altogether different from that in which our faculties act,—it is only in the result that there is any resemblance. A father's peculiar love towards his children is essentially natural and not spiritual ; yet it is not the original : it is only a copy from the Fatherhood of God. It is of no importance, therefore, whether we say that it is the body or the spirit that is like to God, because, strictly speaking, it is neither in the one nor in the other that the likeness appears, but only in the result of both. It is not the spirit alone, therefore, that bears the image of God—it is the body and the spirit combined. The crime of murder is represented in Scripture as exceedingly heinous, " because man was made in the image of God."

If we set aside the symbolic creatures seen in visions, or represented in the sculpture of the sanctuary, we shall find that Scripture affords no warrant for the supposition that angels have any form different from that of man. It is true that poets and painters are in the habit of attaching a couple of wings to the shoulders of angels, and that cherubs are usually represented with the head of a child carried upon the wings of a dove; but we shall look in vain for any Scripture authority for such representations. The angels are represented as the highest created intelligences in the universe; and there is none of them more honoured than Gabriel, who stood in the presence of God, and was upon at least four different occasions entrusted with messages to earth,—twice in the Old Testament and twice in the New Testament history,—and yet the form of Gabriel was a human form, and the angels are uniformly represented as men.

But if we had no other evidence of the supremacy of the human type, the fact of the incarnation of the Son of God would be sufficient. If, in the human form, the Son of God could assume the likeness of a servant, and humble himself even to death, He could, in the same human nature, assume the highest glory and honour. If, when clothed in the natural body, he was made a little lower than the angels, when he was clothed with his spiritual body He was still a man; but He was elevated to the right hand of the Majesty of heaven, "far above all principality, and power, and might and dominion, and every name that is named" not only in this world but in that which is to come. May we not with reverence say, that if the human nature had not been the very highest of all natures, there would have been an evident inappropriateness in investing the great King of the universe with a nature inferior to that of those whose knees were to be bent in homage, and whose tongues were to confess

F

His praise? Surely, among the angels that bow before Him, there cannot be a nature superior to His own.

To some it may be an objection, that the structure of the human body is so like that of the lower animals. Reaching downwards from the dog and the fish, among the vertebrate animals, the same type of being descends to the lowest form of mollusc, in which a speck of nervous matter claims kindred with the human brain. It may seem strange to some that the highest type of being should be so like a beast. But, in truth, this is not a valid objection;—it is rather a confirmation of the doctrine. It is because they are all of them the handiwork of the same Artist that they are so much alike. That which He does is best, not only in its end, but in its means; and if we find that, from the lowest to the highest there is but one principle and one plan, this proves that there are not two which are equally good. Why, then, should the Creator adopt an inferior method even for his lowest creations? If we find that the same type of being is capable of such infinite diversity of development and pattern, from the simple polyp up to the human form, why should we suppose that, after conducting us thus far, it should be imperfect at the end, and that another and altogether different type should be necessary to reach only a little higher?

Some, in the spirit of humility, have ascribed to the angels a nature immeasureably superior to that of man, even in his glorified state; but this is a humility which gives no glory to God, and no honour to the Lord Jesus Christ; because it is based, not upon any revealed glory that belongs to the angels, but upon the supposed inferiority of human nature. Alas! it is but too true that we have so defiled and degraded our bodies and spirits, that it may seem presumptuous for such as we are to claim kindred with the angels.   But that is our work, not God's ; and the enormity of our offence consists in this, that such as we should ever have sinned.   Even now the human body, soul, and spirit constitute a very miracle of beauty and grandeur, fallen as they are ; but we shall be better able to admire their glory when the manifestation of the sons of God shall be complete, and when God himself will look upon us, and "rejoice over us with joy" (Zeph. iii. 17), and the very Son of God will not be "ashamed to call us brethren" (Heb. ii. 11).

CHAPTER VII.

HOLINESS MAN'S NORMAL STATE :

SIN A DISEASE, CONTAGIOUS AND HEREDITARY.

THE Bible asserts that man was originally a holy and sinless being; but that, having been corrupted by the temptation of an alien spirit, he fell into a state of moral depravity which became hereditary, and is now universal among his descendants.   The speculations of modern anthropologists, on the other hand, have been travelling in the opposite direction, and have suggested that man is naturally a savage, and that the change which has taken place is not degradation, but improvement.

There is so much resemblance between man and the lower animals, not only in the structure of his body, but even in his habits and instincts, that many learned natu-

ralists have come to the conclusion that man is a lineal
descendant of the gorilla or some such animal, and that
he has been rising slowly and gradually in the scale of
being. If this be so, then even the present state of the
human race, scientifically considered, cannot be final.
There being no stability in species, and the constant
inclination being to tumble upwards, and to be continually
evolving what was never *in*, we must expect that the
future Man will be as superior to the men of the present
day, as the men of the present day are to the gorilla or
the dog, both in beauty and intelligence.

There are others who, though they reject the doctrine
of development, are nevertheless equally decided in regard to the natural history of man, that it is upward and
not downwards; and that the successive periods of the
stone, the bronze, and the iron ages indicate a gradual
growth of human intelligence from savagism upwards to
civilisation; and, therefore, that the fall of Adam must
be a myth.

We do not blame the votaries of science for pursuing
their investigations independently of the Bible; and would
rather deprecate the idea of anything which it says laying
an arrest upon the most unrestricted examination of all
that nature teaches. Nature and the Bible are of co-
ordinate authority, and if both are of God they cannot
contradict one another. It is the interpretation alone of
each that is fallible, and, therefore, it becomes both theologians and naturalists to observe extreme caution and
reserve in making dogmatic statements, or in arriving at
conclusions which may afterwards be discovered to be
premature or even erroneous. The obvious and proper
course for each to pursue is to follow up their own investigations with their own proper instruments of study;

and, with confidence in the result, leave to the future the reconciliation of their completed testimonies.

The purpose of the present chapter, therefore, is not to impose the authority of Scripture upon the naturalist, but respectfully to suggest the question, whether the view which he has adopted be really borne out by the teaching of his own science; and whether, upon scientific grounds, even though the Scripture had been silent on the subject, we must not come to the conclusion that man's present state and character are exceptional, and that his original and normal condition *must have been* one of stainless innocence.

We would especially call the attention of the naturalist to a fact which has evidently been overlooked, namely, that moral depravity, although, at first sight, it has the appearance of being of the same nature with the dispositions and habits of the lower animals, is in reality entirely different; the latter being the results of true and healthy instincts, the former being morbid and abnormal : in other words, sin is a disease, and not an instinct.

We are apt to be misled by the fact that sin is hereditary, and that, so far as our experience goes, it is universally prevalent in the human family; but we must not allow ourselves to be guided too much by merely local circumstances, or influenced by a superficial view of those things *by which we happen to be surrounded.* The fact that sin is hereditary is no evidence that it is normal and constitutional. There are diseases which are unquestionably hereditary, and whose taint, being in the blood, is transmitted from generation to generation in the family where it has obtained a power. There are diseases, also, which are epidemic; and the fact that they are prevalent, or even universal, in any given locality, does not determine that they belong to the original constitution.

People who have been born in Edinburgh, and never wandered from its precincts, are surprised to hear strangers speak of its surpassing beauty, because they see no reason why it should be so much more beautiful than any other city; the citizens of Venice, if they held no communication with the rest of the world, would be astonished to hear that other cities were planted inland, where no gondola could navigate their streets; and so the inhabitants of this world, cut off from intercourse with every other, naturally but unthinkingly and unphilosophically suppose that, because sin happens to be endemic here and at the present time, it must be the normal condition of the species.

Neither must we be misled by the circumstance that sin is a moral, and not a physical disease. If man were a mere animal, his diseases could be only of a bodily kind; but because he is also an intellectual being, his diseases may be mental as well as bodily; and because he is also a moral being, it is in accordance with this analogy that his moral nature also must be liable to disease. Our pathologists inform us that there are diseases which are unquestionably moral—such as dipsomania, cleptomania, phonomania, and many others; therefore, there can be no doubt that our moral nature also is subject to insanity.

It is true, also, that some of those propensities which are criminal in man are natural instincts among the lower animals, but that is by no means an evidence that they belong to our original constitution. That which is normal in one species may be abnormal in another, and that which is a healthy feature in one animal may be the product of disease in another; therefore, that may be a moral disease in the human subject, which is perfectly healthy and even necessary in the brute.

What, then, is it that constitutes a disease as distinguished from a natural propensity or an instinct? It is obviously this: that an instinct is conducive to the well-being of the individual, or the species to which it belongs; whereas a disease is that which is not necessary, but injurious and detrimental. We challenge contradiction in regard to this test, and ask, Where shall we find an exception? Where shall we find an instinct that is injurious to the individual and the species to which it belongs? and where shall we find a disease that is conducive to their happiness and well-being? We do not ask where there is an instinct which is injurious to the creatures around, because there are many such. The predatory habits of the fox are not conducive to the comfort or well-being of the poultry; nor is the rapacity of the wolf conducive to the safety and happiness of the sheep, but they are certainly conducive to the happiness and well-being of the animals themselves. They are therefore true instincts, and not diseases, notwithstanding their offensive character; but if these dispositions, besides being injurious to others, were also destructive to the animals themselves, they should no longer be called instincts, but morbid and abnormal habits, which could only be ranked in the catalogue of diseases. As instincts' they are a part of the animal's nature, and belong to their original constitution; and notwithstanding their unamiable character, they are a portion of God's fair creation, and He is not ashamed to acknowlege them as His handiwork. He gave talons to the eagle, poison to the serpent, claws to the tiger, and fangs to the wolf; and, having given these weapons of offence, He gave them also corresponding instincts for their use, so as to make them subservient to their own subsistence and comfort. They are necessary to the animal's enjoyment of life, if not to life itself; and the suspension or disuse of them, instead of being an improvement, would be a disease and an abnormalism, producing only suffering, and perhaps death. No amount of improvement would abolish them; on the contrary, the higher the development, the more formidable would be the weapons, and the more deadly would be the instincts.

Can we say the same of sin? Is it necessary to man's existence, or is it conducive to his well-being? The wolf is really the better of the sheep which it has slain and devoured, and the cat is really the better of the mouse which it has caught and eaten; because their preying upon these animals is in accordance with their nature, and is the provision which God has made for their sustenance. The law of the brute creation is obedience to their natural instincts, and they are entitled to take all that they can get, and to keep all that they can. No code of morality would have been at all suitable to the lower animals; and, therefore, the only rule of right and wrong is power and weakness. God has a right to endow his creatures according to his will, and He has given to them all that they can take, and no more; and so long as they can take and keep, they have a perfect right to do so. For that reason, man does no injustice to the lower animals, *so far as they are concerned*, when he enslaves, or kills, and eats them *if he can*. This is the law of the lower creation, and it is right, not only because no other code was possible, but because upon the whole it is the one most conducive to their well-being.

But it is not so with man. He has been created upon a different model, and has received a moral nature, in which might is subordinated to right, and conscience is made to rule supreme. The animal propensities in man are sinless in themselves, and, when guided by conscience, are conducive to the happiness and well-being, not only of the individual, but of the species. But sin is the morbid action of these propensities; and inasmuch as it is morbid, instead of being conducive to the individual's welfare, it is only destructive and suicidal. A man is really nothing the better of sin, of whatever kind that sin may be; murder, robbery, drunkenness, dishonesty, lying, lust, instead of promoting a man's own interest, tend rather to destroy his happiness and increase his misery. It is the natural offensiveness of sin that proves its abnormal character. Unrestrained selfishness and ferocity are healthy instincts among the lower animals, and are not diseases; because, however offensive to those around them, they are not destructive, but useful to themselves; and if unrestrained lust and ferocity were really advantageous to a man's own self, and consistent with a man's own happiness, they would be healthy instincts in human nature also, even though they might be inconvenient and destructive to his neighbours. But God has not made man so, and, therefore, unrestrained indulgence is not conducive to man's comfort or well-being, either in regard to the individual or the species. It is its SUICIDAL character which proves it to be a disease. It is because sin injures the interests, mars the enjoyments, and shortens the days of the individual who indulges in it, therefore it is not an instinct. It has not a single element of goodness in it, or connected with it, so that a moderate indulgence in it might be salutary. It is essentially and entirely evil ; and, what proves most conclusively that it is no part of our normal constitution is, that it injures the individual who sins more than the individual who is sinned against. Where will the anthropologist find anything approaching to this throughout all the wide domain of nature ? Where will he find an instinct, the use of which is destructive to the individual, and injurious to the species to which it belongs ? There is no such thing.

We have, indeed, diseases and abnormalism among the lower animals, monstrosities and unhealthy developments, but these are not the original and normal condition of the creatures as God made them. Unless, therefore, we mean to say that God has planted sin in our nature on purpose, and that man is naturally and intentionally a beast of prey, whose life and happiness depend on lust and rapine ; unless we are prepared to assert this, we cannot assert that sin is not a disease, or deny that innocence, purity, and holiness are the natural and normal condition of the human being as God originally made him.

A second argument against the normal character of sin consists in the antagonism of conscience, which condemns it. We say *condemns,* because there is no other word. It is not that there is merely antagonism between conscience and sin: that would not prove sin to be abnormal. We have plenty of antagonisms in nature which are perfectly normal ; we have the antagonism between the eagle and the dove, between the wolf and the sheep, or even between wolf and wolf, and between dove and dove. There is even an antagonism between the normal instincts of our own nature, between combativeness and caution, or between acquisitiveness and generosity ; but where do we find condemnation ? When the eagle has torn the dove, or the wolf has devoured the lamb, there is perfect self-satisfaction and repose, without any secret misgiving that anything-has been done wrong : in other words, there is no verdict of self-condemnation. Fear there may be, but fear is not condemnation, and a man may fear even when he has done no wrong. We affirm, therefore, that if sin were a normal and natural instinct, which God planted in man's nature, and intended to be gratified, it would not have been condemned by conscience.

A third proof that sin cannot be a natural instinct, characteristic of the undeveloped man, is to be found in its partiality and want of uniformity. In this respect it has all the characteristics of disease. If our race were afflicted with a leprosy, which never attacked the whole person, but only some one or other of our members; if it also varied in the intensity of its loathsomeness, rotting off a finger from one victim, and a foot from another; if some part of the body were generally unaffected, and the healthy portions not always the same, we should have satisfactory evidence in such an affliction that it was a disease, and not the natural condition of our species. Now, so it is with sin; it invades every part of our moral nature, but it varies in the malignity of the attack. In some individuals it settles upon one region of the moral system ; in other individuals it settles upon another. In some individuals it leaves one portion of our moral nature comparatively healthy; while in other individuals the healthy portions are altogether different. One man who, in one respect, is a very bad man, has an unblemished reputation for truthfulness and honesty ; another man, whose domestic virtues are unimpeachable, would cheat his neighbour without any compunction of conscience if he had the opportunity. One man has a tender and compassionate heart, that would feed the hungry and

clothe the naked; but he has no self-denial, and altogether neglects his business. Another man is devotedly
attached to his parents, and would not let the wind blow
upon them if he could help it; but his temper is most
violent, and his vindictiveness almost murderous. We
might go over all the commandments of the decalogue,
at least of the second table, and for each of the commandments we could discover some individual who, if
not altogether perfect, is very nearly so; and in these
very varieties we have illustrations and specimens of
that which is morally healthy and that which is morally
diseased. This proves that there is not a single sin which
is a necessary part of the human constitution; and, therefore, that sin of every kind and of every degree is a real
disease, and is not the normal and natural state of
man.

We have spoken only of the second table of the law,
because we have purposely excluded the theological element; but we should not complete even our scientific
argument if we did not observe that there is one region
of our moral nature which is always diseased, and is
never whole. We refer to that central region which we
call the religious, and which has special reference to our
relations to the Deity. In that central spot we find the
remains of a ruptured relation, the fragments of an um-
bilical cord, as it were, which had been violently severed,
leading to something now awanting, man cannot tell
where; but it is so disintegrated and damaged, that we
even fail to discover what has been its original form and
structure. Every other member and region of our moral
nature can be seen and examined, in at least some specimens more or less healthy; and mankind can scarcely

be said to be divided in opinion as to what is the right and healthy condition of that region; but, in regard to this inner and most central region it is not so. Filial piety, benevolence, chastity, sobriety, honesty, and truthfulness are simple virtues, in regard to which mankind is quite unanimous; and, if not in practice, at least in imagination, we could reconstruct a perfect man. But as we approach this central region—the religious, the sacred, the supernatural—that portion of our moral nature which, even in its ruin, dominates over all the rest, we find a difference. There can be no doubt that it is there —obtrusively and inevitably there—but, in what a state ! so torn, so inflamed, and so mortified, that even its original form and structure cannot be recognised. We appeal to the infidel himself whether it is not so, and we challenge him to account for it. Here is the one diseased member of our moral nature which costs him all his grief, and against which he never ceases to declaim. Even upon his own showing, it is the weak point of humanity, the cancerous spot upon which " superstition " and " priestcraft," " fanaticism " and " bigotry," " hypocrisy " and " intolerance," are sure to fasten, and from which he is for ever and in vain labouring to drive them away. It is the one point upon which all men are disagreed, and upon which the most violent contradictions are expressed. That there is a religious instinct in human nature no man in his senses will deny. That this sense of the sacred involves also a sense of responsibility and obligation to some superhuman authority, is also a self-evident proposition. That it is a most powerful instinct, capable of overbearing, if not of regulating, every other passion of the human heart, must be admitted by all who have studied the history of mankind. How is it, then, that this instinct is, of all others, so diseased and so mangled, that it bids defiance to every attempt to discover even its original structure?

Having thus proved that sin is not an instinct like the offensive propensities of the lower animals, but a disease which, instead of promoting the well-being and ministering to the comforts of mankind, destroys their happiness and shortens their life; unless we are prepared to say that man is AN EXCEPTION TO ALL THE OTHER WORKS OF GOD, and that he alone was created with a diseased constitution, we must come to the conclusion that his original and normal condition was a state of holy innocence, and that he was *not* created in the state of malformation in which we find him. It is no business of ours to explain how the change took place; nor is it material, so far as our argument is concerned, whether the naturalist accepts the testimony of Scripture on the subject or no. We have purposely excluded the theological element, because it was really not needed for our demonstration; and we leave the naturalist to account for the change which we have proved to have taken place, in the best way he can. He may help himself a little so far, because, even in God's creation, so far as he knows it, there is no creature, however perfect, that is not subject to disease. Unfavourable circumstances may produce predisposition to the malady, and it may also be communicated by contagion. It may become hereditary, or it may be epidemic, or it may even be generated or aggravated by an alien and parasitic life, introduced into, and dwelling in, the system. Such are the suggestions of science on the subject, and, if the naturalist chooses, he may legitimately speculate in this direction; but he must do so on his own responsibility: and yet it is interesting to observe that Scripture conducts us to a very similar result.

In one respect the naturalist is very favourably circumstanced in an investigation of this kind : not having to deal with things as they ought to be, but only with things as they are, he is not troubled with any speculations in regard to the origin of evil. It is enough for him that moral disease exists; and he can, from an examination of the laws which regulate diseases generally, determine that the normal state of the human species *must have been* one of sinless purity, and not of hereditary malformation.

But he may do more. The *human* species is only one of many thousands with which he is acquainted, and if he shall set himself to study the subject with a view to investigate the natural history of disease ; that is to say, if he shall, by a purely inductive process, discover what it really is, what is its purpose (for it must have a purpose), and what are the laws of its distribution,* he will throw a flood of light on anthropology. This question he may work out with his Bible shut and his eyes open, because there can be no doubt that it is purely a physical question ; and if, excluding poor fallen humanity and its protégés which have shared his malison, with its consumption and its rinderpest, its smut and its blight ; and, taking into council only nature, *sinless, wild,* and *free,* as God alone has made them—the fowls of the air, and

---

* It is interesting to observe, in connection with this subject, that man, more than any other animal, is subject to disease. Radiating from him as from a centre, it creeps forth upon nature towards every plant and animal which he has subjected to his sway, in proportion as it has been associated with his civilisation. Beyond his pale, death by disease is comparatively rare.

the fishes of the sea, the mountain daisy and the lilies of the field, the coney of the rocks and the wild ass of the desert—he shall ask them what they know of disease and malformation; whatever be the proportion which their answer may indicate as subsisting between their healthy and their diseased, that is the proportion in which he may expect to find in other worlds UNFALLEN MAN.

Let the unbeliever rise above his prejudices, and looking down impartially on his own position, try whether he can explain facts as he finds them, even upon his own principles. If superstition and hypocrisy (religiousness) be an almost universal mania, the unbelievers being the only sane exceptions; and if sin, in a scientific point of view, be not a true instinct but a disease, how is it possible to believe that man alone in all creation is normally abnormal? If the scientist flings away analogy as well as revelation, we may well ask what he has left to guide him. It is the Bible alone that is consistent.

CHAPTER VIII.

THE PHYSIOLOGY OF THE SPIRIT.

THERE is a great deal of the old Gnostic superstition still prevalent in the Christian world, which looks upon matter as a base and degraded form of existence, from which we are to be emancipated at death. There seems to be an impression that, as soon as we die, we enter into a new universe, which is not material, and in which sun, moon, and stars have no existence. It is the old heathen spirit-world, in which not only the persons, but the locality is immaterial—with its spirit-mountains and its spirit fields; in short, a spirit-universe having no relation to the material universe, to which we are supposed to bid an eternal adieu when we close our eyes in death and open them in heaven. The idea of heaven being a material world, with mountains and streams, and clothed with material vegetation, would be considered by many as a profane and materialistic degradation of our heavenly inheritance. The Bible has no sympathy with this semi-pagan transcendentalism; and so little does it harmonise with these popular superstitions, that it has to be smoothed down and explained away in order to enable it to maintain its character for spirituality.

Christianity is the only religion that vindicates the dignity of the material universe, by connecting it with man's future existence in the resurrection from the dead. All heathen religions deal not only in worlds of ghosts, but in ghosts of worlds.

Now, it is quite true that there is a spirit-world, which, although we do not see it, has, nevertheless, a real existence. But it is a spirit-world composed of persons, not of things. There are spiritual beings surrounding us, and going to and fro upon the earth on their unhallowed errands; yet the theatre upon which they act is not a spirit-earth, but a material one; and the reason why we do not see them is not because we do not live in the same universe with them, but because we have not yet that sense developed in us which would receive the impression. There may be rays which they emit or reflect which our optic nerve is unable to recognise, any more than the caloric or actinic rays. Material nature is full of the unseen. Who would have suspected the existence of

G

magnetism, if we had not had iron? and who would have known that there are chromatic rays, had not God made the optic nerve to detect them? We can experiment with the caloric rays and the actinic rays of the sun; but who has ever discovered a substance that would have revealed the rays of colour?

We have the sense of hearing and the sense of sight; but between these there are vibrations which the human ear and the human eye cannot detect. Sound is simply the vibration of our atmosphere and other substances, and we can even tell the number of vibrations which go to make any musical tone. They rise note by note until they have completed the octave, by which time the rapidity has been exactly doubled. If the rapidity of vibration be further increased it ascends octave after octave, until the ear can no longer distinguish it. It has entered a region where it ceases to impress any of our present senses, till, having reached its fortieth octave, it reappears as light. Who knows what senses lie between? for as the retina of the eye distinguishes colour by rays whose existence no chemist can detect, why may not the spirit respond to electric or magnetic emanations, or emanations which are neither electric nor magnetic, but cognisable only by spirit? The caterpillar has not the same senses as the butterfly, but nature has modes of vision for them both; and so will it be with us. The natural body has its senses, the spirit also has its senses; but there is no reason to suppose that they are the same, neither is there any reason to suppose that their perceptions are miraculous— they are all according to law. Now we see through a glass darkly, for the lenses of the eye give but an imperfect vision, compared with the spiritual sight that sees face to face: now we are seen and known by witnesses whom we cannot see; the time is coming when we shall know, even as we are known. Even in our present state we have in embryo these other spirit-senses, and they are sometimes brought into action when the body and the mind are in an abnormal state. Such cases excite our wonder, and seem to be miraculous; but it is not so— they are all according to law, because they merely exhibit the latent capabilities of the human constitution.

It is one of the peculiarities of the human species that it generates a spirit capable of a separate existence, like the seed generated in a plant. The plant dies, but the seed survives; and as the seed contains in itself the germ and elements of a future plant, so do the human soul and spirit when shed from the body, possess not only an independent existence and vitality of their own, but also the power of reproducing another body similar to that in which they were generated, whenever they shall be placed in circumstances favourable to their germination. As in the butterfly when it escapes from the chrysalis, the former organs of sense are no longer available, but new organs, or, it may be, new senses, come into play, specially adapted to its new style of being. It could scarcely be that this peculiarity of our species was impressed upon it in anticipation of a fall: we must rather suppose that these future senses of the spirit already exist, though at present only in an embryonic state, and that their normal development was intended to take place, not at death, but at the time when the natural body, unfallen, should be normally changed into the spiritual body; that is to say, when the man should be developed into the angel.

That these new senses already exist in a rudimentary state, even in the natural body, is abundantly evident from many considerations. Upon no other principle could we account for those extraordinary exhibitions of exalted sensibility which so frequently occur in somnambulism, hysteria, and other morbid and abnormal states of the human body. We do not here allude to mesmerism and clairvoyance, although those who believe in them will at once accept them as evidences of what is here affirmed; for it is well known, that the very same phenomena have presented themselves where there was no mesmerism, and at times, where their exhibition was unexpected and spontaneous. Had there been no spiritual retina upon which these impressions could be received, it never could have been quickened into action; and the mere fact that, in our natural state, that retina is usually dormant, cannot prove that it is awanting, or that it exists only in diseased subjects. What better proof could we have of this spiritual sense than the prophetic consciousness of spiritual vision, and the reception of spiritual communications? Unless there had been an inner person possessed of senses which do not belong to the natural body, but which God occasionally allows to be brought into action, these prophetic powers would have been an impossibility.

We have at least two very remarkable examples, one in the Old Testament, the other in the New, in which the prophet became acquainted with external objects, not by spiritual communication, nor yet by the aid of the bodily senses, but by what might be called spirit-perception. These were Elisha and the apostle Paul; Elisha especially appears to have been endowed with this wonderful faculty, It was most remarkably exhibited in the affair of Naaman the Syrian, when Gehazi followed the chariot to obtain money fraudulently in the name of his master. Elisha said, "Went not mine heart with thee, when the man turned again from the chariot to meet thee ?" from which it appears that Gehazi's conduct was not revealed to Elisha by a third party, but was seen by Elisha himself.

After this he was present in spirit at the consultations of the king of Syria in Damascus, and revealed his plans to the king of Israel, who was thus enabled to defeat them. "Therefore the heart of the king of Syria was sore troubled for this thing," feeling assured that some of his own courtiers must have been in correspondence with the enemy : "Will ye not show me," said he, "which of us is for the king of Israel? And one of his servants said, "None, my lord, O king ; but Elisha, the prophet that is in Israel, telleth the king of Israel the words that thou speakest in thy bed-chamber" (2 Kings vi. 8).

Subsequently also, Elisha appears to have observed the coming of the king of Israel's messenger to arrest him ; the king himself being immediately behind : " Elisha sat in his house, and the elders sat with him ; and the king sent a man from before him : but ere the messenger came to him, he said to the elders, See ye how this son of a murderer hath sent to take away mine head ? Look, when the messenger cometh, shut the door and hold him fast at the door : is not the sound of his master's feet behind him ? And, while he yet talked with them, behold the messenger came" (2 Kings vi. 32).

Paul also gives some indication of this extraordinary faculty—first in his Epistle to the Corinthians (1 Cor. v. 4) : " For I verily, as absent in the body, but present in spirit, have judged already, as though I were present, concerning him that hath so done this deed, in the name of our Lord Jesus Christ, when ye are gathered together, and my spirit, with the power of our Lord Jesus Christ, to deliver such an one unto Satan."

Also, in his second Epistle to the same Church, he says (chap. xii. 1-4), "It is not expedient for me doubtless to glory. I will come to visions and revelations of the Lord. I knew a man in Christ about fourteen years ago, (whether in the body, I cannot tell; or whether out of the body, I cannot tell: God knoweth;) how that he was caught up into paradise, and heard unspeakable words, which it is not lawful for a man to utter. Of such an one will I glory; yet of myself I will not glory, but in mine infirmities."

The circumstance that he could not tell whether it was in the body or out of the body that he heard these words, proves, that whatever were the facts of the case, he at least possessed the faculty of hearing by his spirit words spoken in paradise, while his body was present on earth, whether the faculty was exercised in this particular instance or not. He would not by inspiration express an uncertainty regarding a thing which was impossible in its nature.

It has been generally supposed that when our Lord said to Nathaniel (John i. 48), "Before that Philip called thee, when thou wast under the fig-tree, *I saw thee,*" he indicated the divine omnipresence of His person. It is more probable that in this as well as upon other occasions when he wrought miracles by the power of the Holy Ghost, it was his humanity that is presented to our view in its prophetic power after being anointed with the Holy Ghost. We may therefore regard this incident as another instance of spirit-vision.

While we are in the flesh, the five senses are the chief instruments by which we receive information from the world without, and that which we have seen and heard constitutes the greater part of all that we know. But the bodily senses are not the only means by which we acquire knowledge or receive impressions from without; there is a spirit within lodged in the body, though not a part of it, which has been developing its own peculiar faculties, and which is not without its own senses and sensations which are independent of the body.   Even when the body is laid to rest in the darkness and silence of solitude, when no sound or sight either helps or hinders, there are busy senses within, examining and judging, approving, and condemning, joying and grieving, hoping and fearing, after a fashion of their own, which no bodily sense can imitate.

Like a seed which has been growing in a plant, and is ready to be shed, we feel that there is a spirit within which we call ourselves, and which is perfectly distinct from the body in which we dwell ; and, although we had never heard nor read of immortality, we already know it in those unexplored depths of our own consciousness where our intuitions lie, so that its announcement does not startle us as a fresh discovery would do.   Like the memories which lie buried in the deep world within, and which might never be awakened into recollection, it is known, although it is not known, and is believed before it is consciously realised. Our being is not only a wonderful phenomenon, it is also a mysterious and unfathomable deep.

When the body dies, and the spirit is shed, then only will it be conscious of what it is not.   Like the butterfly when it escapes from the chrysalis, its former organs will be thrown off only to unscale the interior senses, which had all along been there, although their existence had never been suspected.   Sensations and perceptions will be recognised as old acquaintances which were formerly supposed to belong to the body, but which will then be discovered to be the experiences of the spirit only ; so that, when we have " shuffled off this mortal coil," we shall be surprised to find how very much of our former self remains.

That spirits can communicate with spirits is a self-evident necessity, which scarcely needs to be proved, because without this the spirit would be isolated, and practically would have ceased to exist. It is more to our purpose to show that spirit is capable of impressing and being impressed by matter. This may not be very obvious to our reason, but it is happily much more obvious to our senses. Were the spirit incapable of impressing matter, its command over the body would be an impossibility; and, on the other hand, if matter had not been capable of impressing spirit, the bodily senses would convey no intelligence to the mind. It may be that nervous tissue is of all substances the most sensitive of spirit-action, as iron is of all substances the most susceptible of magnetism; but it may also be that all substances are more or less in communion with spirit, impressing and being impressed.

This correlation to matter seems to be one of the primary attributes of spirit, which analogy traces downwards even to the inorganic kingdom. Throughout the whole of God's varied administrations, there is one feature which persistently presents itself as characteristic of his government, and that is the subjection of material substances to immaterial agencies, and the corresponding ascent of the immaterial agency with every ascent of organic structure, or rather the corresponding ascent of organic structure with every ascent of immaterial agency. Inorganic matter has got its inorganic spirit to begin with, before it commences its ascent into the vegetable and animal worlds. Without gravitation, without electricity, without magnetism, or light, or heat, or chemical affinity, matter would be inorganically dead, and incapable of ascending into organic life. It is this inorganic spirit, if we may so call it, that gives life to inorganic nature, as well as accompanies it in its ascent.

To say that spiritual phenomena emerge according to law, is to assert that there is a physiology of the spirit; and, although it has not as yet been formally admitted into the list of sciences, it is by no means unlikely that we have already broken ground upon the subject in the recent discoveries of the convertibility and indestructibility of *force*—doctrines most valuable, not so much on account of their own importance, as because of their being the avenue to an entirely new field of research.

What is meant by the *convertibility* of *force* is this— light, heat, electricity, magnetism, and momentum (possibly also, chemical affinity, gravitation, and elasticity)— are all of them different modes or forms of one essential *force*. This *force* can assume any of these forms, and change from one to another without losing its identity. For example, if we have it in the form of heat, we may change it into light by concentration, or into momentum by the steam-engine. If we have it in the form of electricity, we may change it into light by the electric spark, or into heat by the attenuated wire, or into magnetism by the artificial magnet, or into momentum by the electro-magnetic engine. If we have it in the form of momentum, we may change it into light by percussion, or into electricity by the electric machine, or into heat by friction, and so on.

What is meant by the *indestructibility* of *force* is, that, as it cannot be generated from any source, so neither can it be spent, lost, or destroyed. For example, if it exist in the form of momentum, the momentum can never be destroyed, although it may be changed into some of its other forms, such as heat or electricity. If one elastic ball be struck by another of equal weight, it will fly off in the same direction, and with the same velocity, after having received its momentum; while the other ball which communicated the impulse will be at the same instant put to rest; the force being transferred from the one to the other. But if a leaden ball be shot against a rock, and thus arrested in its course, without communicating motion to the rock which it strikes, the force is not destroyed,—it is converted into heat, and the amount of heat produced will be an exact equivalent of the force expended in producing it.

There is yet one other quality of force which we must notice, and that is, its capability of being stored up in a latent or quiescent state. For example, latent force which may be stored up in steam and water, may again be developed as an active force by the steam becoming water, and the water becoming ice. Electricity also may store up force in a latent state by decomposing water. It then resides in the oxygen and hydrogen, of which the water was composed, under the form of chemical affinity, and is developed in the form of light and heat when they are again united in combustion.

But this is not all : the forces which exhibit themselves in the phenomena of inorganic matter are found to be related to the forces which are in action in living organisms. There is, therefore, another convertibility of which force is capable, by which light, heat, and electricity can be converted into another, or living force, possessing perfectly different properties, and in the production of which the original force disappears. This is proved by the fact that the new force may be reconverted into the old ; that is to say, light, heat, and electricity may be converted into living force, and living force may be re-converted into light, heat, and electricity.

The ascent which thus takes place in the translation of inorganic into organic force does not end in its vegetable form.   The force peculiar to vegetable life undergoes a still further translation into the force peculiar to animal life, and yet the same law operates ; there is no generation of force, and there is no destruction of it.   All the forces in operation in an animal body were originally light, heat, and electricity ; but it was necessary that they should undergo an intermediate change by means of the vegetable kingdom, in order to render them accessible to animal life, because animal life is unable to draw its supplies of vital energy directly from the inorganic kingdom.   Vegetables can live on light and heat—animals require the intermediate action of vegetable life to make these forces available for their support.

So far as we have gone, we are guided by observation and experiment ; another step in the same direction leads us directly to the physiology of spirit ; for if the original force of light and heat ascend by translation, first into the vegetable kingdom, and after that, by a second translation, into the animal kingdom, we have strong reason to conclude that the forces of spirit-life are only a third translation of the original force, and not the generation or creation of a new one.

It has long been an interesting question among scientific men, whether light be a material substance, or no substance at all, all its phenomena being capable of being explained on the hypothesis that it is nothing more than the effect of vibrations, or undulations, communicated to a medium supposed to exist throughout the universe. May it not be, that neither of these views is the true one, but that God has created another kind of *substance*, altogether different from matter, of which light, heat, and electricity are some of the forms—a substance which is as subject to law, as varied and invariable in its properties, and as indestructible in its essence, as matter itself?

Even supposing that light is nothing more than mechanical undulations or vibrations in the medium through which it passes, and that heat is nothing more than a mechanical rotation of the particles in which it resides, this would merely bring two of the forms into which force can be translated, under the head of mechanical momentum, which would then include sound, light, and heat. But this does not exhaust the catalogue; for besides sound, light, heat, and momentum, all of which *may* be varied states of the same form, we have also electricity, magnetism, and chemical affinity, which cannot be included in momentum. Therefore, there must be something else besides momentum or motion, because force may exist where there is no motion, and motion cannot cease to exist until it is converted into something else. There must, therefore, be a *substantive* existence under these phenomena which we attribute to force,—a substance which is quantative and divisible, as well as possessed of properties which form the laws of its being.

It is difficult, indeed, for us to conceive of force being an actual substance, distinct from matter; and, were it not for its indestructibility and transmutability, and still more for its being capable of existing for any length of time in a latent or quiescent state, it would not be necessary that

we should; but the undoubted existence of spirit substance forces us to grope in this direction; and groping,
we come upon its outskirts where nothing else can be;
and so we guess that it is there.   It is only a guess, it is
true, but it is a precious guess; because in the absence
of theory an uncontradicted hypothesis may be the pioneer
of discovery; and because it presents an opening and
avenue of thought altogether new, the contemplation of
which is itself an expansion of the mind.   Our studies in
nature are continually bringing us into contact with new
conceptions, the unexpected nature of which fills us at
first with curious surprise; which, however, after more
mature experience, ripens into reverential admiration.
The nature of spirit phenomena, leads us to anticipate
some such discovery as this; and whether force be or be
not the substance of which spirit is composed (supposing
force to have a substantive existence), spirit substance
cannot differ very widely in its attributes from those
which we have described as belonging to force.   In its
ascent from its inorganic forms into organic life, where
it assumes a *quasi* organic character (beginning with
its action in the vegetable cell of the red snow plant,
and rising upwards into the vital forces of the animal
economy), we discover a line, which, though we fail to
trace it further, points significantly to the nature and
powers of the human spirit.   It resembles spirit in being
correlative to matter without being matter itself, and
in being void of those two great characteristic properties of matter, gravitation, and impenetrability; and if
force be not only incapable of being destroyed, but also
incapable of being generated, may we not at least suspect that the physical energy possessed by the human
spirit, and exercised upon the nervous system, is elabo-

rated, first by vegetation, then by animal life, and at last receives its full development as spirit-energy?

But whether "force" be a substance or not, we have not done with the inquiry, because we must distinguish between vegetable *force* and vegetable *life*. When the *inorganic* forms of force have ascended into the higher sphere, and have been transformed into *organic* force, it never assumes more than one form at a time. But there is in the plant something more than organic force; there is *organic life*, which receives and wields that force, like a master builder, who has in his mind the entire building in all its several parts; and although he does not lay a single stone himself, there is not a single stone laid by any of the individual masons which he does not *cause to be laid*. In the plant, therefore, we have not only the organic forces, we have also the individual life which animates it, and carries on its operations according to a type of its own. It is itself the cause of organisation.

It is said that the human spirit is an immaterial substance, which is homogeneous, and not organic—that is to say, not composed of parts; and when we ask how a homogeneous substance can be capable of performing a multiplicity of functions, the answer is, that *it is itself intelligent*. But what shall we say about this vegetable life? this immaterial individuality which superintends the economy of life and growth in every plant, determining not only its structure but its habits. It cannot be homogeneous, *because it is not intelligent*. It must consist of parts; and it must itself be organic after its own fashion, in order to be the cause of organisation.

Under any hypothesis, therefore, we come to the conclusion that there is a vaiety of immaterial substances, just as there is a variety of material substances; and these substances may be either simple, or compound, or both; and, as it is much easier to suppose that there is an infinite variety of collocations than an infinite variety of elemental substances, every one of them different from every other, there is no reason why the human spirit may not be organic, notwithstanding its being immaterial.

If our spirits, then, which are generated in or with our bodies, are elaborated from *immaterial* substances into separate existences, constituting individual *spirits*, quite as truly as our bodies are elaborated from *material* substances into separate existences, constituting individual *bodies*, there appears to be no greater reason for affirming that our spirits are homogeneous than for affirming that our bodies are so.   These individual spirits must be presumed to be composed of spirit substance or substances, and possessed of different faculties, which are generically alike in all, although individually different in each. In some individuals one function is healthy and another diseased, one function strong and another weak.   Our very language implies that the human spirit is an organism composed of parts mutually related, which, though individually different, are generically the same, unless we suppose that the brain is itself the intellect, and that there is no spirit at all.   And why should the spirit not be an organism?   Matter is not the only subject capable of organisation ; because whatever is composed of parts having a mutual relation, and constituting an individual subject, is really organised.   A syllogism is organised, a poem is organised, and if even abstractions be capable of organisation, why should not a spirit, although not material, be also organised ?

It is true that in physical science we have no means of obtaining force except in and by means of matter, and,

therefore, so far as experiment is concerned, we have
never been able to organise force into a separate entity ;
but that does not prove that the thing is impossible.
There are many things done in nature which cannot be
done by art.   For example, we have never been able by
any artificial apparatus to use up more than a fraction of
the force that is lodged in fuel, whereas nature uses up
the whole.   A pound of oats eaten by a horse will give
out mechanical power far beyond what it would supply if
used as fuel.   If, therefore, in the ascent into the vegetable kingdom *matter* undergoes organic changes which
we in vain attempt to imitate by experiment, why should
we think it impossible that nature should have the power
of organising *force*, so as to constitute the various types
of vegetable and animal *life?*   If these types exist in
endless variety, as we know they do, and if they be the
appropriate causes of corresponding material organisations,
how can they themselves be inorganic ?

CHAPTER IX.

DEMONIACAL POSSESSION AND INSPIRATION.

THE light which Scripture sheds on the natural history
of the human race may be still farther increased by
an examination of the structure of the human body.   It
is a well-established doctrine of Scripture, that the body
is animated by an intelligent and immortal spirit, that
feels and acts by means of its material mechanism,
without being itself material.   We also learn from Scripture that at death the spirit is not destroyed with the
body, but separated from it, and that it is capable of

maintaining an independent existence; so that in its disembodied state it possesses a measure of consciousness and intelligence, sufficient to preserve its identity of person.

It may be desirable, but certainly it is not necessary, that we should be able to prove a doctrine by means of two distinct processes; and therefore, although our researches in anatomy might never conduct us to the necessary conclusion that there is an immortal spirit resident in every human body, it is sufficient that such a conclusion is warranted by Scripture, and is, at the same time, quite consistent with all the teachings of natural science. It may be that this admission would also involve the probability that every animate object, however low in the scale of creation, has some immaterial substance connected with it, corresponding to the human spirit; but it does not follow that these substances are immortal : on the contrary, Scripture speaks of the lower animals as "the beasts that perish," and affirms, that while the spirit of a man "goeth upwards" and returns to God who gave it, the spirit of a beast "goeth downwards." It may be that anatomy might never be able to prove such a distinction between the two natures—it is enough that it does not disprove it; and, therefore, Scripture testimony is sufficient for our purpose.

Taking for granted, then, that there is an immortal spirit distinct and separable from the body, we next inquire what light anatomy throws on their connection and action one upon the other.

On examining the human body, we find a canal running through the back-bone, filled with nervous matter, which, reaching from the brain at the top, sends out, at different places, through its entire length, cords and fila-

H

ments, which branch out, like the ramifications of a tree, over the whole body : this is called the cerebro-spinal system. It has also been found that this nervous matter consists of two distinct columns, different from one another, and discharging totally different functions. One of these columns, the posterior, consists entirely of sensitive nerves, by means of which the spirit receives impressions of things without; the other consists of motor nerves, by means of which the spirit is able to set the body in motion, by energising the muscles. It is by means of the former of these, spread over the whole body, that the spirit within receives intelligence of what is taking place without; because, by means of them the sensations of heat and cold, resistance and pain, are experienced ; and it is the same kind of nerves that communicates with the eye and the ear, although they do not pass through the vertebræ. The optic nerve passes directly from the brain into the back of the eye-ball, and spreads itself over the whole of what is called the retina, to receive the light that comes through the pupil.

The second, the anterior column of nerves, is of a totally different nature : these do not convey intelligence *to* the spirit, but they convey energy *from* the spirit to the muscles in order to produce action; they are called the motor or moving nerves, and it is by their means that the spirit is able to set the body in action.

We may regard these two columns as like the double line of rails on a railway; one line of rails carrying the trains in one direction, the other carrying them back in the opposite direction : the column of the sensitive nerves carrying despatches upwards and inwards,—the column of the motor nerves carrying the despatches downwards and outwards.

Supposing, then, that we cut across the first of these columns, the immediate consequence is, that sensation in all the parts beneath the section ceases; but while the motor column continues whole and healthy, the power of the body remains as before. It is like the cutting of the telegraphic wires, by which communication is interrupted. If, however, instead of cutting the first, we cut the second column of nervous matter, a very different result is experienced. Sensation continues as before, but voluntary motion is now impossible; the limbs are paralysed and hang loose upon the body, because the spirit has ceased to have any control over, or communication with, the muscles.

Here, then, we have a view of the residence of the human spirit, with all its furniture and conveniences provided. By means of the brain and the spinal cord, the spirit becomes an embodied person, observant and active, holding converse with external nature. Without such an apparatus it would be an agent mysterious and unknown.

The spirit that is generated with or from its own body will naturally fit it best; and yet we find that other spirits are capable of affecting, or even taking possession of, bodies, which are not their own. This susceptibility gives rise to different kinds of phenomena, which have been observed in all ages and in all countries, but which have been so mixed up with fable and imposture, that it would be difficult to obtain any certain information regarding them, were it not that in Scripture we have sufficient materials for the purpose; and these being authenticated by inspiration, may be used to throw light upon the corresponding passages of ancient and even modern history.

DEMONIACAL POSSESSION.

The most aggravated form of spirit influence is that of demoniacal possession, in which the alien spirit usurps the place of a man's own spirit, receiving impressions from his nerves of sensation, and throwing the body into action by means of the motor nerves and muscles. This kind of possession appears to have been prevalent and of no ordinary severity during the ministry of our Lord and His apostles, attacking alike men, women, and children.

1. The first thing we have to notice in regard to demoniacal possession, is the name uniformly given to the unclean spirits. The word devil, which occurs so frequently in our English Testament, is the translation given to two very different Greek words, which have not the same meaning, and which are never used interchangeably, the one for the other. The first is *daimōn* or *daimonion*, or, as we call it in English, *demon ;* the other is *diabolos*, which is truly translated "devil." The word *diabolos* is never used in the plural. It is the name of an individual, not a class. There are many demons, but there is only one devil. In all the cases of demoniacal possession, the unclean spirit is called a demon, never a devil. This distinction is important because of the word demon being found in profane history, as the name given to spiritual beings, which are not so repulsive nor so malignant as those described in the New Testament.

2. Another observation presents itself in regard to the comparative malignity or wickedness of these spirits. Some, probably, were comparatively harmless, such as the spirit of infirmity by whom Satan had bound a poor daughter of Abraham eighteen years (Luke xiii. 11 ; or the blind and dumb demoniac (Matt. xii. 22), whose only

sufferings appear to have been the inability to see and speak. A difference in wickedness is expressly asserted in the case of the demon who took seven other spirits *more wicked than himself*, to the house which he had previously left; and in the case of the demoniac whom the disciples could not cure, we have a fearful instance, not only of the desperate malignity of a particular kind of demon, but of his power to resist all efforts to expel him, unless accompanied by great faith as well as fasting and prayer.

3. It would appear, that in the more violent cases of possession (and it may be more or less in them all) the attacks came on in fits, after intervals of comparative repose. In that remarkable case to which we have just referred, we find the father saying, " Lo, a spirit *taketh* him, and he *suddenly* crieth out; and it teareth him, that he foameth again; and, bruising him, hardly *departeth from him* " (Luke ix. 39); and again, "Wheresoever he taketh him, he teareth him; and, he foameth, and gnasheth with his teeth, *and pineth away* " (Mark ix. 18). We have also indirect evidence of these alternations in the case of Legion : " He had often been bound with fetters and chains " (Mark v. 4), evidently when prostrated by exhaustion after the fits; " but oftentimes the demons *caught him* " (Luke viii. 29), and then " the chains were plucked asunder by him, and the fetters broken in pieces " (Mark v. 4).

4. We next observe the symptoms which these possessions exhibited :—*First*, There were hatred and enmity towards mankind, living without clothes night and day in the mountains, or dwelling among the tombs, " exceeding fierce, so that no man might pass that way." *Second*, There was fear and antagonism towards God and Christ

as in the case of the demoniac who, seeing Jesus, ex-
claimed, " What have I to do with thee ? "   " Art thou
come to destroy us ? "   Art thou come to torment us before
the time ? "   " I adjure thee by God that thou torment us
not."   *Third,* There was passive misery, exhibited in
howling, even when the spirit was dumb, wallowing on
the ground, foaming, gnashing the teeth.   *Fourth,* There
was extreme violence of action.   One was driven into the
wilderness—no man could tame him ; and the swine into
which the legion entered ran violently down into the sea.
Fifth, There was malignant cruelty towards the person
possessed.   Nearly all the victims appear to have been
" sorely vexed : " one was in the habit of cutting himself
with stones ; another was thrown down, and torn, and
bruised, besides being ofttimes cast into the fire and into
the water, that he might be destroyed.   And *sixth,* It
appears that when the devils were cast out, the immediate effect in two cases was exhaustion.   The daughter
of the Canaanitish woman, although made whole at the
very moment when our Lord said, " The demon is gone
out of thy daughter," was so prostrated, that when the
mother arrived at her own house, she found that the
demon had indeed gone out, but her daughter was " laid
upon the bed."   And again, when our Lord cast out the
malignant demon from the boy, we are told, " he was as
one dead, insomuch that many said, He is dead."

5. A remarkable doctrine is brought out regarding
what may be called the physical constitution of these
unclean spirits.   They were able to occupy the same body
or nervous system, in considerable numbers.   Besides the
proper spirit of the man himself, not only do we find one
demon sharing or disputing the habitation or government
of the body, but, in the case of Mary Magdalene, seven

demons; in another case, eight; and in a third, not fewer than several thousands. It is interesting also to observe the physiological effects produced by the concentrated spiritual influence of these demons, first on the man, and afterwards on the two thousand swine.

6. The circumstance that they were able to possess the nervous system of the swine, leads us also to conclude that if the nervous system of the lower animals be so constructed as to be capable of receiving impressions from spirit, there is probably some spiritual substance connected with the lower animals, though it may not be capable of separate existence.

7. We are informed that the demons earnestly desired that Christ would not send them out into the "abyss," but allow them to enter into the swine. From this it would appear that there is some kind of gratification enjoyed by a spirit in the habitation of a body. This is illustrated in the parable of the unclean spirit, which, when it went forth from the man, is said to have walked in dry places, like a wanderer in a thirsty, barren land. On returning, however, to its old habitation, it took with it seven other spirits, and they entered and dwelt there. This natural appetite for a bodily tabernacle may probably proceed from one of two causes: either that the functions of the spirit cannot rightly be exercised, except upon, or by means of, a nervous system; or because the incubation of a nervous system provides some kind of nourishment or vitality elaborated by the body, without which possibly the spirit may lapse into a dormant or suffering state.

DEMONIACAL INSPIRATION.

Another kind of possession is prophetic ecstasy, or demoniacal inspiration. It does not appear to differ very much in its nature from simple possession, perhaps not at all, except in the disposition of the indwelling spirit and the periods of its manifestation.

There does not seem to be any malevolence exhibited by the demon in the transports into which the prophet is thrown; and although there may be a peculiarity of constitution which makes him more susceptible of spiritual influence than others, it appears as if there must be some sort of consent, or even solicitation, on his part to permit or induce the spirit to deliver his responses or manifest his presence.

It is the fashion of the present day to ascribe to imposture or fanaticism all pretences to spiritual manifestations of whatever kind; and it is somewhat remarkable that this Sadducean philosophy is most prevalent among scientific men. This is to be accounted for, not by any natural tendency which the inductive philosophy has towards materialism, but by the lingering influence of the old " a priori " method of disposing of a question, not by impartially balancing the evidence, but by anticipating a conclusion, and then endeavouring to explain the phenomena in accordance with it as best they can.

It is by no means improbable that many, perhaps the great majority, of pretenders to spiritual communications in ancient or modern times are imposters or fanatics; but it does not follow that all of them are so. We may indeed believe that Divine inspiration ceased at the close of the apostolic age; but it would be difficult to show that demoniacal inspiration had any canonical period, or that any age has been exempt from its influence.

If soothsaying be an imposture rather than in its own nature a crime, Scripture certainly does not say so; but, on the contrary, speaks as if there were only too much reality in the profession.

Perhaps the most remarkable instance of this species of demoniacal influence is that recorded in Acts xvi. 16:—"And it came to pass, as we went to prayer, a certain damsel possessed with a spirit of divination (*pneuma Puthōnos*) met us, which brought her masters much gain by soothsaying.

The same followed Paul and us, and cried, saying, These men are the servants of the Most High God, which show unto us the way of salvation.

And this she did many days. But Paul, being grieved, turned, and said to the spirit, I command thee, in the name of Jesus Christ, to come out of her. And he came out the same hour.

And when her masters saw that the hope of their gains was gone, they caught Paul and Silas, and drew them into the market-place unto the rulers."

It is evident that, in the case of this woman, there was no deception nor collusion. The woman and her masters professed that she had a spirit of divination; this fact was not denied, but acknowledged by Paul; the spirit (like others mentioned in the Gospels) bore testimony to the truth; Paul, in expelling him, exorcised him in the name of Jesus Christ; and, lastly, the spirit came out the same hour, so that the hope of her masters' gains was gone.

The name given to this spirit (for it is called a spirit of Python) invests this narrative with a deep interest, inasmuch as it forms a sort of connecting link between the heathen oracles of profane history and the demoniacal possessions described in the New Testament. The name Python is not a Scripture name, but, like Jupiter and Mercury mentioned in the Acts, belongs to the heathen mythology of Greece and Rome; and therefore we must turn to the classic writers of those countries for an explanation. From them we learn that the spirit of Python was no other than the Pythian Apollo, whose temple was at Delphi, not very far distant, and whose inspirations there brought much gain to the priests: in other words, the Pythian Apollo was the great spirit of divination or soothsaying, celebrated throughout the heathen world, and his responses were given by means of a woman, who was called the Pythia. The following is the account given by Lemprière in his Classical Dictionary :—

"PYTHIA, the priestess of Apollo at Delphi.—She delivered the answer of the god to such as came to consult the oracle, and was supposed to be suddenly inspired by the sulphureous vapours which issued from the hole of a subterraneous cavity within the temple, over which she sat. Vapour was inhaled by the priestess, and at this divine inspiration her eyes suddenly sparkled, her hair stood on end, and a shivering ran over all her body. In this convulsive state she spoke the oracles of the god, often with loud howlings and cries, and her articulations were taken down by the priest, and set in order. Sometimes the spirit of inspiration was more gentle, and not always violent; yet Plutarch mentions one of the priestesses, who was thrown into such an excessive fury, that not only those that consulted the oracle, but also the priests that conducted her to the sacred tripod, and attended her during the inspiration, were terrified, and forsook the temple; and so violent was the fit, that she continued for three days in the most agonising situation, and at last died. The Pythia, before she placed herself on the tripod, used to wash her whole body, and particularly her hair, in the waters of the fountain Castalis, at the foot of Mount Parnassus. She also shook a laurel-tree that grew near the place, and sometimes ate the leaves with which she crowned herself. The priestess was originally a virgin, but the institution was changed when Echecrates, a Thessalian, had offered violence to one of them, and none but women above the age of fifty were permitted to enter upon the sacred office. They always dressed in the garments of virgins, to intimate their purity and chastity; and they were solemnly bound to observe the strictest laws of temperance and chastity, that neither fantastical dresses nor lascivious behaviour might bring the office, the religion, or the sanctity of the place into contempt. There was originally but one Pythia, besides subordinate priests, and afterwards two were chosen, and sometimes more. The most celebrated of these is Phemonoe, who is supposed by some to have been the first to give oracles at Delphi. The oracles were always delivered in hexameter verses, a custom which was sometime after discontinued. The Pythia was consulted only one month in the year, about the spring. It was always required that those who consulted the oracles should make large presents to Apollo, and from thence arose the opulence, splendour, and magnificence of that celebrated temple of Delphi. Sacrifices were also offered to the divinity, and if the omen proved unfavourable, the priestesses refused to give an answer. There were generally five priests who assisted at the offering of the sacrifices, and there was also another, who attended the Pythia, and assisted her in receiving the oracle."

With this historical explanation, we have no difficulty in understanding the circumstances of Paul's miracle in exorcising the woman. As the event did not take place in Delphi, and as the spirit was called, notwithstanding, a spirit of Python, which, according to the Greek idiom, may be as well translated a Pythian spirit (indeed, some readings give us *pneuma puthōna*), we must conclude that this woman was possessed in exactly the same manner as the Pythoness at Delphi, although she was not connected with that institution. The description given by Luke corresponds sufficiently with the statements collected by Lemprière, to show that the one was related to the other in something more than the name; and if so, we are not warranted in supposing that the oracle at Delphi was a trick or an imposture; it was a demoniacal inspiration, and the responses which were given were the deliverances of demons. This opinion is confirmed so far by the fact, that at least upon the one occasion mentioned above by Lemprière, on the authority of Plutarch, the possession was very much akin to the demoniacal possessions described in the New Testament.

Paul himself appeared to entertain no doubt regarding the demoniacal nature of the heathen gods; for although he says that an idol (*eidōlon*), or image, is nothing in the world (1 Cor. viii. 4), yet he affirms (1 Cor. x. 20), that the things which the Gentiles sacrifice, they sacrifice to demons, and not to God. The following passages in the Old Testament present the same explanation :—

Lev. xvii. 7. And they shall no more offer their sacrifices unto devils, after whom they have gone a whoring.

Deut. xxxii. 17. They sacrificed unto devils, not to God; to gods whom they knew not, to new gods that came newly up, whom your fathers feared not, See also 2 Chron. xi. 15, and Ps. cvi. 37.

Even the heathens themselves identify their gods with demons. For example, in Herodotus we find the following passage :—

Ye Scythians ridicule us because we celebrate the Bacchanals, and the god possesses us (*ho theos lambanei*), but now the same demon (*houtos ho daimōn*) hath taken possession of your king.

The following passages of Scripture, besides many others of the same kind, appear to bear upon this subject :—

A man also, or woman, that hath a familiar spirit, or that is a wizard, shall surely be put to death (Lev. xx. 27).

There shall not be found among you any that . . . useth divination, or an observer of times, or an enchanter, or a witch, or a charmer, or a consulter with familiar spirits; or a wizard, or a necromancer. For all that do these things are an abomination unto the Lord : and because of these abominations the Lord thy God doth drive them out from before thee (Deut. xviii. 10-12).

And Manasseh . . . used enchantments, and used witchcraft, and dealt with a familiar spirit, and with wizards (2 Chron. xxxiii. 6).

Thou shalt be brought down, and shalt speak out of the ground, and thy speech shall be low out of the dust, and thy voice shall be, as of one that hath a familiar spirit, out of the ground, and thy speech shall whisper (*Hebrew*, peep or chirp) out of the dust (Isa. xxix. 4).

But there was a certain man, called Simon, which beforetime in the city used sorcery, and bewitched the people of Samaria (Acts viii. 9).

When they had gone through the isle unto Paphos,

they found a certain sorcerer, a false prophet, a Jew,
whose name was Barjesus (Acts xiii. 6).

Many of them also which used curious arts, brought
their books together, and burned them before all men :
and they counted the price of them, and found it fifty
thousand pieces of silver (Acts xix. 19).

Now the works of the flesh are manifest,—idolatry,
witchcraft (Gal. v. 19, 20).   See also 2 Kings xxiii. 24,
and Micah v. 12.

The scientific value of these passages is much increased
by the account given of the Pythoness in the Acts of the
Apostles, chap. xvi. 16, which establishes the following
propositions :—

First, Soothsaying and possession, or inspiration by a
familiar spirit, is not necessarily or in all instances an
imposture.   The damsel really had a familiar spirit, and
Paul really cast him out.

Second, By means of the familiar spirit the soothsayer
is able to communicate information, known to the demon,
though it may not be known to men.   This is proved.
not so much by the damsel crying out, "These men are
the servants of the Most High God, which show unto us
the way of salvation," as by the lucrative business which
her masters had established by her means, and its entire
failure when the spirit was cast out.   "Her masters saw
that the hope of their gains was gone," whereas, previously, she had brought them much gain by soothsaying:
and,

Third, The name given to this spirit, "a spirit of
Python," and the place where the event occurred—viz.,
Greece, connect this instance of inspiration with the other
heathen oracles of Greece, particularly the Delphic oracle
and its Pythonesses.

If these propositions be established, the other passages which refer to soothsaying and familiar spirits assume a scientific importance which they would not otherwise possess. Instead of having reference to impostures and superstitions, they stand out before us as evidence of the existence of real crimes; so that the details which are given regarding them may be considered as truly descriptive of their nature and their objects. As regards the other practices of charming, enchanting, necromancy, and prognostication, we have no means of knowing whether or how far they were connected with demoniacal agency, and how far they were fictitious—the products of deceiving and deceived minds. No doubt the spirits with whom intercourse was cultivated, did know many things, and guessed many things, which superior knowledge, and even moderate ingenuity and foresight, might pass off as pretended prophecy; there might even be physical effects which disembodied spirits were able to produce, the nature of which we cannot understand, so long as we do not understand the nature and functions of spirits. All this might be so combined and played off by wicked men, in concert with wicked spirits, as to deceive and impose upon an ignorant and depraved population. But to conclude that there must be *in these cases* any such thing as miraculous foreknowledge or magic, or astrology, as we understand them, would be to impose upon the passages referring to them an interpretation which they do not necessarily bear.

We must next observe that not every one was capable of being a soothsayer or prophet—a certain peculiarity of constitution or temperament being required. In some, this peculiarity might be natural, in others it might be acquired; in all, the exercise of it appears to have been

more or less subject to the will; otherwise the punishment of death would have been not only barbarous, but
futile.

It would appear that, generally speaking, the familiar
spirit did not inspire the soothsayer, or give any response,
unless he was invited or solicited to do so; and it would
also seem that, for this purpose, some act or process was
necessary; and on this act or process being completed, the
inspiration was expected to follow.

It was evidently a knowledge of these methods that
constituted the art and literature of soothsaying, prescrib-
ing how the intended soothsayer might render himself
more susceptible of spirit influence, and also how he might
invite, or perhaps even command, the services of particular
spirits. No doubt, there must have been great proficients
in the art, and many books must have been written upon
the subject. May we not suppose that the books burned
by the Ephesian converts (Acts xix. 19) were of this kind?
for, had the "curious arts" which were so assiduously
cultivated in Ephesus been merely feats of legerdemain
and imposture, their converted owners would rather have
published them to the world, and thus have exposed the
deceit that had been practised. Their burning of these
books proved that the knowledge of these arts would not
abolish them, but rather spread the contagion of their
influence.

The state of the soothsayer, while under inspiration,
appears to have been one of great excitement, or even of
frenzy. The imaginative faculties were exalted, the utter-
ances being highly figurative and poetical. This, indeed,
appears to have been to some extent, the natural origin
of poetry, which was an imitation of spiritual inspiration.
The Latin word *vates* means both a prophet and a poet,

and probably there was, at one time, something more than fiction in the customary invocation of the muse or the god of poetry. It is an interesting circumstance that the responses of Apollo at Delphi were, at one time, always delivered in hexameter verses—not very polished, and not always intelligible. Even the heathen critics remarked that the god of poetry was decidedly the worst poet of the age ; and it was in consequence of this fact becoming somewhat notorious that the practice was discontinued.

CHAPTER X.

ANGELS AND MEN ONE SPECIES.

IN the book of God we are introduced to three, and only three, great types of intelligent and moral beings, Angels, Devils, and Men; and these, though possessing many attributes in common, differ very widely in their physical constitution. A careful examination, however, of the various statements regarding them, contained in Scripture, leads us to the conclusion that, like the worm, the chrysalis, and the butterfly, they are only different states or stages in the development of the same species ; and that throughout the universe there is but one type and one law of development among the sons of God.

In Adam we have a specimen of the species in its primary state, possessing the natural or animal body, the *corpus animale* or " *sōma psuchikon* " of Paul, by means of which propagation takes place; and in this state man is capable of undergoing one of two transformations, according to circumstances. As one alternative, he is

I

capable of throwing off the body by death, and becoming a disembodied spirit, like the devils; or he is capable of being changed either gradually, or " in a moment, in the twinkling of an eye," into his complete development, possessing a spiritual body (the " *sōma pneumaticon* " of Paul), like the celestial bodies of the angels of heaven.

The peculiarity of the Adamic race seems to be, that in its two sections it experiences both changes; because in the case of the lost, the naked spirit is cast forth into the deep, like the demons; and in the case of the saved, the attainment of the spiritual body is accomplished, not by a spontaneous and normal development according to its original constitution, but by an exceptional arrangement, through which the children of the resurrection become " equal to the angels."

When, therefore, God said, Let us make man in our own image, sin and death did not form any part of his original programme. Adam was, indeed, created with the natural body, but Paul tells us that there is also a spiritual body, and that the progression is—" first, the natural body, and afterwards that which is spiritual."

Although the Bible was not given to us to gratify curiosity, or to give lessons in natural science, it could not deliver its message without informing us of this; and, in order to give us *some* idea of the spiritual body which Christ has promised us, He has, on various occasions, sent *perfect* men to show us what they are like, and to enable us to lift up our thoughts above our present humiliation, and contemplate the glorious change that awaits us when we shall be equal to the angels.

Beyond the fact that the angels have spiritual bodies, and are from heaven, the Scripture does not warrant the supposition that their nature is in the slightest degree

different from our own.   The word angel does not imply
any constitutional difference, as in our language it seems
to do.   It expresses an office, not the distinction of a
species, and is applied to men in the natural body as well
as in the spiritual.   The word " messenger," when it
occurs in the New Testament (except in two passages,
where it should not be so translated), is no other than the
word " angel."   John the Baptist is thrice called an
angelos—Matt. xi. 10 ; Mark i. 2 ; and Luke vii. 27 ;
and the messengers whom he sent to Christ when he
was in prison were called *angeloi*, Luke vii. 24.   The
spies that were lodged in Rahab's house were *angeloi*,
James ii. 25 ; and when Christ set His face steadfastly
to go to Jerusalem, He sent *angeloi* into the village of
the Samaritans to make ready for Him, Luke ix. 52.

But if men are called angels in Scripture, angels are
much more frequently called men.   They were not mere
optical illusions, deluding men's senses, and appearing
to be what they really were not.   Scripture, it will be
observed, never casts doubts on the evidence of the senses,
because it is the highest which we possess.   It does indeed inform us that there are many things around us
which we do *not* see ; and, in order to reveal that which
cannot be perceived by the senses, visions and dreams are
superadded : but we never find any suspicion cast on the
evidence of the senses.   Their testimony is sacred, and
is always appealed to as the basis on which all revealed
religion rests, so that if that be shaken, all must go.
" That which we have heard, which we have seen with
our eyes, which we have looked upon, and our hands have
handled, of the Word of life ; that which we have seen
and heard declare we unto you."   This was the ground
of the beloved apostle's testimony, and Christ Himself

appeals to the evidence of sense in proof of His resurrection, when He says, " Handle me and see, for a spirit hath not flesh and bones as ye see me have." What better proof, then, can we have that the angels have flesh and bones, than that they were handled, and seen, and heard by men and women, who could not be mistaken as to the reality of their bodies, although for a time they were mistaken in supposing that they were ordinary men?

It will be hereafter shown that the devils are disembodied spirits; and though we are informed that they are the " angels" that kept not their first estate, this does not prove that angels are spirits only. We must not hastily conclude that angels are unembodied spirits, like the devils, because in one passage it is said that they are all " *ministering spirits.*" The emphasis lies not on the word " spirits," but on the word " ministering," just as in the corresponding passage Christ is said to be a " *quickening spirit* "—the emphasis lying on the word " quickening," not on the word " spirit." In both cases the word spirit is not without deep meaning, although that meaning is shrouded in our English translation. It will be observed that in the case of Christ, He is contrasted with Adam, and as Christ is called a spirit so is Adam called a soul, and yet both had bodies. The angels are called spirits, Christ is called a spirit, and Adam is called a soul; but a soul is as immaterial as a spirit, and therefore any argument drawn from the expression "ministering spirits," to show that angels have no bodies, would be equally effectual to prove that Adam was a soul without a body, and that Christ was a spirit and nothing more. In the verse immediately preceding, we have the key to both passages, 1 Cor. xv. 44—" It is sown a natural body, it is raised a spiritual body. There is a natural body, and there is a spiritual body." The word "natural body" ought to have been translated "soul-body," because we have no adjective in English for *soul* corresponding with the adjective spiritual for *spirit*. Perhaps the most intelligible rendering which we could give to the passage would be by converting the words soul and spirit into adjectives in the 44th verse, and then reconverting them into substantives in the 45th, thus,—" It is sown a *soul*-body, it is raised a *spirit*-body. There is a *soul*-body, and there is a *spirit*-body. And so it is written, The first man Adam was made a living *soul*, the last Adam was made a quickening *spirit*." Here, then, we have an explanation of the words "ministering *spirits*" as applied to angels. It means that they have not soul-bodies, but spirit-bodies; so that as Adam was a *living soul*, because he was possessed of a soul-body, the angels are called *ministering spirits*, because they are possessed of spirit-bodies.

This shows the danger of building scientific conclusions on the mere words of Scripture : it is the facts and arguments alone that will safely bear them; and turning to facts, we have the most convincing proofs that the angels are possessed of bodies as real as our own. We have said that angels are much more frequently called men than men are called angels; because if we look at those passages in which the missions of angels are recorded, we shall find not only that the acts and experiences of the angels are sufficient to prove that they are real men, but that the very name "men" is applied to them, as being appropriate to their nature.

For example, the first recorded visit of angels to the Old Testament saints is to be found in the 18th chapter of Genesis, and there they are introduced at once as men :—" Abraham lifted up his eyes and looked, and lo,

three *men* stood by him;" and throughout the whole
narrative they are uniformly called men, and never angels.

Their actions, too, proved that they were men, and if
in any of their actions a super-natural power is exerted,
it was only because they had super-natural bodies—that
is to say, they had " spiritual bodies; " for as our natural
bodies are sown in corruption and weakness, and raised
in incorruption and in power, so these " men " possessed
of spiritual bodies, were already endowed with incorruption and with power. And yet these spiritual bodies
spoke and walked, and ate and were handled, like other
men. They rested under the tree; they permitted
Abraham to wash their feet; they allowed Sarah to bake
upon the hearth cakes of three measures of meal, and
Abraham to kill a calf, tender and good, for their refresh-
ment; and when all was prepared, Abraham brought the
calf and the cakes, and butter and milk besides, and set
them before them, AND THEY DID EAT. We must be
careful how we reject evidence of this kind, lest in doing
so we destroy the evidence of by far the most important
dogma of the Christian faith. What evidence have we
of the resurrection of Jesus Christ, if the testimony of the
senses be rejected? and if Christ be not risen, then is our
faith vain. What evidence have we of the resurrection
of Christ but that of the senses? He was seen, He was
heard, He was handled; what more convincing proof
could there be? He said, " Handle me and see, for a
spirit hath not flesh and bones as ye see me have." And
while they believed not for joy, He said unto them,
" Have ye here any meat? " And now comes the crown-
ing evidence. " They gave Him a piece of a broiled fish
and of an honeycomb, AND HE DID EAT BEFORE THEM."
And why did He eat? Not because He was hungry or

needed food, but to give the most convincing evidence that could be given that He had a real body. They might be foolish enough to think that a spirit might speak and walk and be handled like mortal men, but none of them could be so foolish as to suppose that a spirit could eat a piece of a broiled fish and honeycomb. Surely that which was sufficient to prove that Christ had a real body of flesh and bones, was sufficient to prove that angels also are possessed of the same.

We have not the slightest warrant in Scripture for believing that there are any created spirits without bodies where there has been no death; and there can be no death where there has been no sin. We do not affirm that there are no unfallen spirits; we merely say that we have no warrant in Scripture for believing that there are. Heaven is not a phantom locality, like the heathen Elysium or the Mohammedan paradise. It is a real locality, to which Christ ascended with a real body, accompanied with the saints that rose after His resurrection. It is the world upon which the angels with their spiritual bodies have been dwelling for thousands of years, with Enoch and Elijah, and it is yet destined to receive a multitude of resurrection saints whom no man can number. The popular superstition which converts the metaphoric language of Scripture into something between substance and nonsense—spirit mansions and spirit fields and spirit golden streets, and spirit palms and spirit harps and spirit trees of life—is a delusion and a travestie on majestic realities revealed in metaphoric language, only because they could not otherwise be communicated. A spirit heaven and a spirit hierarchy are a dream and an impossibility. There never were spirit mountains or spirit

rivers, or anything out of which could be manufactured
spirit harps that would give out spirit sounds. There are
spirits, but God did not make them so : they became
spirits because of their sin; for if they had not sinned
they should never have died. As a human skeleton is
the produce of sin and death so also is a disembodied
spirit, because neither of them could have existed if sin
and death had been unknown. There are unembodied
spirits, but instead of being of a higher order, they are in
reality of a lower, or rather, they are the abnormal products of a fall. Who will say that the devils belong to a
higher species than the angels, or the resurrection saints,
or the Son of God Himself, who sits, a real and living man,
the son of Abraham, the son of David, upon the throne of
the universe ? If an unembodied spirit be higher in the
scale of creation than a being having a spiritual body,
then the dead are higher now than they shall be hereafter,
and would be reduced to an inferior state of existence
by means of the resurrection.

  Observe how the argument stands. Angels and devils
were once alike in nature; how unreasonable is it to suppose that the unclean spirits alone have kept their first
estate, and continued to be spirits; whereas the angels of
heaven have fallen from their high estate, and having become like men with bodies, have been mistaken for men,
and been entertained unawares? If the constitution of
the angels and the devils was at one time identical, and
if the angels have not been degraded in their constitution,
then it necessarily follows that the devils at one time had
bodies, and that they walked, and spoke, and ate like men
—and this is something very near the truth; but it must
be supplemented : the bodies which they had were soul-
bodies, like our own; and because they sinned, they died;

and now their disembodied spirits remain upon the planet which their sins defiled; and those geological discoveries of ancient humanity which have recently awakened so much interest in the scientific world, may have also a theological value in confirming this view of Satanic natural history.

But besides the positive evidence of the non-spirituality of angels, there is also negative evidence, which is even more conclusive. We never find an angel inhabiting the bodies of men, either for good or evil. It is somewhat remarkable that the unclean spirits are found to fit into the organism of our natural bodies exactly in the same manner as our own spirits do, influencing their actions, and in many instances using the bodies of living men as if they were their own: in fact, a disembodied spirit, ejected by death from its own proper "habitation," and earnestly desiring to be clothed upon, could not be conceived to be in any respect different from these unclean spirits, either in their nature or their habits. Their physical correspondence with the vertebrate physiology of the human body is further illustrated by their entering and energising the bodies of the swine at Gadara; although it is evident, from the catastrophe that followed, that the difference was too great, and that the attempt was a failure. They succeeded in obtaining a lodgment, but they found that the bodies of the swine did not sufficiently correspond with their spirit functions to enable them to direct or control their movements. They got into the saddle, as it were, but could not grasp the reins. Spirits such as they fitted the human body, but not the bodies of the swine; and accordingly, the moment they took possession, the frightened animals ran down a steep place into the sea, and were choked in the waters—a consummation which the unclean spirits evidently did not anticipate, and which would issue in their being again unclothed. Here, then, we see that the natural constitution of the spirits fits them for entering into the bodies of men, and sharing with their own proper spirit the government and use of the body. It is, in fact, an appetite which their imperfect nature must ever feel : fearing to be cast out into the deep; seeking rest in human organisms, and disappointed when they cannot find it. This is according to the nature of a spirit, but where do we find anything of this kind in the angel?　There is no more appearance of an angel being able to possess a man, than of one man being able to dwell in the body of another.

It is of great importance to ascertain that the angels have spiritual bodies, because we are told that at the resurrection we shall be " equal to the angels;" and unless we had testimony regarding the appearance, powers, and capabilities of the angels, we should not have been able to form any conception of the nature of the resurrection bodies of the saints. It is true that we have, in the resurrection body of Christ, a little information upon this point; and yet it is only a little. It is well that it should be supplemented by all that the Old Testament and New Testament history tells us of the angels; and it is the more valuable, because there is a remarkable coincidence in the phenomena. We are told that our resurrection bodies are to be like His. " Our mortal bodies shall be fashioned like unto His glorious body," and " we shall be like Him, for we shall see Him as He is." His entering the room where the disciples were assembled for fear of the Jews, when the doors were shut, corresponds with the entry of the angel into the prison where Peter lay bound. His vanishing out of the disciples' sight corresponds with the vanishing of the angel from the sight of Gideon ; and His ascent into heaven from the Mount of Olives corresponds with the ascent of the angel in the smoke of the sacrifice of Manoah.

What a glorious prospect does this present of the future inheritance of the redeemed ! With bodies possessed of angelic powers and immortality, and, like Gabriel, capable of passing from world to world in the service of their Master, the whole universe in all its grandeur and beauty is thrown open to them during the endless ages of eternity.[*] How do our present attainments and opportunities sink into insignificance when compared with this ! and how sad the case of those men of science who, after having got a glimpse of the glories of creation, have to bid them an eternal adieu when they lie down to die !

CHAPTER XI.

THE DISEMBODIED STATE.

IT is very remarkable that, although Scripture speaks very plainly and very fully regarding the coming of Christ and the resurrection of the saints, so that we have no difficulty in understanding the general character of the changes which are to take place on that great day, there is no such information accorded to us regarding the spirit in its intermediate state between death and the resurrection. It would appear that, however blissful may be the experience of those who die in the Lord, we are at present altogether incapable of understanding its nature. The resurrection state, with its spiritual body, though

* See Appendix.

grandly superior to the mere animal state in which we at present exist, is nevertheless perfectly intelligible in its high powers of life and immortality; and we have in the resurrection body of Christ, and the spiritual bodies of the angels, examples and illustrations of what we shall hereafter be when mortality is swallowed up of life. But the disembodied state with its sensations and longings, its modes of communication and employments, its incubations and joint possessions—in short, its whole style of being—is so utterly unknowable in our present state, that to have described it, would only have been to alienate our sympathies, without conveying any true understanding of its nature. For this reason, metaphor and parable alone are employed to convey to us information; and yet these are so evidently figurative as to forbid any attempt to apply to them a literal interpretation. The parable of the rich man and Lazarus, for example, is drawn in lines of light and fire that dazzle and terrify, yet forbid the profanation of a literal understanding of its truths. The feast and the flames, the tongue and the finger, the water and the gulf, are all evidently borrowed from the things of time and sense; but they have their counterpart in realities of which we are entirely ignorant. Nor need we wonder that it should be so, when we consider, that the intermediate disembodied state is abnormal in its nature, and in that respect different both from our present state of existence in the animal body, and our future state of existence in the spiritual.

In the previous chapters we have endeavoured to trace the natural history of the human species, or rather, we may say, the natural history of the sons of God created in His image; for there is reason to believe that the Adamic race is only one of a large class of intelligent and moral beings scattered over the universe, whose constitution is everywhere the same, although their history may be different. The first state of each individual is the animal or soul state—which was the state in which Adam was created, and continued to exist up to the time of his death. We have found that this natural or animal state provided for the propagation of the species, and also for the ripening for, and ultimate development of, the spiritual state which is immortal. "He who hath wrought us for that self same thing is God." But in all this there was no provision made for such an event as the fall; so that, when sin entered into the world, and death by sin, it was a calamity all the more frightful because of the immortality of the spirit. Death among the lower animals was a physical and constitutional necessity, clothed in no terrors and armed with no sting; but when death broke out among the sons of God, and wrecked their constitution, by degrading it to a level with that of the beasts that perish, their immortal spirits shrank from the dreadful thought that, when this earthly house of their tabernacle was dissolved, they should be cast out naked and abject from its ruins into a state of homeless and hopeless destitution. The misery of a fallen spirit is an inevitable necessity, even though there were no hell and no judgment to come.

From the information contained in the New Testament regarding unclean spirits, we discover that the disembodied spirit does not, as many suppose, fall into a state of sleep or unconsciousness, from which it awakes only at the resurrection. The disembodied spirit is evidently a personal and conscious being; as personal and as conscious as when it was in the flesh; perhaps more so. Throughout all the narratives of the New Testament they are represented as personal and active agents, communicating with one another, and acting with much energy on their own behalf. "When the unclean spirit is gone out of a man, he walketh through dry places, seeking rest, and findeth none. Then he saith, I will return into my house from whence I came out; and when he is come, he findeth it empty, swept, and garnished. Then goeth he, and taketh with himself seven other spirits more wicked than himself, and they enter in and dwell there : and the last state of that man is worse than the first " (Matt. xii. 43). This passage is, indeed, a parable; but it must be understood literally. It stands in the same position as the parable of the sower, or the barren fig-tree, or the hiring of the labourers, and must, therefore, be an incident of common occurrence. We learn from it, *firstly*, that the spirit in its disembodied state is capable of conscious existence and locomotion; *secondly*, that it is able to communicate with other spirits by means of which we have at present no conception; *thirdly*, that the human body is a dwelling-place naturally fitted to give rest and shelter to disembodied spirits; and *fourthly*, that more than one spirit can reside in it at the same time. These we must suppose to be the attributes not of the demons only, but of all disembodied spirits, whether of our own race or of any other.

The little that Scripture does reveal regarding the intermediate state between death and the resurrection has been obscured, not only by the various names given in Scripture to the abodes of the disembodied spirits, but by the very loose way in which our English version has translated them, sometimes translating one Greek word by different English words, and at other times translating different Greek words by the same English; so also with the Hebrew. We shall endeavour to explicate them;

and in order to do so, we must, in the first place, discard
the English word " hell," which our translators have
ruined by applying to no less than three different Greek
words—Hades, Gehenna, and Tartarus,—all of which are
different from one another.

In the first place, Our Lord's reply to the penitent
thief supplies us with a valuable key to the interpretation of other passages. " This day," said He, " shalt
thou be with me in Paradise." Paradise, then, was the
name which He gave to the place where He was to meet
the redeemed spirit of the suppliant thief; and from this
we infer, that after death our Lord went to the same
place where the redeemed spirits of the Old Testament
saints went after death: consequently all the names which
are given to the place where our Lord went after death,
may be applied to the place where the Old Testament
saints went.

Now there are four names given to the place where
our Lord went after death : (1.) *"The heart of the earth,"*
or *"The lower parts of the earth."* " So shall the Son of
man be three days and three nights · in *the heart of the
earth,"* Matt. xii. 40. " He descended into *the lower
parts of the earth,"* Eph. iv. 9. (2.) *"Hades."* " Thou
wilt not leave my soul in *hades,"* Eph. ii. 27. (3.) *"The
Abyss."* " Who shall descend unto *the abyss* (that is to
bring up Christ again from the dead)," Rom. x. 7. (4.)
" Paradise." " To-day shalt thou be with me in *paradise,"* Luke xxiii. 43.

But we are also informed that the rich man went to
Hades, and that when there he lifted up his eyes being
in torment; so that until the resurrection of Christ both
the righteous and the wicked went to Hades in the heart
of the earth after death.

But, again, we are told that the unclean spirits, before being cast out, besought our Lord that He would not command them to go away " into the abyss," showing that the unclean spirits also had their dwelling in Hades under the earth.

Still further, we find that Tartarus is the name given to the place where the unclean spirits were cast when they sinned, " God spared not the angels that sinned, but cast them down to Tartarus " (2 Peter ii. 4).

We thus discover that *Hades* or the *Abyss* was the general name given to the place to which the disembodied spirits went after death, both of the righteous and the wicked; but that in Hades there were two different regions, one called " Paradise," which was the abode of the redeemed, and the other called " Tartarus," which was the abode of the unsaved.

There can be no doubt, then, that until the resurrection of Christ, the disembodied spirits of the Old Testament saints went *down* to Paradise in Hades after death; they did not go *up* to heaven.   Nowhere in the Old Testament Scriptures do we find it stated that the righteous dead went to heaven : uniformly they are represented as going *down* to Sheol, which is the Hebrew word for Hades.   For example, when Jacob said, " I will go down into Sheol unto my son," he could not mean " the grave," because Joseph was not supposed to be buried.   It is a serious fault in our English translation that the word Sheol is sometimes translated Hell, and sometimes " the grave," so that English readers are prevented from knowing what the Scriptures really teach on this important subject.

In consequence of the figurative language in which Scripture speaks on this subject, we cannot be positively certain that Hades is a *locality* under the earth, and not the disembodied *state* after death. But when we observe the persistency with which Scripture reiterates the idea, and as we must be assured that every spirit must be in some locality, we know of no reason why Hades should not be a locality as well as a state, more especially as we find the unclean spirits beseeching our Lord not to send them to the abyss, which could not mean the disembodied state, because they were in that state already.

We have said that our English Bible has translated three different Greek words by one English word. These three words are, Hades, Gehenna, and Tartarus. Hades and Tartarus are names given to places to which disembodied spirits descended after death; but Gehenna is the lake of fire into which Satan and the wicked are to be cast, soul and body, after the resurrection.

The passages in which the word Gehenna occurs are these :—

Matt. v. 22. But whosoever shall say, Thou fool, shall be in danger of *gehenna* of fire (or fiery gehenna).

Matt. v. 29. For it is profitable for thee that one of thy members should perish, and not that thy whole body should be cast into *gehenna*. (See also ver. 30, and chap. xviii. 9 ; and Mark ix. 43, 45, 47.)

Matt. xxiii. 15. Ye compass sea and land to make one proselyte ; and when he is made, ye make him twofold more the child of *gehenna* than yourselves.

Matt. xxiii. 33. Ye serpents, ye generation of vipers, how can ye escape the damnation of *gehenna* ?

James iii. 6. So is the tongue among our members, that it defileth the whole body, and setteth on fire the course of nature ; and it is set on fire of *gehenna*.

The spirit went to Hades, at death, but when Hades

K

shall give up its dead, then the re-embodied spirits of the wicked will be cast into Gehenna. It is the body that is cast into Gehenna; it is the spirit only that went down to Hades.

Every careful reader of Scripture must have observed that in the parable of the rich man and Lazarus, there appears to be much that is figurative in the narrative. Abraham presiding at a feast, with Lazarus as his most honoured guest; and the rich man intreating that Lazarus might be sent to dip the tip of his finger in water to cool his tongue. There are evidently post-resurrection elements here, and the flames of Gehenna are evidently borrowed for Hades, so that we cannot, even though we would, interpret the parable literally. A spirit could not convey a drop of water on the tip of its finger, neither could the tongue of a spirit be cooled by its application. We would reverently suggest an explanation, but it is only a suggestion; and that is, that the parable anticipates Gehenna as if it were in Hades, and the sufferings of the body after the resurrection, as if they were immediately after death. If it be so, the actual sufferings would be much more literal than is generally supposed, although the narrative itself is only a parable.

We must observe that throughout the whole of Scripture the punishment of the wicked is represented as a thing which does not take place till after the day of judgment, and this holds true with regard to both men and devils.

In regard to the devil and his angels there can be no doubt. Tartarus was not a place of punishment, but only the condemned cell in which the culprits are chained, "God cast them down to Tartarus, and delivered them into chains of darkness to be *reserved unto judgment*" (2 Peter ii. 4).

The same thing is evident from the cry of the unclean spirits when they saw their judge approaching, " Art thou come hither to torment us *before the time?*" (Matt. viii. 29.)   Nowhere do they appear to be in a state of torment when either Satan or the unclean spirits pass before us in the sacred history. At the time of Job Satan, though no doubt miserable, was certainly not in torment; and when he encountered our Lord in the wilderness, he certainly had no appearance of being in pain.   As for the unclean spirits, their terrors were all for the future.

Nor do we find any evidence that it is otherwise with wicked men.   All Scripture represents the day of judgment as a necessary preliminary to execution.   To suppose that the wicked shall be taken out of the lake of fire in order to stand before the judgment-seat of Christ, and then sent back again for a continuation of their punishment, is not consistent with such passages as 2 Pet. ii. 9, " The Lord knoweth how to *reserve* the unjust unto the day of judgment to be punished," or with Matt. xi. 22, " It shall be more tolerable for Tyre and Sidon *in the day of judgment* than for you," besides many others to the same effect.   If our Lord in this parable (for we must keep in mind that it was only a parable) chose to speak of the state after death coinciding with the day of judgment, and so mingle the terrors of Gehenna with the gloom of Tartarus, it is in perfect keeping with other parts of His teaching; as when He blended His references to the destruction of Jerusalem with those of His coming at the day of judgment, revealing and yet not revealing that which was yet to come.

If it be so, it is not inconceivable that the spirits of the unsaved may be placed in exactly the same circumstances as the unclean spirits of the New Testament history, and that they too are not tormented before the time. Still we confess that there is a difficulty, but the only other way out of it is to suppose that the parable is a literal history, and that this carnally-minded Jew was earlier and more severely punished than Satan himself.

As death is the punishment of sin, and Hades was the abode of the dead until the ransom of the prisoners was paid, we find everywhere in Scripture that Hades is represented as a prison with its gates and bars, so that even Paradise, although it was a rest for the people of God, was certainly not the inheritance of the saints.

Still, the very name Paradise implies that it was not without its enjoyments. To us who are still in the flesh, and are so largely dependent on the things of time and sense, it is difficult to understand how the spirits of just men made perfect could find a paradise in the heart of the earth; and yet we are so differently constituted that this is no more than what we ought to expect. A deaf man cannot understand the charms of music, neither can a blind man revel in the beauties of nature, although there are other luxuries to which they are not insensible. So we, whose spirit-senses are at present sheathed in the clay tenement of a fallen body, can have no conception of the enjoyments that are possible in the disembodied state.

And yet the saints on earth have sometimes experienced some of these joys; and the revelation of God's presence and love has been sometimes vouchsafed to a degree that the frail body was scarcely able to endure it. When the veil of flesh, therefore, was dropped by these Old Testament saints, such an experience might well be called a paradise to them. "When they made their bed in Hades, there would Jehovah lead them, and His right hand sustain them ; and instead of darkness covering them, the night around them would be as light."

The view continually presented to us in Scripture of this intermediate state of the blessed is that of rest, not the rest of unconscious sleep, but the Sabbatic rest of ceasing from labour, and communion with God. To many the idea of such a rest may not be at all attractive, more especially to the young and enterprising; and yet even to them the sweet consciousness of unclouded communion with God, the absence of all care and anxiety, the freedom from all pain and distress, and more especially the ceasing from sin and all possibility of discord between God and the soul, would make the rest that remained for the people of God an internal paradise. Even though nature were shut out, God is a universe to live in, larger and richer and grander than nature.

It would also be a mistake to suppose that in Hades there could have been any monotony or want of incident. Certainly there would be none in Tartarus among the miserable, whose only occupation would be to make others more miserable than themselves; neither would there be any want of incident in Paradise.

What meetings would there be of loved ones never to be again separated by death.! ` What friendships renewed, what histories related, and what mysteries solved ! The circles of acquaintance, also, would be continually enlarging, and new intimacies formed.

But it would not be with the past only that these dwellers in Paradise would be occupied : every fresh arrival would bring with him tidings of the present and the prospects of the future. What a thrill would pass through Hades, for example, when Simeon and Anna were ushered in among them, bringing the welcome tidings that the Messiah had at length been born, and that they had actually held the infant Saviour in their arms. From that day forward the expectation of His arrival would be continually increasing; and when at length the shout of victory that came from Calvary rang through the regions of the dead, and "It is finished." resounded to the utmost limits of Tartarus, all Hades would be moved at His coming.

What a retrospect does this open up to our view, first in His reception by His glad people in Paradise, both He and they in the disembodied state in the heart of the earth, but He with the keys of death and Hades in His hands.

The idea of Hades being a prison even to the redeemed meets us everywhere in Scripture. If there had been no sin, there would have been no death, and if there had been no death, there would have been no Hades. But it was to ransom His people from the power of Hades that the atoning work was necessary.

It is by overlooking this great fact that the promise in Matt. xvi. 18 has been so much misunderstood, "Upon this rock will I build my church, and the gates of Hades shall not prevail against it." This does not mean, as Romish theologians believe, that the council of Satan will not succeed in overthrowing the Papacy, but that the gates of Hades would not be able to retain the Church of God in prison when the price of her redemption had been paid. If the gates of Hades had been able to retain their great Head as prisoner, they would have retained His members too, but as it was impossible that He could be holden of them, so neither was it possible that its gates should prevail against His Church. He was the Son of the LIVING God, and this was the Rock on which the Church was to be built.

For three days and three nights our Lord is withdrawn from our view, and the scene of His operations is transferred from earth to Hades, where in imagination alone we can follow Him. He was put to death in the flesh, but while His body was lying silent and still in the tomb of Joseph, in spirit He was alive and active, carrying forward His mediatorial work. When He reappears, He reappears alone, and yet what a change has taken place during the interval. Paradise has been emptied of its inhabitants.

What took place during these three days and three nights Scripture has not informed us, unless we apply to it that difficult passage in 1 Pet. iii. 18, regarding which we offer no opinion; and yet what could be more likely than that He went and preached to the spirits in prison, "proclaiming liberty to the captive, and the opening of the prison doors to them that were bound."

What a grand and magnificent meeting would it be between Jesus and His ransomed myriads, the patriarchs and kings, the prophets and the martyrs, of whom the world was not worthy, and who had been waiting and wearying for His coming; and when He at length descended among them, and announced that the victory had been won and their redemption completed, how would the adoring host exult in His triumph, and prepare to follow Him to His Father's home.

From the death of Abel till the time when Christ Himself descended to Paradise there had been gathering for four thousand years a multitude which no man could number, prisoners of hope; these He was about to carry with Him to heaven as the trophies of His victory and the purchase of His blood. When Israel came out of Egypt under Moses, they came out, not in haste, nor in disorder, but marshalled like an army and in squadrons. Were no preparations needed for the great exodus that was about to take place? and, when the Leader and Commander of the people arrived among them, had He no proclamations to make, no orders to issue, no marshalling of their ranks, previous to issuing the signal for their departure?

We are very unwilling to believe that the three days and three nights so expressly specified as the period during which our Lord was to be in the lower parts of the earth, were only two nights and one day, with only three hours of the second.* For, although there was no necessity laid upon Christ Himself, yet when we consider the innumerable multitudes that were about to migrate, and the importance of thorough organisation in the removal, so that there should be no misunderstanding or confusion on their part, three days and three nights do not seem too

---

* The tradition that our Lord was crucified on Friday must have arisen at a time when the Jewish reckoning of the Sabbath, "from even to even" (Lev. xxiii. 32) was forgotten, so that the expression "when the evening was come," did not suggest to them that another day had commenced. There is the most perfect unanimity in Scripture in testifying that Christ was *buried* on the "preparation," that is, the day before the Sabbath; but as no steps were taken for the purpose till "the even was come," the crucifixion must have taken place on *the day before the preparation*, that is, on the Thursday. The moment we admit that every evening was the commencement of a new day, we have not even the shadow of a reason for supposing that our Lord was crucified on a Friday. That the Jews would crucify three men within nine hours of the Sabbath, when none of them were expected to die before the evening; or that all the events connected with the burial of our Lord took place in the twinkling of an eye, between the coming of the evening and the coming of the Sabbath, which were simultaneous, is incredible. All the learning that has been expended in proving that three days and three nights means less than two days and two nights has been wasted, because it attempts to remove a difficulty which never existed. It is better to acknowledge that Good Friday is a mistake.

long for preparation. Not that there would have been any difficulty if a shorter time had been mentioned, but neither would it have been surprising if it had been much longer.

In regard to those who die in the Lord now, we have positive assurance, that at death the spirits of believers go to Christ in heaven; so that, when they are absent from the body, they are present with the Lord. Whatever darkness, therefore, rested on this matter before the work of Christ was completed, life and immortality have now been brought to light through the Gospel.

When the work of Christ was completed, and a new and living way opened to the holiest of all by His blood, the kingdom of heaven was opened to all believers, because the union between Christ and the members of His body is such that, whenever the earthly house of their tabernacle is dissolved, they must needs go home to Him. Until the time of Christ's ascension, the many mansions in His Father's house were not ready for their reception, even though they themselves had been prepared; and therefore it was needful that He should go away, that He might "prepare a place" for them, which up to that time had not been prepared. In this manner Christ was the true ladder of Jacob's dream because He was the road to heaven. "Thomas saith unto him, Lord, we know not whither thou goest, and how can we know the way? Jesus saith unto him, I AM THE WAY."

If this be the case, the spirits of the redeemed do not now remain upon this earth or under it after death, but are carried to heaven, there to be with Christ. But heaven is not an ideal locality, or an immaterial spirit-land, as many erroneously suppose it to be. The body of Christ, being a material body, must needs be lodged somewhere; and the angels which are sent from heaven to earth, having real bodies, must also have a real world to dwell in. The resurrection bodies of the saints have to be accommodated in some real locality; and, if our Lord, when He went up into heaven to prepare a place for them, was seen to go away in a bodily form, the spirits of His saints must needs also travel by the same way that He went, for where He is, there must they be also.

We are informed in 2 Cor. v. 1, that the spirits of those that die in the Lord now are not unclothed at death, but clothed upon with their house which is from heaven, so that it may be truly said that he that believeth in Christ never dies; that is to say, he is never unclothed as all the Old Testament saints were, and as Christ Himself was unclothed, when He descended to Hades.

"For we know, that, if our earthly house of this tabernacle were dissolved, we have a building of God, an house not made with hands, eternal in the heavens. For in this we groan, earnestly desiring to be clothed upon with our house which is from heaven: if so be that being clothed, we shall not be found naked. For we that are in this tabernacle do groan, being burdened: not for that we would be unclothed, but clothed upon, that mortality might be swallowed up of life. Now he that hath wrought us for the self-same thing is God, who also hath given unto us the earnest of the Spirit. Therefore we are always confident, knowing that, whilst we are at home in the body, we are absent from the Lord: (for we walk by faith, not by sight:) we are confident, I say, and willing rather to be absent from the body, and to be present with the Lord" (2 Cor. v. 1-8).

From this passage we infer, *first*, that the spirits of the saints are not cast out naked at death, but are clothed upon with a house or body which is from heaven; *secondly,* that this body in which the redeemed spirit is lodged at death is not a frail tabernacle or movable tent, like the body which has been put off, but an immortal body, which is eternal in the heavens; and, *thirdly,* that this spiritual body is not the spiritual body which is to be raised up from the earth at the resurrection, but one which is "from heaven." *

In connection with this subject there is a remarkable passage (Heb. i. 14), which we must re-translate, as the English version does not accurately represent it :——"Are they not all ministering spirits, sent forth for service on behalf of those *about to* † inherit salvation?" We take this in connection with Matt. xviii. 10 : "Their angels in heaven are always observing the face of my (Christ's) Father in heaven;" and Luke xvi. 22 : "And was carried by the angels into Abraham's bosom." From these passages combined we infer, *first,* that the saints——ay,

---

* May not the "building of God, the house not made with hands, eternal in the heavens," be the glorious person of the Lord Jesus Christ? In verses 6 and 8 there is an evident antithesis between the mortal body in which the spirit dwells before death, and the person of Christ after death ; but much of the force of the passage is lost in our translation. Were we to render the words *endēmountes* and *ekdēmountes* by the corresponding English in-dwelling and out-dwelling, we should have a clearer view of Paul's train of thought. "Knowing that, whilst we are in-dwelling in the body, we are out-dwelling from the Lord : we are confident, I say, and willing rather to be out-dwelling out of the body, and to be in-dwelling with the Lord." At the same time there is a difference. The in-dwelling of the spirit is said to be *in* (en) the body, and the out-dwelling *out of* (ek) the body : whereas the in-dwelling of the spirit is said to be *with,* (pros) not *in,* the Lord, and the out-dwelling is said to be *from,* (apo) not *out of,* the Lord.

† The same word (*mellō*) is used in Acts xx. 3, 7, where it is translated "*about to* sail," and "*ready to* depart."

even little children—have angels appointed to them, who are called "their angels;" *secondly*, that the chief employment of these angels is service (*leitourgia*), and waiting for commands; and, *thirdly*, that on every needful occasion, and especially when the saints are about to enter on their inheritance, these angels are sent forth on service to carry them to heaven.

When a man dies, if he have no ministering angel sent forth for the occasion, what is it but that he must be unclothed without being clothed upon, and he descends, as others descended before him, into the deep, there to await the judgment. But the Lord knoweth them that are His, and if an angel has been sent forth to be in waiting, the saint is not unclothed, but clothed upon with his house which is from heaven. God always works according to law, and by the use of means, and such appears to be the means that conveys the saint to glory.

It would appear then that the Old Testament saints were not so well provided for as the New. But this was a necessity of the case, because the stream could not rise above the fountain-head, and if Christ, when he died, descended to Paradise, it was enough for the servant to be as his Master, more especially as there was no other place as yet prepared to receive them. "These all having obtained a good report through faith, received not the promise, God having provided some better things for us, that they without us should not be made perfect" (Heb. xi. 39, 40). But at Christ's resurrection they were admitted to the same privilege with ourselves.

In reading our Bible we never think about these Old Testament saints, how they got to heaven. But Christ was not unmindful of them. "I am the good Shepherd, and know my sheep, and am known of mine. As the

Father knoweth me, even so know I the Father : and I lay down my life for the sheep.   And other sheep I have, which are not of this fold : them also I must bring, and they shall hear my voice : and there shall be one fold, and one shepherd" (John x. 14-16).   During the three days and the three nights in which he was in Hades, his attention was wholly occupied with their affairs ; and during the forty days of interval between his resurrection and ascension He was similarly employed; because it was only occasional glimpses of His presence that His disciples in the flesh were permitted to enjoy.   There were transactions going on on earth of which they knew nothing, nor was it necessary that they should.   His attention must have been chiefly engrossed by the preparations for His triumphant entry into heaven, attended by the whole of the Old Testament Church which He had just brought forth with Him from Hades.

But how, it may be asked, were they to be conveyed to heaven ?   Our Lord had said : " He that believeth in me, though he were dead, yet shall he live, and whosoever liveth and believeth in me shall never die."   Were these Old Testament saints to enter heaven unclothed ? Were there no ministering spirits sent forth for them, no chariots provided to convey them to heaven ?   We cannot tell how they were conveyed; but there does seem to be an allusion to this in the 68th Psalm, which is quoted by Paul as descriptive of our Lord's ascension : " The chariots of God are twenty thousand (myriads), even thousands of angels : the Lord is among them, as in Sinai, in the holy place.   Thou hast ascended on high, thou hast led captivity captive : thou hast received gifts for men" (Matt. xxvi. 53).

Another remarkable passage in Daniel is interesting,

taken in connection with this subject (chap. ix.).   When
Daniel set apart a day for supplication and prayer on
behalf of Jerusalem and the Jews, the angel Gabriel was
sent to him to give him information regarding the future
history of his people and the time when the Messiah was
to appear.   Now we know, from what Gabriel said to
Zacharias (Luke i. 19), that he was one of those ministering spirits that stood in the presence of God.   "I am
Gabriel," said he, "that stand in the presence of God;"
and we are told that upon the present occasion he was
commanded to fly *swiftly* upon the errand on which he
was sent.   But we should not have known how long the
angel took to fly from heaven to earth, were it not that
Gabriel incidentally mentions the time when he set out,
and Daniel mentions the time when he arrived.   *"At
the beginning of thy supplications,"* said Gabriel, "the
commandment came forth" (ver. 23); and Daniel says
(ver. 21), "Yea, whiles I was speaking in prayer, even
the man Gabriel, whom I had seen in the vision at the
beginning, being caused to fly swiftly, touched me *about
the time of the evening oblation."*   The journey, therefore, occupied probably between six and nine hours.

If the material world to which our Lord ascended from
the Mount of Olives was some distant orb of heaven, to
which He began to direct his flight when He entered the
cloud and disappeared from the gaze of his disciples; and
if Gabriel took between six and nine hours to make the
passage when he was "caused to fly swiftly," we are left
to conjecture what time would be occupied in the passage
upon ordinary occasions, when the ministering angels are
sent forth to conduct us home.   It is very evident that
the journey is a long one, and that the departing spirit
would need not only a guide, but a conveyance, because

how otherwise could we know the way ?   Can it be that one of these angels will receive us into his own person, and clothe the naked spirit in his own body, so that we shall see with the angel's eyes, hear with the angel's ears, and speak with the angel's tongue ?   We cannot tell. Physiologically speaking, it is not impossible, because the spirit of the saint is as capable of "entering" the body of the angel as an unclean spirit is of entering the body of a man.   But, whatever be the conveyance, the angels will show the way ; and, during those intervening hours between earth and heaven, what sublime views of celestial scenery will present themselves, and how intensely interesting will be the conversation !   What questions to be asked ! what misconceptions to be removed ! what hopes to be kindled ! what scenes to be prepared for !   And, when at length we near the happy world, where, perhaps, upon some Mount of Olives, expectant friends are gathered to catch the first glimpse of our appearing, far up in the deep blue of that sunny sky,——We leave them there ; because "eye hath not seen, nor ear heard, neither have entered into the heart of man the things which God hath prepared for them that love Him."   For a time, at least, there will be nothing seen but the smile of Him whose love is heaven, and who will be the first to welcome us to the mansion which He has prepared for us in "HIS FATHER'S HOME."

CHAPTER XII.

THE SPIRITUAL BODY ACCORDING TO LAW.

THE BIBLE bids us believe that, at the resurrection, we shall have bodies differing from our present bodies, not so much in their appearance as in their capabilities. They are to be fashioned like to Christ's resurrection body which our Lord informs us was composed of flesh and bones (Luke xxiv. **39**), and which was seen by Mary at the sepulchre, and by the two disciples on their way to Emmaus, without appearing to be different from those of other men. They are also to be "equal to the angels" who had been entertained as strangers unawares, as by Abraham and Lot as well as by Manoah and others without being suspected to be different from mortal men. But whatever might be their outward appearance they were possessed of powers of which our natural bodies are altogether incapable. They could become invisible to the natural sight (Luke xxiv. **31**). They could pass through material obstacles (John xx. **19**; Acts xii. **7**); and they could rise in the air in apparent opposition to the laws of gravitation, besides exercising other powers which we call miraculous, for no other reason than that they are supernatural; that is to say, they are beyond the power and capabilities of our natural bodies. It is usual to say that, in all such cases, the laws of nature were suspended, and that what was done was contrary to law. This is a grievous mistake, and pregnant with mischief in whatever way we view it. For example, it gives a handle to the infidel to reject all testimony on the subject, because he tells you that what you ask him to believe is simply an impossibility.

Even a miracle is not necessarily a violation or suspension of the laws of nature. Nowhere does Scripture represent it to be so; nor does the purpose of a miracle require that it should be so defined. A miracle is the super-natural act of a super-natural agent acting according to law; that is to say, acting according to the super-natural laws; and the purpose of a miracle is to prove the intervention of a super-natural agent, or (as is not at all impossible) that super-natural powers are exercised by a natural agent. It is a great mistake to suppose that God alone works miracles. We cannot even be certain that anything which Scripture calls a miracle was done without some intermediate agent. If, then, a miracle be defined to be the super-natural acting of a super-natural agent, according to law, then any super-natural agent can work a miracle. Miracles may, with God's permission, be wrought by Satan and other unclean spirits, as well as by angelic power; and we are informed that in the last times these miracles will be wrought (2 Thess. ii. 9; Rev. xiii. 14; xvi. 14; xix. 20). To suppose that Satan or any other creature has the power of suspending God's laws, which are God's special agency, is to suppose an impossibility. There may be some super-natural agents who have greater power than others, but in every case this power is limited, and must act according to law. We do not, and dare not say that God cannot suspend the natural laws—we cannot even affirm that He never did. But as *Scripture does not say that miracles are a suspension of these laws*, no man is entitled to found an argument against miracles on the supposition that it does. It is nothing more than a supposition resorted to in order

L

to explain what our present faculties cannot understand, and cut a knot which, in our present state of being, we feel ourselves unable to unloose. Analogy leads us to infer that as vegetation is a super-inorganic effect produced by a super-inorganic agent, acting according to super-inorganic law, so may it be with the super-natural : and as the organic laws are *over and above* the inorganic, without violating or suspending them, so are the super-natural laws superadded to the natural, and may co-operate with, without suspending them. It is for those who deny the possibility of miracles to prove the *non-existence* of super-natural agents, and the impossibility of any laws higher than those with which we are already acquainted. No true philosopher would ever attempt it.

We ought not to throw unnecessary stumbling-blocks in the way of scientific men who believe in the inviolability of the natural laws. We should remember that their whole system is based upon it. Of what use would their observations, or their experiments, or their calculations be without it? There may be anomalies and apparent contradictions in nature, and scientific men are often perplexed and disappointed in their expectations and experiments : residuary differences are left in their hands where they expected all things to agree; but, they account for all such cases, either by the imperfection of their instruments, or by errors in their calculations, or, by what sometimes is found to be the true cause, the introduction of a new element of whose existence they were not previously aware; but they never allow even the shadow of a suspicion to rest on their minds as to the infinite perfection of God's physical administration. To ask them to believe in the instability of law and its occasional suspension, is to ask, not faith, but, *as they think*, the surrender of their faith in the very intuitions of their nature.

It is not necessary to suppose that the super-natural acts of super-natural agents are violations of law. They may be acting quite as much according to law in their spiritual bodies as we in our natural bodies. Their action may appear miraculous to us, but that is only because we do not understand the super-natural condition of the spiritual body, and the super-natural laws according to which it acts.

Approach them upon another tack, and you will at once observe a change. Tell them that there is another administration higher than any with which they are acquainted, and that that administration is also according to law; you at once engage their attention; and, although they may not believe you, they will never say that it is impossible. In fact, to true philosophers there is not anything impossible, except the violation of law. This higher administration is the very thing of which they are in quest, and which all the analogies of nature would lead them to expect. They have found that above the inorganic administration there is the vegetable, above the vegetable there is the animal, and above the animal may may there not be the spiritual, with laws as truly distinct from those of the animal, as those of the animal are from those of the vegetable administration?

Nor does it present itself only as a possibility; even already they find that they have approached the confines of a mysterious region unknown to their philosophy, and from time to time are startled by the occurrence of phenomena which do not belong to any known administration. In the language of an eloquent writer (Sir David Brewster), we may say that "there exists in every human

being a vast, dimly-lighted region, of unknown extent and
unascertained resources, a world of which we as yet know
too little even to define its boundaries. . . . Far off
there is a murmur as of the ocean; and we hear, far
inland, the rush and roar of a mighty cataract; dark un-
tracked woods are around us, and through them the
river of life flows down.   All that we as yet know of our
nature tends to awaken surmises as vague and wild as
were those of Cortez when he gazed, ' Silent upon a peak
of Darien.' "

In God's works of creation and providence, there are
what may be called different administrations, each of
which has this in common, that it carries on its own
government distinct from, and independent of, the others.
It is the co-ordinate jurisdiction of these independent
administrations that gives rise to what appears to be
inconsistency and miracle; but that is only because our
present natures are incapable of grasping the idea of a
unity so grand, or appreciating the harmony of a chord
so profound.
     Some of these administrations we know, but who would
be so presumptuous as to say that we know them all, or
that those which we do not know must be intelligible to
our present capacities.   Might we not learn a lesson of
humility from a review of those administrations which
have successively appeared?   For example, let us go
back in imagination to the time when the earth was a
stranger to either plants or animals, when the inorganic
laws were the only administration which had yet appeared.
Even then, nature was grand and lovely, and even then
there were sciences which, in their height and depth, are
even yet not perfectly explored.   Astronomy, geology,

inorganic chemistry, mineralogy, optics, electricity, and others, were all at that time complete, and independent of any creation which might yet be superadded. Already had the exhaustless resources of creative power been displayed in the glorious mechanism of the heavens; and even our own world was at that time replete with beauty and grandeur, with its rolling ocean and its everlasting hills—now lit up with golden sunshine, and then quietly sleeping under the gentle radiance of the moon; with the iceberg and the glacier, the avalanche and the thunderstorm, to give variety to its scenery. Let us imagine an intelligent being to have been introduced to the world at such a time, and told that a new creation was about to appear; how would it have been possible for him to conceive or imagine the vegetable kingdom? It is easy for us now to imagine and comprehend it, when we have seen it; but it would have been utterly impossible for us to do so then. Now that we have a vocabulary of plants and trees, of roots and stems, of leaves and flowers, of fruits and seeds, of life and death, we can describe what vegetation and vegetable life might mean; but before that vocabulary was formed, how would it have been possible to do so! The nearest approach of inorganic to organic structure is the crystal; and were we to attempt to describe the coming creation of the vegetable kingdom by the inorganic vocabulary, how very unintelligible would be the description! We should tell of a whole kingdom of crystals about to be formed, in which the deoxidising power of the sun's rays was to be turned to account in forming strange substances hitherto unknown to chemistry. We should say that systems of these crystals would secede from the catholic unity of nature, and set up for themselves independent interests, forming each for itself a little universe of its own; that presently existing substances would be absorbed into cycles of mysterious sequences, whence they would again be expelled in forms in which they could not be recognised. Water, without losing its power of gravitation, would ascend in microscopic streams five, twenty, fifty, or even a hundred feet high, and there, spread out, would be decomposed, its oxygen dismissed, and its hydrogen united to carbon found in the air, forming a hydro-carbon; and to complete the mystery, "force" would ascend into another and higher sphere, obey different laws, and form an entirely new administration. We ask, Could any creature have conceived such an idea before it was revealed? And when the actual realisation was presented for the first time, how completely would any created being be lost in wonder and admiration at the new universe that had sprung up around him!

But we must allow fancy to take yet another flight, and consider how the same intelligence would be exercised if, upon the basis of the vegetable kingdom, he were called to expect another and higher administration to rise from this higher platform. The vocabulary is now enlarged, and plants, not crystals, must furnish the nomenclature of the new creation. He is told that an entirely new kingdom of plants is to be called into existence, having an equally luxuriant variety of form and character, but built upon an entirely different type. Instead of living by the direct power of the sun's rays, these new plants are to live by reoxidising that which has been deoxidised; that the plants, instead of being fixed in the ground, are to move upon their branches, or fly upon their leaves; that they are to carry about with them their roots, gathered up into a sack filled with the juices ready made, intended to be absorbed into their systems. Again, we ask, Who could have conceived the existence of such an administration before the animal kingdom had been actually seen?

We might continue the ascent from the beast to man, in which there are new elements, such as reason, science, conscience, and fellowship with God. The ascent in each case is so sudden, so great, so unimaginable, that in each case it requires a higher power of conception to receive it. New regions are discovered, where no region was suspected to exist; and when wisdom and imagination had been overwhelmed by the exuberance of creative power, another height suddenly opens above our head where all had seemed immeasurably high, and another profound opens beneath our feet where all had appeared immeasurably deep. When God seemed to have exhausted creation's resources in the endless profusion of beauty and grandeur in the vegetable kingdom, suddenly there bursts forth a fresh eruption of magnificent conception and creative glory in the animal kingdom. And when above that again there rises into existence a moral universe displayed in the creation of man, in this, as in each previous ascent, we appear to have acquired new faculties in order to rise to its conception; and after being lost in wonder, we are again doubly lost in our helpless incapacity to wonder more.

The effect of all this on the higher intelligences is to make them cover their faces with their wings, and say, "Holy, holy, holy, Lord God of Hosts! the whole earth is full of thy glory." The effect upon other minds is—simply atheism. Not that their intellectual and moral perceptions are different, but one of the springs of their moral nature has been broken, and lost its hold; so that their wonder goes round and round without ever finding a God.

Now, there are two things which inevitably press themselves upon our attention here; the first of which is the
extreme likelihood of the existence of another and higher
administration beyond those of which we are already cognisant; and the second is, that all analogy would suggest
that this higher and unknown administration should be as
unlike the present known administration, in its subjects
and its laws, as the organic is unlike the inorganic, or
as the moral and intellectual are unlike the vegetable
and the animal. It is under these circumstances that
the "super-natural" administration presents itself to our
notice.

We might perhaps object to the word "super-natural,"
as not altogether a fair representation of that which the
Bible reveals as spiritual; as, if being super-natural, it
implied a suspension or violation of the natural laws. But
we accept the word as a convenient one, and not untrue,
although, at the same time, we protest against the assumption, that the super-natural is not according to law. The
organic world is not one whit less subject to law than the
inorganic, and the moral and intellectual is not one whit
less subject to law than the organic. If there be, then,
another administration called the super-natural, there is no
reason why it should not be as subject to law as the
others.

It is true that the laws may be different; but that is
no more than is to be expected. The organic administration does not administer the inorganic laws, and the moral
and intellectual administration does not administer the
organic laws. Each administration has its own laws, and
therefore we should expect that the super-natural would
possess a code of its own, and that these should be as inviolable as any of the laws of the administrations below.

The word "super-natural" is not an inconvenient word, not only because it expresses that which is popularly understood to be its meaning, but also because it has something like Scripture authority for its adoption; and being indefinite in its application, and only relative in its definition, it is well suited to express either one or more administrations which may happen to be above the "natural."

According to St. Paul's teaching, the resurrection body is called a *spiritual* body, and is distinguished from our present bodies, which are called "*natural*" bodies, by its super-natural powers and functions. Adopting, therefore, the phraseology of Paul, the laws and administration under which all our present experiences take place may very properly be called "natural;" whereas the laws and administration under which the resurrection bodies, corresponding with the angelic, will be placed, may very properly be called the "super-natural;" and it is this, the possibility of which is denied. Now, we affirm that the "super-natural" is not only *not impossible*, as some scientific men affirm, but, looking at the matter in the light of analogy, it is most probable and most likely. Of course, we admit that the possibility of a thing, or even its extreme probability, does not prove its existence; and we also admit that very conclusive proof of the existence of the super-natural is required: but what we complain of is, that these men will not even admit it into court, because they say that it is "impossible;" and, instead of collecting, examining, and weighing proofs, they first declare that the proofs *must be* false, and then exercise their ingenuity in trying to dispose of them. Loyalty to their creed demands that each proof must somehow or other be broken; their only anxiety, therefore, is to find the point at which the fracture may most conveniently be made.

Is it the apparent mystery and miraculous nature of the super-natural administration that repels them? We have seen how the phenomena of the vegetable kingdom wore an air of mystery and apparent miracle when the vocabulary of the inorganic kingdom was used to describe them; and how the phenomena of the animal kingdom wore an air of mystery and miracle when the vocabulary of the vegetable kingdom was used to describe them; how then should we expect it to be otherwise when we rise from the natural to the super-natural. Having to use the vocabulary of the natural administration (for we have no higher) to describe the phenomena of the super-natural, how could it be otherwise than that it should invest with an air of mystery and apparent miracle an administration in which there is in reality none?

Why should we suppose that we are already acquainted with all God's administrations? We detect, even in the theory of Darwin, an aspiration after, and expectation of, something higher than the present man. Even he sets no limit to development, because all analogy teaches him that there must be something higher. But he forgets that in previous elevations there were not only successive developments, as he calls them, but also succcessive platforms, rising one above another by abrupt and lofty transitions. Between the inorganic life of oxidation, and the vegetable life of deoxidation there was a gulf, because there was antagonism; and between the de-oxidation of vegetable life and the re-oxidation of animal life there was a second gulf, because again there was antagonism. These were not developments, but antagonisms; and, therefore, the successive elevations were accomplished by successive

platforms, not by gradual ascents. He must also acknowledge that not only the subjects, but the administrations
are different. With each successive platform there arose
a new administration, so that their substances and their
immaterial forces were not more different than their laws.

As regards the present, therefore, even though every
thing were conceded to Mr. Darwin that he demands, he
has only accounted for one-half of the phenomena, by his
hypothesis of development without abrupt transitions,
whereas Scripture accounts for the whole ; and in regard
to the future, the Scripture theory of a higher platform,
as that which is above the natural, has this advantage
that, besides being more conformed to the analogy of
nature, its existence is supported by actual proofs and
examples, whereas Mr. Darwin's is supported by none.

This higher platform, the SUPER-NATURAL, is not a
hypothesis, but a fact. It is a fact that is evidenced by
a thousand testimonies ; and the superiority of its laws,
and the independence of its administration, instead of
being evidences of its incredibility, are corroborative of
its truth. It would not be in accordance with analogy if
its laws and administration were not higher than, and
independent of, the natural; and it is nothing more than
was to be expected that we should not at present be able
to understand them. The naturalist objects, that it is
contrary to the law of gravitation that a body should rise
from the ground and ascend into heaven ; but how does
he know what the law of gravitation is ? It may be
no more a miracle than the magnetic pendulum, which
is attracted or repelled according as it changes its polarity;
for, although we have not as yet discovered any polarity in
gravitation, it does not follow that no polarity exists. It
may be of the very nature of spirit to dominate gravi-

tation, and we actually have conclusive evidence that it does so.

Again, as regards the passage of the spiritual body through material obstacles, if you tell a philosopher that, upon one occasion the laws of nature were suspended, and that a body of flesh and bones entered a room in the presence of eleven people, while both the doors and the windows were shut, he will tell you that it is impossible. But if Professor Poey, in the London Meteorological Society, mentions an instance of "lightning falling down a chimney and passing into a trunk, in which was found an inch of soot, which must have passed through the wood itself,"* he is listened to with respectful attention. He might not convince his audience, and it is quite open to question whether the fact be sufficiently authenticated; but so little do we know of the fundamental laws of matter that he would be no true philosopher who would say that the thing was impossible.

The only other difficulty in regard to the spiritual body is, that it is immortal. We find that the natural body, like those of the lower animals, grows to maturity, and after that, decays and dies; and this is actually the case with the animal body after it has lost its normal constitution; but if there be a higher sphere into which it is capable of ascending, we know of no law which would be broken were the body to be maintained in a state of per-

* The following is a report of a meeting of the Meteorological Society in the spring of 1858:—"PHOTOGRAPHIC EFFECTS OF LIGHTNING.—At the last meeting of the Meteorological Society there was read a paper on the Photographic Effects of Lightning. . . . To corroborate this view, Mr. Poey mentioned an instance of lightning falling down a chimney and passing into a trunk, in which was found an inch of soot which must have passed through the wood itself."

petual youth or maturity; and the only reason why we expect decay and death is, not because we see any necessity for it, but because we invariably find it so. Physiologists are agreed in this, that there is not a single action of the system necessary to produce immortality, which has not been found to be already in existence in some portion or another of the animal economy.

CHAPTER XIII.

THE ANGELS THAT SINNED.

WHEN a historian like Luke speaks of "all the world," we understand him to speak from his own point of view, using the phrase which was current at the time to signify the whole Roman empire, to which a decree of Cæsar would be applicable. It may be more questionable, but it is equally legitimate, to apply the same rule of interpretation to the passage in Genesis vii. 19, where it is said that "all the high hills which were under the whole heaven were covered." But that would depend on two things—*first*, that the statement should not be literally true; and, *second*, that it should be the testimony of an *eye-witness*, and not the absolute assertion of a *historian;* in other words, that it should be Noah, and not Moses, who gave us the information, as we have endeavoured to show in the second chapter.

But such a rule of interpretation is clearly not applicable to any statement in Scripture made by God Himself. Now, we have shown that the first chapter of Genesis was not written by any human eye-witness, but is a pure revelation; and, therefore, when it is said, " In the beginning God made the heavens and the earth," we are not at liberty to restrict its meaning, as if it only affirmed that God was the maker of part of the universe, and not of the whole.

In like manner when, in Exod. xx. 11, God Himself says, "For in six days the Lord made heaven and earth, the sea, and all that in them is," we have an inspired commentary on the first chapter of Genesis, which determines that the six days do not refer to this world's creation only, but to the whole universe and all that it contains. It follows, then, that every creation must find its place in that sacred vision which professes to announce it; and that if there be angels in heaven or unclean spirits upon earth, their birthday also must have been upon one of the six.

It has been supposed that the angels were created on the first day, along with God's first-born light; but this would be inverting the order of creation, by making the highest first instead of last; and in order to give sanction to such an anomaly, we should require some authority from Scripture, which is entirely awanting. The angels of heaven are uniformly called men; and as man was made in the image of God on the sixth day, the angels must have been made in the image of God on the sixth day.

In the interests of Scripture it is very undesirable to restrict its interpretation *in any one direction*. We do not, therefore, assert, that angels *must* have been created on the sixth day; but we do assert, not only that the Scripture is capable of such an interpretation, but that this is the one which is most natural and obvious to those who do not allow their judgment to be influenced by preconceived opinions.

If, then, we have rightly interpreted the character and purpose of the first chapter of Genesis, it is not necessary to suppose that all worlds were made at the same time, or to infer a chronological parallelism in the days of creation in all the different worlds. It *may* be so, and, in that case, the creation of plants, trees, animals, and man, must have taken place simultaneously in all worlds. We do not insist on limiting the interpretation, but we think it more likely from the apocalyptic character of the chapter, that it should present to us, as it were, the TYPE of all creation, including that of our own world; so that the creation of man in the first chapter refers to the creation of man in all worlds, wherever such a creation takes place; whereas the history contained in the second chapter has a more limited subject, being a narrative of the creation of our own Adam only, from whom the Messiah was to be descended. If this view be correct, the first chapter of Genesis does not supply what might be called a chronological history of creation, but rather reveals its style and order, commencing with the formation of the different worlds, the raising of the land above the water, and the successive orders of organic life, commencing with the formation of plants, and terminating in the creation of man. Without doubt our own world finds its history there, yet not our own world only, but every world in which there is a man. Judging from what we see around us, there is not one of the fixed stars visible in the firmament that is fit even for vegetable life;* and judging from what we find of the past history of our own planet recorded in the rocks, millions of years must pass even in the most favoured worlds with nothing higher than gigantic reeds and reptiles. But this we learn above all

* See Appendix B.

that man is the last link of the chain, and that by that link we become related to God. When it is said, therefore, " Let us make man in our own image, after our likeness," "and let them have dominion over the fish of the sea, and over the fowl of the air, and over every living thing that moveth upon the earth," it is spoken not only of Adam, the progenitor of Christ, but of every other man created, either in this or in any other world ; because they were all created in the same image, and invested with the same dominion over the creatures.

But when God created man, the immortal spirit was lodged in a body which never would have died so long as that immortal spirit retained its allegiance to God. Creative power had been luxuriating in unbounded multiformity of types, and each successive ascent witnessed some new idea of creative beauty and luxuriance, till in the last ascent of all He fashioned a glorious image of Himself. It was the connecting link between Deity and dust; the culminating point of that great pyramid of life whose broad base traversed both earth and ocean, and in its upward sweep pointed at each successive stage to a coming man. Hidden within each type there always lay the mysterious germ of some higher thought brooding in the mind of God, and giving promise of its ultimate development ; and even in the lowest form of animated nature there were not awanting prophetic hints of that which was to be the last ascent of all. The transformation of the pupa worm into the psyche butterfly was the distant and faint rehearsal of the "change "* of the psyche man into the pneuma angel.

* " We shall all be changed. . . . For this corruptible must put on incorruption, and this mortal must put on immortality."—1 Cor. xv. 51, 52.

But with all this there was no provision made for sin. The last ascent of creative power was sharp and sudden, rising at once into a new order of beings, leaving all that had preceded them immeasurably far beneath and behind. Between the brute and the man there lay an infinity of distance, which could not be bridged over by any intermediate organism. Creation had entered into the moral sphere, and the product was an image and likeness of the Creator. It was more than a creation, it was a birth; and therefore man is called a " son of God " (Luke iii. 38). Hitherto there had been no sin, because there was no conscience and no law among creatures not possessed of moral responsibility ; and hitherto death had been the termination of a life, the purposes of which had been completed. After rising to its highest point, it could really rise no more ; so that an immortal brute would have been really a monster. To the lower animals death can have no terrors, but, on the contrary, is the kind friend that relieves them of their sufferings when life could be only a burden or a pain ; but when man was created in the image and likeness of God, he became both a moral and an immortal being, and sin and death became an awful possibility. So long as the moral creature maintained his moral integrity, the course of nature would run on until the natural body became developed into the spiritual, and man became an angelic creature ; but if, through moral guilt, the natural body became dispossessed of the faculty of transformation and died, the spirit would be cast out naked into the deep, a demon man.

Leaving out of view the great " I AM," whose nature is infinitely different from, and superior to, all created in-

M

telligences, an essence not a substance, there are only two classes of beings revealed in Scripture which are purely and altogether spirits. These are, first, the spirits of the departed dead, who were once in the flesh; and, second, the unclean spirits, called also devils, or rather demons. Besides these, there are really no other spirits of which we have any knowledge.

Regarding the unclean spirits or devils, as well as regarding the angels, we have a large amount of information in the sacred narratives; but there is a very remarkable contrast between them. Unlike the angels, the unclean spirits were never mistaken for men ; they are represented as really spirits, and nothing more, never assuming any visible form, nor eating, drinking, or being entertained, as were the angels in Scripture history. In the garden of Eden, Satan is represented as speaking to Eve as a serpent ; but, whatever might be his reason for addressing her by such means, it is sufficient for our present purpose to know that Satan is not a material serpent. He is again introduced to us in the book of Job, and afterwards in the prophecies of Zechariah; but in neither case is there any evidence that he appeared in any visible form, as the angels invariably do. It is generally understood that, in the book of Job, Satan is represented as presenting himself in heaven among the angels, and, in that case, it is supposed that, if the angels appeared in a visible form, so must also have Satan. But Scripture does not say that it was an assemblage of angels in which he appeared, or that the incident recorded took place in heaven; on the contrary, it is much more likely (as will be afterwards shown) that the society into which he intruded himself was a company of worshippers on earth, where he was much more likely to be present than to be absent.

In 1 Kings, ch. xxii., we have also a statement, by a prophet called Micaiah, of a vision which it would be impossible to interpret into a historical fact, and in which a
spirit volunteers to inspire the prophets of Ahab; but his
offer was to be a lying spirit in their mouths, not to
appear to them in any visible shape or form.   Besides all
this, we have mention made of evil spirits and familiar
spirits in the Old Testament; but they correspond with the
evil and unclean spirits of the New; and in no case have
we the slightest intimation that they were seen or spoken
to under any form, as appears invariably to have been the
case with the angels.

In every respect there is an entire correspondence
between the unclean spirits of Scripture and the disembodied spirits of men.   Their very capability of inhabiting
the bodies of men, and energising them in the same manner
as the spirit of the man himself, is presumptive proof of the
identity of their physical constitution.

It is also a remarkable confirmation of the identity of
the two natures, that the unclean spirits of Scripture are
represented as having their present dwelling in the same
place (*hades*) with the departed spirits of men, and that
men shall have their future dwelling in the same place
(*gehenna*) that was prepared for the devil and his angels.
It is a still further confirmation, that both devils and men
are awaiting the great day of judgment; and that they
shall stand together to be judged before the same great
white throne.   We must come to the same conclusion,
whether we suppose *hades* to be a state or a locality.   If
it be a state and not a locality, the doctrine is proved
without further investigation; because, if *hades* be the
state of the dead, and if the devils be in *hades*, then the
devils are in the state of the dead.   If, however, *hades*

be a locality as well as a state, it is a confirmation, though not a proof, when we find the departed spirits of men and the unclean spirits of devils sharing the same temporary prison.

It is interesting also to observe the converging testimony of Scripture on this subject, although obscured by the defect of our English version. In Acts (ch. ii. 27) our Lord is represented, after death, as going down to "*hades*," and remaining there till His resurrection : "Thou wilt not leave my soul in *hades*, neither wilt thou suffer thy holy one to see corruption;" and in ver. 31 it is said, "He, seeing this before, spake of the resurrection of Christ, that his soul was not left in *hades*, neither his flesh did see corruption."

But *hades* is not the only name given to the place or state to which Christ went when He died; it is called also "the lower parts of the earth," and "the abyss" (*abussos*): "Now that he ascended, what is it but that he also descended first into *the lower parts of the earth?*" (Eph. iv. 9). "Who shall descend into the *abyss?* that is, to bring up Christ again from the dead" (Rom. x. 7).

Now this last is the name given in several passages to the residence of the unclean spirits, as in Luke viii. 31, where we are informed that the devils "besought Christ that he would not command them to depart into the *abyss.*" So also, Rev. xx. 1, 2, 3, 7, 8 : "And I saw an angel come down from heaven, having the key of the *abyss* and a great chain in his hand. And he laid hold on the dragon, that old serpent, which is the devil, and Satan, and bound him a thousand years, and cast him into the *abyss.*" For our purpose it is not necessary to determine the meaning of these passages. It is enough that we discover the identity of the prison in which the unclean spirits and the spirits of the wicked dead are confined until the judgment-day.

There is one passage in Jude which must have cost our translators much anxious thought, not only because the words are capable of a considerable variety of interpretations, but because, in one of the sentences, the grammatical construction of the Greek implies that the angels that kept not their first estate are classed with the cities of the plain, both in their sin and in their punishment. To the translators the idea of the angels being guilty of crimes similar to those of Sodom would be inadmissible so long as they believed the angels to be incorporeal spirits, and therefore they have translated the passage thus—"And the angels which kept not their first estate, but left their own habitation, he hath reserved in everlasting chains, under darkness, unto the judgment of the great day. Even as Sodom and Gomorrha, and the cities about them, in like manner, giving themselves over to fornication, and going after strange flesh, are set forth for an example, suffering the vengeance of eternal fire " (Jude 6, 7). The English adjectives and pronouns here employed differ from the Greek in having no gender, so that in translating them we are not able to express distinctions which exist in the Greek, except by inconvenient circumlocutions. In this passage the genders of the Greek pronouns would naturally suggest the following as a more literal rendering—"And the angels which kept not their first estate, but left their own house, he hath reserved in everlasting chains, under darkness, unto the judgment of the great day. Even as Sodom and Gomorrha and the cities about them (*feminine*, the cities), in a manner like to them (*masculine*, the angels), giving themselves over to fornication, and going after strange flesh, are set forth for an example, suffering the vengeance of eternal fire." This is not only the grammatical meaning of the original,* but also the order of the members of the sentence.

Our translators have rendered the expression "*apolipontas to idion oikētērion*," as "leaving their own habitation;" and, perhaps, this may be a good translation of the phrase; but it is susceptible of another, which is at least worthy of examination. The word "*oikētērion*" is a diminutive form of the word "*oikos*," a house or household, and would be quite inapplicable to heaven, or a locality of any kind. Its natural meaning is *a little house*. It occurs in *only one other passage* of the New Testament, and in it it is translated "house."

2 Cor. v. 1. For we know, that, if our earthly house (*oikia*) of this tabernacle were dissolved, we have a building (*oikodomē*) of God, an house (*oikia*) not made with hands, eternal in the heavens. 2. For in this we groan, earnestly desiring to be clothed upon with our house (*oikētērion*) which is from heaven.

The apostle is here speaking of the body as a dwelling in which the spirit resides, or a clothing which it puts off or on. This is somewhat remarkable, as in either case the apostle is speaking of spirits. Paul speaks of the spirit

---

* Commentators have been sorely puzzled with the grammar of this passage, because, as it stands, it implies that the angels that fell were guilty of aggravated fornication. The most plausible supposition which has been suggested is, that it was the cities round Sodom and Gomorrah (*feminine*) that sinned in a manner like to Sodom and Gomorrha (*masculine*), meaning the *men* of Sodom and Gomorrha. The difficulty is certainly very great so long as we reject the natural interpretation, because in mending the grammar, we spoil the sense. To compare the sin of the *cities round* Sodom and Gomorrha, with the sin of the *men in* Sodom and Gomorrah, is a waste of words.

putting on the *oikētērion*. Jude speaks of the spirit leaving it behind. This appears more distinctly, by an examination of the word, translated "leave," *apoleipō*. This is a word which occurs in only two other passages of the New Testament, in which it is rendered "left," with a very significant meaning.

2 Tim. iv. 13. The cloak that I left (*apoleipō*) at Troas with Carpus, when thou comest, bring with thee.

Ver. 20. Erastus abode at Corinth, but Trophimus have I left (*apoleipō*) at Miletum sick.

The "leaving," in these passages, it must be observed, is not to be understood as the *going away* from a place or a habitation, but the *leaving behind* of some *article* of which he was in possession; or some *person* with whom he was in company. If we are to allow Scripture to interpret Scripture, and if Jude used the word in the same sense as that in which Paul used it, we must understand that the prince of this world, and those who fell with him, when they were cast down in chains under darkness, *left behind* them their *oikētēria*—that is, their bodies in which their spirits dwelt or were clothed—in the same way as Paul *left behind* his cloak at Troas with Carpus.

It may be objected that *oikētērion* is singular, while the persons who left them are plural; and that, if bodies had been meant, Jude would have said that they left behind their *oikētēria* (in the plural). But it is somewhat remarkable that Paul also keeps *oikētērion* in the singular, while the persons who put them on are plural: "*We* groan, earnestly desiring to be clothed upon with *our oikētērion* (not *oikētēria*) which *is* from heaven.

If this be a just inference, and, if these views be consistent with a legitimate interpretation of Scripture, we are entitled to hold that the recent discovery of ancient human remains, supposing them to be ultimately proved to be pre-Adamic, instead of shaking our confidence in Scripture, supplies additional proof of its veracity.

CHAPTER XIV.

THE FIRST PRINCE OF THIS WORLD.

THERE are, at the present time, as is well known, very learned ethnologists who assert that the existing varieties of the human race can only be accounted for by the creation of several Adams—a white Adam and a black Adam, a red Adam and a yellow Adam, as the case may be; each deriving his existence from his Maker independently of the others. Not that naturalists are at all agreed among themselves upon the subject; on the contrary, another and very formidable school has arisen, which affirms that this plurality of Adams is not only unsupported by evidence, but is contradicted by all analogies of nature. This school loudly proclaims the unity of the human race—with the proviso, however, that time must be allowed, not only for the gradual divergence of one family from another, but of man himself from his forefathers of the brute creation.

Between these two schools of modern ethnology the Bible student seems to have little comfortable choice, if it were really necessary to choose between them; which, happily, is not the case. But, meantime, a new difficulty has arisen unconnected with either; for, first in one locality, and then in another, it was positively asserted that human remains had been discovered in such positions as to indicate an antiquity of the race far beyond the six thousand years of canonical history.   More perplexing still is the undoubted fact, that, to whatever age these remains belonged, they indicate a state of savage degradation more consistent with the theory of gradual development, than with that of an original righteousness.

At first these announcements were received with the fullest measure of orthodox incredulity; because, although the strata, in which they were said to be found, are the most modern of all the earth's formations, still, their testimony seemed so contrary to all that Scripture had been understood to say about the creation of man, that nothing but the most conclusive evidence could be sufficient for their proof.   This incredulity, however, has been gradually melting away before accumulating facts, all tending in the same direction; and although they have not as yet amounted to absolute proof, and may not do so for a long time, there can be no doubt that they have already become very formidable; so much so, as to make it a question of the deepest interest how they may be explained in a manner consistent with the inspiration of the Bible.

Sir Charles Lyell has, with great ability, and yet with great caution, marshalled the facts in order without committing himself to any theory; and the result to which they lead us is evidently this, that although the proof in favour of the inspiration of the Bible is far more conclusive than the evidence in favour of the antiquity of man, yet they are both so powerful as to suggest that they cannot be really inconsistent with one another.   No one can read Sir Charles Lyell's "Geological Evidences of the Antiquity of Man" without acknowledging that these evidences are very strong indeed; and that they point to an antiquity far beyond the six thousand years which have hitherto been regarded as our age. Nor is this conclusion weakened by his evident reluctance to commit himself to any chronological measurement of the geological changes which have taken place since these relics were deposited, or to admit the absolute certainty of the conclusions which have been drawn. In this he displays the characteristic caution of the true philosopher, the want of which has produced so many scientific blunders among those who have allowed their devotion to cherished theories to hurry them into false, or at least premature, conclusions. It may be safely asserted, that, notwithstanding the powerful and accumulated evidences which appear to assign a more remote antiquity to the human remains which have been discovered, they are neither individually nor collectively so strong as those by which the inspiration of Scripture is attested; so that if the Bible really asserted that man did not exist at any period before the last six thousand years, there is stronger evidence to show that the Scripture is true, than to prove that the statement is false. But, reserving all this, we are bound to admit that the evidences of a much higher antiquity are not only very strong, but so cumulative in their character as to bid fair, at no distant day, to become conclusive.

Let us suppose, then, that these early relics of primeval man are really what they are supposed to be, the remains of a savage, or at least an uncivilised race of human beings which existed many thousands of years ago; the question arises how such a discovery can be made to harmonise with Bible history. The Scripture is generally understood to affirm that Adam was the first human being that ever existed on this planet, that he was originally a holy and sinless creature, and that it was only because of his fall in the garden of Eden, that death and its attendant miseries obtained admission to the world. According to Scripture chronology, the creation of Adam took place only about six thousand years ago; and yet here is apparent evidence, not only of man's existence, but of man's degradation and misery thousands of years before Adam's creation and fall.

Now it is quite true that, so far as Adam is concerned, the popular understanding is fully borne out by Scripture statements in which these facts are positively affirmed. But it is not so conclusively asserted that Adam was the first man, or that no previous race existed before his time; for, although an uncareful reading of the Bible might lead us to suppose that when Adam was created the sun and moon were only two days old, we cannot avoid observing that we require a whole chapter of unwritten history to be interpolated, to account for the presence of Satan in the garden of Eden. The fall of the angels *must* have preceded the fall of Adam, and, therefore, the popular idea cannot be correct, because it is really inconsistent with itself.

We have already shown that Scripture *history* commences in the second chapter of Genesis, not in the first; and that it is the story of the Messianic family only, commencing with the creation of Adam, who was its first ancestor. We must also bear in mind that, besides the narrative of the creation of Adam in the second chapter, we have another perfectly distinct account of the creation of Man in the first; and, although we are entitled to conclude that the creation of Adam as described in the second chapter, took place somewhere about six thousand years ago, we are not entitled to accuse the Scripture of falsehood, on the ground that the one narrative can be nothing more than a repetition of the other. On the contrary, if it shall be proved that long before the creation of Adam there was another race of men existing on the earth, we are entitled to conclude that their creation is recorded in the first, and not in the second chapter of Genesis; and that they may have lived and become extinct[*] thousands of years before the time of Adam.

And, then, in regard to the evidently savage state in which these early inhabitants of our planet lived, it is too confidently presumed that they must always have been savages, and never anything higher. This is altogether a gratuitous speculation, as it implies either that God created them originally in a savage state, or that they had been developed from some brute. If that be a legitimate conclusion from the premises, we do not need these pre-Adamic remains to prove the falsehood of Scripture, because the existence of savages in our own time would be equally conclusive in proving that no such person as Adam existed. Until it be proved that man never *can* degenerate, the statements of Scripture are entitled to as much respect as the speculations of philosophy; and, if the existence of savages in our own day is not inconsistent with a state of original righteousness in Adam, it is not impossible that these primeval men were in like manner the degenerate descendants of a progenitor originally holy and sinless.

We might even assume stronger ground, and say not only that it might, but that it must have been so. In a previous chapter it has been proved that sin is a disease, and not the natural and normal condition of rational and

* The statement in Gen. ii. 5, that "there was not a man to till the ground," pushed to its extreme length, would only prove that the previous race or races were at that time extinct.

moral beings; and therefore, these primeval men could not have been created as we find them. They must have been originally pure and sinless, when they came from the hand of their Maker; and there must have been a period in their history when the change took place. Natural science has now attained such proficiency, that even a single bone is sufficient to enable the naturalist to tell, within certain limits, not only the size and the form, but the very habits of the animal to which it belonged. These inferences are not considered presumptuous or fanciful; and, although to the unlearned, it may appear marvellous that so much may be read where so little appears to be written, the naturalist himself feels persuaded that not one-half has been deciphered of that which may yet be read. May we not, with equal confidence, from these relics of pre-Adamic man, restore their moral, as well as their natural history? If they were really men, they must have been possessed of immortal spirits like our own; and these spirits must necessarily be still in existence, either wandering upon this earth, or confined in " chains under darkness," waiting for the judgment of the great day. We also infer that where there has been death, there must have been sin, and that where there is sin, there must have been a fall. We read in these records of pre-Adamic man another tragic history not unlike our own, and there rises up before us in the dim distance a first created man, who must have been formed after God's own image, a princely being, created in knowledge, righteousness, and holiness, and exercising dominion over a world subjected to his sway.

If Satan and his angels were created in the image of God, and if, falling from their original righteousness, they died, and are now disembodied spirits, they must have

lived and died before the time of Adam; because, even in
the garden of Eden, Satan was a disembodied spirit, and
had to use the organism of a serpent in order to communicate with Eve. The only novelty to which these
discoveries introduce us is the important fact, that this
earth must have been the place of their abode, and the
theatre upon which their history transpired; and that their
remains consist not only of a parasitic spiritualism which
has haunted and afflicted our race in all ages, but also
of their material bodies, and other remnants which have
been found in Denmark, England, France, &c., to attest
the degeneracy at which they had arrived before they
became altogether extinct. Instead of fearing or regret-
ting these discoveries, we ought rather to hail them as
most opportune, not only in the interests of truth, but in
the interests of theology; because they afford a key to a
number of interesting but hitherto perplexing facts, which
may, by their means, be satisfactorily explained.

First of all, we obtain a key to the history of Satan,
who figures so largely in Scripture story, and whose nature
and origin have hitherto been shrouded in impenetrable
mystery. Who and what is Satan? In nature and constitution he differs, in no respect, from the unclean spirits,
his angels. He is himself an unclean spirit, and, therefore, must at one time have possessed a body in which he
died, and, from which, at death, he must have been cast
out. Here, then, was the original prince of this world,
who, in addition to the authority which he wielded as the
patriarch of his race, and the monarch of the whole earth,
would possess also a physical and intellectual grandeur as
the immediate creation of God, which must have been
perfect of its kind, and noble even in its ruins; and as
Adam and his antediluvian nobility, who counted their

ages by centuries, and survived the successive generations that descended from them, would tower above the savage bushmen of the present day, so would the prince of this world, and probably the first few generations of his race tower above their degenerate descendants, who, wanting the conservative and life-sustaining influence of a dispensation of mercy, such as that which has been in our times the salt of the earth, would at length lapse into a state of utter degradation such as is indicated by the Danish shell heaps, or the bone caves of the continent.

In the second place, these remains bring us face to face with a pre-Adamic fall. Sin, misery, and death are written in very legible characters on these memorials of the ancient world, and as they must have come from the hand of their Creator very good, we infer that there must have been a fall. As regards our own race, the Scripture has transmitted to us a very circumstantial history of the fall of Adam. He and his wife were lodged in the garden of Eden, and received as the test of their obedience the command that they should not eat of the fruit of a certain tree which grew in the middle of the garden. It seems very probable that, had they been left to their own inclinations, and not been tempted by Satan, they would have continued to obey the command, and at length, when the time of their probation was happily ended, a transformation to an angelic state would have taken place either gradually or in the twinkling of an eye. Mortality would have put on immortality, and the animal body, the *sōma psūchikon*, would have been changed into the spiritual body, the *sōma pneumatikon*.

In regard to Satan we have no such history, and, therefore, we can only reason by analogy. It may have been that, like Adam, Satan received some positive command, which was to be the sacramental test of his obedience; or it may have been that natural conscience, and the precepts of the moral law, were the only restraints imposed upon his perfect freedom; we cannot tell. The result alone we know; he sinned, and fell from his original righteousness.

If it be asked how it was possible for Satan to sin if he was created with a holy nature, and with no tempter to tempt him, we can only answer by analogy. A man may be created healthy, and yet not be proof against disease. There is a very great difference between a healthy state and a state of disease, and a man may be created in the one state and afterwards fall into the other. So it is quite possible that Satan may, and it is quite certain that he must, have been created in a perfectly healthy moral state, with an instinctive reverence for God's law, and an intense desire to do His will. It may be that, like Hazael, he would have said—"Is thy servant a dog that he should do such things," if it had been told him in a state of innocence, what he would do in a state of sin. It may be that it was an error of judgment, and not an error of heart, that led him into circumstances unfavourable to moral healthfulness; for it does not by any means follow, that because his moral nature was unsoiled by sin, his intellectual nature was incapable of error. It may be that he over-estimated his own power of maintaining his integrity in circumstances of great moral danger; and as holy Adam was ruined by a lie, so might holy Satan have been the victim of his over-confidence in his own moral strength.

There can be no disease where there is no susceptibility, but there may be susceptibility where there is no disease. In like manner, there can be no sin where there is no fallibility, but there may be fallibility where there is no sin.   A man may have naturally a healthy constitution, but he may imprudently expose himself and induce disease. In such a case the disease is caused, not by any weakness of the constitution, but by the imprudence of the exposure.

But we do not propose to attempt the solution of the origin of evil.   Our only purpose in making these re-marks is to show that an existing state of corruption is quite consistent with the fact of a previous state of original holiness, just as a man's being consumptive is quite con-sistent with his having previously enjoyed a robust con-stitution and healthy lungs.   To put the question, why God made Satan and Adam fallible is equivalent to asking why He conferred on intelligent and rational beings a moral nature at all (in which the possibility of sinning, as well as of continuing in holy obedience, is implied).   The fatalistic arguments that are used in order to charge God with the origin of sin, involve no greater difficulty in regard to the unknown circumstances of Satan's fall, than in regard to all the events that are taking place around us.

What an interesting chapter does this open up to our view in the early history of our planet, thousands of years before the story of Eden began—unwritten, it is true, but not altogether unknown.   The immutable principles of God's moral government on the one hand, and the out-going of the human character and instincts on the other, are the warp and woof in which might be woven histories, romances, and even biographies wonderfully like our own. The earlier ages of the Satanic race, and more especially during the life-time of Satan, may have been a period of patriarchal civilisation and comparative repose—a time of Tubal-cains and Jubals, when both sciences and arts

N

attempted to strike their roots into the accursed ground ; but for want of a Seth and a Noah, violence and lust would blast the budding hope, and century after century of hopeless degeneracy and degradation would mark the remaining history of that ruined race, until it became altogether extinct, and left the world a solitude again. What a subject for an epic, different from Milton's, or rather for many epics, with scenery that still survives! There are inevitable incidents which must have occurred. We see before us, as clearly as if a thousand ages did not intervene, the gay primeval lover wooing his blushing bride at dewy eve under the Danish oaks that then grew where now no oaks will grow. Another picture presents us with the primeval mother nursing her sickly child, or, it may be, the gray primeval patriarch bending under his load of years with his primeval offspring innocently gamboling by his side. Who can tell how many moral heroes may have risen in different ages of that ancient world, combating the wickedness, and struggling to turn back the tide of advancing degeneracy and approaching ruin, but all in vain ? A thousand such pictures rise before us, and although individually they are fictitious, in the aggregate, they were all there.

Many features, no doubt, would appear in those landscapes which are never seen in ours, and although by far the greater number would be common to both, there are some which must be peculiar to our race, which could not have been seen by theirs. There may have been an Eden, but there never was or could be a Calvary. There must have been many Gilboas, but never a Penuel or a Moriah. Cains and Nimrods there must have been in abundance ; perhaps also a Jannes and a Jambres, or it may be even a Balaam, but there never was an Abel or an Abraham,

or an Isaiah or a Daniel, to light up the gloom of that
old world's history.

Nor must we suppose that God was altogether a stranger
to them either as a lawgiver or a judge. They probably
never listened to the thunder of a Sinai, but the fires of a
Sodom may not have been altogether unknown; and the
same God who remonstrated personally with Cain, and
held converse even with Satan, was not unlikely to have
had personal dealings with primeval man. As the missionary recognises in the Red Indian a brother having an
immortal soul, where the soldier would see only a warrior,
the merchant a trader, or the traveller a guide, so does
the Christian recognise in these earliest tenants of our
world, not merely intellectual, but moral and religious
beings, where the naturalist discovers only ancient specimens of the *genus homo*, and the antiquary nothing more
than the denizens of the stone, the bronze, or the iron age.

CHAPTER XV.

SATAN NEVER IN HEAVEN.

CHRISTIANS have a mythology of their own, although
whence they got it, it would not be very easy to
tell. Much of it, no doubt, is of heathen origin, and has
been unconsciously absorbed into our creed by Christian
poets, weaving Scripture into the creations of their own
fancy, until they have ceased to distinguish the one from
the other. Milton, especially, is our great Christian
mythologist; and, although no one imagines that his
" Paradise Lost " is a historical representation of facts,
the splendour of his genius has done more to mislead the

Christian mind on the subject of angels and devils, and heaven and hell, than all the other poets put together.

It is remarkable how much the Miltonic theory, so grossly material in its ethics, and so fancifully spiritual in its physics, underlies the popular conceptions of heaven, with its spirit hills and spirit vales, its spirit trees, and spirit mansions, having no locality in God's material creation, with which our resurrection bodies having flesh and bones can have any connection. " Farewell sun, moon, and stars," said a dying saint, as if he should never see them again, or as if the heaven which he expected to enter were far beyond the nebulæ, or not in space at all.

It is also the prevailing belief, that Satan once dwelt in heaven; but that, having seduced a countless host of the celestial inhabitants, and having raised the standard of rebellion, he encountered in battle the angelic armies that remained faithful to their allegiance. As the result of this angelic war, he and his fellow-rebels being defeated (though without slaughter), were hurled from the battlements of heaven, and from thence sank into hell. Such is the Miltonic interpretation of the passage in 2 Peter ii. 4, where we are informed that they were cast down to hell.

We will search in vain throughout Scripture for any foundation on which to rest the idea that Satan ever was in heaven. He is called an angel no doubt, and probably that has afforded the ground upon which the fancy has been built; but we must distinguish between the " angels of heaven," and the angels which belong exclusively to this world—between the "angels of God " and the " angels of the devil." There are, it is true, a few passages which *seem* to say that Satan was once in heaven; but these need only to be quoted, in order to show how incapable.

they are of affording ground for such a supposition. They
are as follows :—

Isa. xiv. 12. How art thou fallen from heaven, O Lucifer,
son of the morning ! how art thou cast down to the ground
which didst weaken the nations !

Luke x. 18. And he said unto them, I beheld Satan
as lightning fall from heaven.

Rev. xii. 7. And there was war in heaven : Michael and
his angels fought against the dragon ; and the dragon
fought and his angels, and prevailed not ; neither was
their place found any more in heaven. And the great
dragon was cast out, that old serpent, called the devil, and
Satan, which deceiveth the whole world : he was cast out
into the earth, and his angels were cast out with him.

Whatever may be the general impression which the
reading of such passages produces upon an unthinking
mind, a very slight examination of each is sufficient to
satisfy us, that not the faintest indication is afforded in
any of them of Satan having ever been really in heaven.

The first passage has no reference whatever to Satan,
but applies to the king of Babylon, whose power and
dignity are represented as exalting him to heaven ; and
when that power and dignity were overthrown he is represented as being cast down to the ground. It need
scarcely be remarked that the king of Babylon never was
in heaven. Even if the passage, therefore, had referred
to Satan, the figure which is employed would not have
been sufficient to prove that he was in heaven ; but it
has palpably no reference to him at all.

The second passage is not more conclusive than the
first ; because our Lord was speaking not of what had
taken place before the time of Adam, but of what he
saw as the result of the preaching and mission of the

seventy disciples. The seventy returned with joy, saying, Lord, even the devils are subject to us through Thy name. And he said unto them, I beheld Satan as lightning fall from heaven. Moreover it was not Satan, but the lightning that fell from heaven. The words are, " I saw Satan, like lightning from the heaven falling." But even though it had been Satan, and not the lightning that came from heaven, it could only be the same heaven from which the king of Babylon fell; it was the heaven of power and influence upon earth, not the heaven which is inhabited by the angels. A few verses before, the same figurative language is applied to Capernaum : " And thou, Capernaum, which art exalted to heaven, shalt be thrust down to hell ;" not that either Satan or Capernaum, ever was in heaven, but the power of the one and the privileges of the other were so great, that they are said to be exalted to heaven ; and when they are said to fall, we are not warranted in supposing that anything more is meant than their degradation and ruin. This passage, therefore, as well as the other, refuses to countenance the idea of Satan having been expelled from heaven.

The passage in Revelation is even less available than any of the others ; not only because, like the others, it is merely figurative, but because it speaks of events which were then in the future, probably the downfall of the pagan empire in Europe ; and for this reason it cannot represent what took place before the time of Adam.

Probably the supposition that Satan and his angels were once in heaven may have had its origin in the name which Scripture has given them as "Angels;" and, as the devils are immaterial spirits, it is presumed that heaven must have been their original habitation. But we have already shown that the word angel simply means a messenger, and is applied to the inhabitants of earth as well as the inhabitants of heaven. We must not, therefore, attach too much importance to the circumstance that the devils are called angels. Besides, we must keep in view that there is a difference between the angels of God and the angels of the devil. The angels of God are called the angels of heaven, evidently to distinguish them from those who are not the angels of heaven; and we have no evidence to show, that the demons were angels in any other sense than that of being angels of the devil. As for Satan himself, he is always represented as exclusively and emphatically belonging to this world, and to this world only.

We must not forget, even in reading the Bible, that this world is a planet of the solar system; and that when our Lord ascended into heaven from the Mount of Olives in the presence of his disciples, his departure was as distinctly seen, when he sailed off into intersolar space, as that of any ocean-bound vessel that ever left our shores. To what place, or in what direction he went, is another question; but there can be no doubt of this, that He well knew the way; and as He directed His flight towards His Father's house of many mansions, which He went to prepare for His resurrection saints, His eye would be directed to one particular point in the heavens, and to some orb, as material in its nature as the body it was about to receive. Christ knew that this earth was but a planet circling round the sun, because He made them both. He knew that the sun was but a single star in the bright nebula which we have called the Milky Way; but whether His flight was directed to one of those stars, or whether His pathway lay far beyond, toward some other nebula, of this we may be assured, that it lay in some particular direction of the starry heavens; and that often previously, during His weary pilgrimage on earth, His eye would be turned upon it with a loving and longing gaze, so that He had an astronomic meaning when He said (John viii. 14), "I know whence I came, and whither I go."

This heavenly relationship is much dwelt on by our Lord. "Ye are from beneath, I am from above; ye are of this world, I am not of this world" (John viii. 23). "Doth this offend you? What if ye shall see the Son of man ascend where He was before" (John vi. 58-62). Speaking of the angels also, the same heavenly relationship is continually presented to us. They are called "the heavenly host," "the angels of heaven," and "the angels that are in heaven." They are "sent from heaven," and they go away "again into heaven" (Luke ii. 15), so that whatever part of the material universe they may call their home, they do not belong to this planet.

But in striking contrast with this heavenly relationship of the angels, we must mark the earth-bound habitat of Satan. He is the "prince of this world;" the astronomic meaning of which is, that he is the prince of this planet.* He is described as "the ruler of the power of the air, the spirit which now worketh in the children of disobedience" (Eph. ii. 2). The spirit that now worketh in these children of disobedience denotes the unclean spirits, which are his angels, and which are represented to us in Scripture as going to and fro on the earth, walking through dry places, earnestly desiring to be clothed upon, seeking rest, and finding it only in the persons of fallen men under his rule.

* When Scripture speaks of Satan as the "*prince* of this world," he is called the prince of this "kosmos," speaking of it *astronomically:* when he is spoken of as the "*god* of this world," he is called the god of this "aiōn," speaking of it *morally.*

Why should we not take an astronomical view of the question? Our earth is a planet, and theology does not deny it. Let us look, then, at this world, of which Satan is said to be the prince, from the distance, say, of Mercury, or Venus, or the sun, and what do we see?—a brilliant star. On that star Abraham, and Isaac, and Jacob were born. On that star the Son of God became incarnate and died; and on that star Satan and his thousands of unclean spirits are going to and fro over its whole surface, doing what they can to establish the kingdom of darkness, and oppose the kingdom of Christ. Now, if that be the case, we naturally ask, Whence came the thousands of unclean spirits that haunt our polluted earth if they were not natives of the soil?

Let us suppose, for a moment, that Satan was once in heaven, wherever that may be; we might well inquire, what would bring him to this particular planet of the solar system, if he did not originally belong to it. Formerly, when the heavens and the earth were considered a very fair and exhaustive division of the universe, nothing could be more natural than to suppose, that if Satan was cast out of heaven, there was no other place than the earth to receive him. But looking at the world in an astronomical point of view, and supposing that Satan was cast out of heaven, it seems hard to believe that he and his angels should have been able to make the journey to our planet from so great a distance; or supposing them to have been able to make the journey, it is difficult to understand what would make them think of coming here, and remaining so long. So that if Satan be the prince of this planet, and of this planet only, it seems quite unaccountable how he and his subordinate host should have come into possession and lordship of this earth, on any other supposition than that of its being the place of their nativity.

How much more natural is it, and how much more consistent with all that Scripture tells of the devil and his angels, to suppose that our planet was for millions of years the abode of successive tribes of animated creatures, and that at length, this series culminated in a moral and intellectual race of beings, who, though created holy, kept not their first estate, but fell. That such a race existed we have now a considerable amount of proof in these pre-Adamic remains which geologists have lately discovered; and when, in addition to this, we find the earth, at the time when Adam was created, already tenanted by a host of parasitic spirits, we have every reason to conclude that the one fact is the counterpart of the other.

There is in reality nothing in the Bible which ascribes to Satan a nature higher than that which we suggest; and although an unguarded and predisposed interpretation of certain passages has led some to infer a kind of semi-deity, possessed of universal presence, or an abstract personality of evil, in Satan; a careful examination will convince us, that there is really ascribed to him nothing higher than chieftainship over his angels; and, if what is done by *them* be occasionally ascribed to *him*, it is nothing more than a common figure of speech, which we daily apply to the acts and policy of men.

No doubt, there are millions upon millions of these fallen spirits, the accumulated outcome of the successive ages of sin and misery, during which they existed upon earth; so that if there be anything like organisation among them, by which the genius and generalship of the head are made to direct and regulate the whole, we may well say, with Paul, that "we wrestle not with flesh and blood, but with principalities and powers, with spiritual wickedness in high places, with the rulers of the darkness of this world." The position of eminence which Satan is represented as occupying in Scripture, corresponds in every respect with the idea of his having been, like Adam, the immediate "son of God" by creation, and distinguished above others by the high intellectual powers which he received directly from his Maker's hand. To him was given the sovereignty over the subject world, long before the creation of Adam. He was made the prince of this world, having "dominion over the fish of the sea, and over the fowl of the air, and over every living thing that moveth upon the earth." After Satan's fall, and probably after his race had become extinct, Adam was created, and, in turn, became prince of this world; and may we not here discover a motive for Satan's seeking to ruin man by the temptation of Eve? Up till that time he had no rival upon the earth; but when Adam appeared, it was no longer so; and hence his malignity and cunning. Could he but succeed in tempting man to sin, he should obtain fresh subjects for his own kingdom, and, at the same time, snatch the crown from his rival's brow. What the nature and terms of Satan's sovereignty may originally have been, we cannot tell. Neither can we tell how that sovereignty was exercised over his own posterity, either as a living patriarch or a disembodied spirit, when he died. That he should be the prince of this world, and exercise patriarchal authority over his own descendants as long as he lived, is no more than we should naturally expect, even though we had no revelation; but it also appears that, after his death, he continued to be the prince of the power of the air, and that he even now exercises authority over his angels, which, we have reason to believe, are the disembodied spirits of his race. The dim light that falls upon the subject may not be sufficient to bring out all the details; but it is sufficient to reveal the grand outlines of a history which we are only now beginning to understand.

It would appear, then, that when through Satan's machinations, Adam was seduced from his state of happy innocence, he lost his princely crown, and nature refused to recognise his sovereignty: the earth brought forth briers and thorns; and the beasts of the field, the birds of the air, and the fishes of the sea, disowned his sway. The sovereignty reverted to the older dynasty, and Satan again became the prince of this world, not merely in virtue of his superior power and intellect, but in virtue of his original authority and the absence of a superior power.

According to Jude (ver. 8) even Michael the archangel acknowledged his standing and "dignity," and dared not bring a railing accusation against him, and therefore he only said, "The Lord rebuke thee." Paul also speaks of him and his subordinate princes as the principalities and powers (*archai* and *exousiai*) that rule the world (*kosmocratores*). In the case of Adam, his posterity at once degenerated, and yet the early patriarchs lived many hundred years. Satan and his immediate descendants may, in like manner, have lived long patriarchal lives; and although, for want of that Messianic element, which tended, like salt, to preserve the earth after the days of Adam, there must have been a sad and rapid degeneracy in the succeeding generations of the Satanic race; yet, like the antediluvian patriarchs, there must still have been a superior order of his more immediate descendants, which would supply the principalities and powers, and rulers of the darkness of this world, which form the intervening link between Satan and his angels.

In the tenth chapter of Daniel we obtain a casual glimpse of a remarkably perfect organisation of the principalities and powers which rule the darkness of this world, and against which, not men only, but angels have to contend. Besides the rank and file of inferior tempters and oppressors, there appear to be superior intelligences, having the oversight of kingdoms and communities, and exercising authority over subordinate spirits, though themselves subject to their great chief, whose angels they are. See verses 13 and 20.

It cannot but strike a thoughtful observer that there is a remarkable similarity between the way in which God speaks to Satan, and the way in which he would address a man. "Whence comest thou?" said he to Satan one day, in an assembly of worshippers, very much in the style in which he put a similar question to Elijah in Horeb, "What doest thou here, Elijah?" and the reply which Satan gave does not suggest that he considered the inquiry as at all remarkable or uncommon. Although popular opinion has laid the scene of this interview in heaven, on the occasion of an assembly of the angels, as if he had never been cast out from their company; a more sober consideration would suggest that Satan was not likely to be admitted there; and that a congregation of God's children on earth was a gathering at which he would be more likely to be present, either in person or by proxy. The question, "Hast thou considered my servant Job? that there is none like him in the earth, a perfect and an upright man, one that feareth God, and escheweth evil," brings out another peculiarity in Satan's character as the accuser of the brethren; and this is quite in keeping with the other incident which is recorded of him in Old Testament history, in the days of Zerubbabel. There he is introduced to us, standing before the angel of the Lord, at the right hand of Joshua, to resist him; when the Lord said, "The Lord rebuke thee, O Satan." And again, the third time, at the temptation of our Lord, when he plies his treacherous arts, but fails. In none of these, certainly, is he presented to us as a very amiable character; yet if we are to be guided, not by popular tradition or superstitious fancy, but by the unvarnished statements of the word of God, we will have to confess that there are men of our own race drawn by the hand of inspiration in blacker colours than even Satan. With so much power, with so much license, and, at the same time, with so much experience, and with such deep despair, perhaps the best of us would be no better than he.

And then, in regard to God's condescension and forbearance in speaking to, and acting towards Satan, is it at all greater than, or even so great as, His condescension and forbearance towards the impenitent of the children of Adam, whose guilt is certainly greater? The day of judgment has not even yet arrived; and all God's dealings with him, as with us, are as yet only providential and natural, not judicial and final. He might have said to Satan, as He said to Israel, "O Satan, thou hast destroyed thyself," though He might not add "but in me is thy help." The necessary and inevitable consequence of sin was, that when it was finished it should bring forth death; and, therefore, death must needs pass upon him, and upon his posterity, because they all had sinned : but we still recognise the heart of the Father, even in speaking to, and dealing with, His unworthy and disobedient children.

We think too lightly of God's condescension to Israel, when He said, "How shall I give thee up, Ephraim? How shall I deliver thee, Israel? How shall I make thee as Admah ? How shall I set thee as Zeboim ? " and we sometimes think it very natural, and very proper, that the Redeemer should weep over Jerusalem when her day of grace was past, even though she killed the prophets, and was at that very moment seeking how she might destroy Himself. Why, then, should we suppose that in His dealings with the elder race, there should be no compassions, and no regrets? To those who compare the guilt of the one race with the privileges and guilt of the other, the language of God to Satan must appear less wonderful than His condescending language to impenitent men ; and yet neither of them is inconsistent with the doom that awaits them both.

The popular estimate of the nature and character of the devils is so very dark, that it would be considered a libel on the human family to suppose that any of us are nearly so bad : the very name suggests the concentrated essence of wickedness; and, on that account, our suggestion that they are the disembodied spirits of pre-Adamic men will seem by far too favourable an explanation of their origin ; and yet, when we inquire into the grounds on which this popular estimate is formed, we might find it difficult to discover anything which would justify it, beyond the limits which our theory would prescribe. Much of it, no doubt, is due to the instinctive dread with which our nature regards the mysterious world of spirits, and which clothes with imaginary terrors an agency which is both unhallowed and unknown.

That there is great diversity in the character and disposition of the demons, appears very evident from Scripture. One is described (Luke xiii. 11), as a "spirit of infirmity," whose only influence was to produce a state of body, in which the woman who was afflicted with it, "could in no wise lift up herself." We are prevented from supposing that this was a merely figurative description of her disease, by the words of our Lord, who evidently intended us to understand, that this was something more than merely physical deformity or disease. He says, in answer to the ruler of the synagogue, who found fault with Him because the cure was performed on the Sabbath day, "Ought not this woman, whom Satan has bound, lo, these eighteen years, to be loosed from this bond on the Sabbath day?" In contrast with this comparatively harmless spirit of infirmity, we have another case of possession, in which the infliction was peculiarly malignant (Mark ix. 18), "Wheresoever he taketh him, he teareth him; and he foameth and gnasheth with his teeth, and pineth away." On coming into the presence of Jesus, "the spirit tare him, and he fell on the ground, and wallowed foaming." "Ofttimes," said the father, "it hath cast him into the fire, and into the waters, to destroy him." This is, perhaps, the most malicious of the demons of which we have any account in Scripture; and yet it would not be difficult to match it with many a devil in human form, even in our own day: and our Lord evidently intimates, in the answer which He gave to the question of the disciples, "Why could not we cast him out?" that this was a peculiar and extraordinary case: "This kind can come forth by nothing, but by prayer and fasting." If we examine the other cases of demoniacal possession, we will find that, with this exception, and, perhaps, also that of Legion in Gadara, in which not one, but thousands, were in possession of their victim, there is nothing more wicked, or more malicious, in their character than in that of many of our own race. The very fact of being possessed by them was itself a great calamity; and if, as was frequently the case, not one, but seven, and it may be thousands, were joint occupants of the same person, we should not require the further aggravation of peculiar wickedness and malice in the possessing spirits, to make the possession a very terrible calamity.

<hr />

CHAPTER XVI.

ANTEDILUVIAN THEOLOGY.

WHEN Adam was created, Satan and his angels were fallen spirits, who, according to our hypothesis, were the former possessors of this world; and it seems a most natural explanation of the conduct of Satan to suppose that jealousy, hatred, and revenge were the motives which induced him to seek the ruin of our race, by tempting Eve to eat the forbidden fruit. Until Adam was created, Satan was the prince of this world, whether there were any remnants of his race surviving or not; so that, when a rival appeared to occupy the throne which he had once possessed, it was not at all likely that he would patiently look on, if it lay in his power to prevent it.

Satan was permitted to tempt Eve to eat the forbidden fruit; but whether that permission was asked or not, we cannot tell. In the case of Job, and perhaps also that of Peter, permission was expressly asked and formally granted; and so it may have been also in the case of Eve. The punishment awarded to him for his success, shows that the permission did not lessen the guilt of his malignity, nor save him from the penalty of his sin. Balaam received permission to accompany the messengers of Balak; but the asking it was a sin, and, there-

O

fore, he received no protection from its punishment. The sinful request may be granted for the very purpose of defeating the malignity which prompted it; and this was really the case both in the one instance and in the other. As the journey of Balaam and the malice of Balak were overruled for good to the people of God, by converting the threatened curse into a blessing, so may it have been in Eden : the temptation may have been permitted without having been approved ; and when it was successful it was amenable to the penalty of its own success.

The story of the serpent in Eden is one which we do not as yet possess the means of fully explaining, although the day may not be far distant when we shall; but our hypothesis creates no difficulty which did not exist before. If the demons at Gadara were able to enter into the swine, the prince of the devils might surely enter into the serpent; and if that old serpent, the devil, was more subtile than any of his degenerate descendants, the feat which he performed of using the organs of his mouth to produce articulate sounds, needs no metaphorical interpretation to make it credible.

There was also cunning, if not wisdom, in making the experiment on Eve before making the attempt on Adam. Every distinctive quality of her sex rendered her more liable to be persuaded and deceived than Adam, and more likely than the serpent to persuade and deceive her husband. Whether the plan laid by Satan was permitted, by God or not, the result was the same : not only did Satan succeed in ruining our first parents, but in ruining them he overthrew the dynasty that had been established on the ruins of his own.

But he was not permitted to enjoy in comfort the triumph of his cunning. The conqueror was to become the conquered, and the author of his defeat was to be the seed of the very woman who had been the victim of his wiles : in the language of the prophecy, the seed of the woman was to bruise the serpent's head, although the serpent was to be permitted to bruise his heel.   The serpent, however, was again the prince of this world, since his rival was cast down ; and yet from that moment he was destined to be dethroned by the Coming Man.

The events of the succeeding sixteen hundred years form a portion of the world's history of which very few remains have come down to us.   That there were prophets during those sixteen hundred years, and that God communicated with mankind by their means, is nothing more than we should naturally expect ; and we have already, in our second chapter, shown that this probability is converted into certainty by the language of Zacharias, when he said :—" *Blessed be the Lord God of Israel ; for he hath visited and redeemed his people, and hath raised up an horn of salvation for us in the house of his servant David ; as he spake by the mouth of his holy prophets,* WHICH HAVE BEEN SINCE THE WORLD BEGAN."   The same truth is also asserted in Peter's address on Acts iii. 21. " Which God hath spoken by the mouth of all His holy prophets since the world began."   It is remarkable that in Genesis Moses has preserved to us none of these pro- phecies of a coming Messiah.   Adam, and Seth, and Enoch were in all probability the great prophets of the antediluvian age ; but where are their prophecies?   Jude has preserved to us a portion of the book of Enoch, and there indeed we find that Christ and His coming victory over His enemies form the subject of this prophecy ; but this has not come down to us through Moses ; and the omission suggests to us the possibility that there may have been a whole literature which has now perished, filled with prophecies of the person and work of Christ.

Tradition, however, as well as the Apostle Jude, has supplemented the records of Moses by preserving to us some at least of these antediluvian prophecies in the symbols of ancient astronomy. Antiquity with one voice pronounces these to be of antediluvian origin; and the result of modern investigation by astronomers themselves confirms the tradition, by showing that there is internal evidence of their having been constructed upwards of five thousand years ago. Cassini thus commences his History of Astronomy:—"It is impossible to doubt that astronomy was invented from the beginning of the world; history, profane as well as sacred, testifies to this truth." Bailly and others have asserted that astronomy must have been established when the summer solstice was in the first degree of Virgo, and that the solar and lunar zodiacs were of a similar antiquity. This would have been about 4000 years before the Christian era. They suppose this science to have originated with some ancient and highly civilised people who lived at that time in about latitude 40°, but who were swept away by some sudden destruction, leaving, however, traces of their knowledge behind them. Sir William Drummond says:—"The fact is certain that at some remote period there were mathematicians and astronomers who knew that the sun is the centre of our system, and that the earth, itself a planet, revolves round it;" and Mrs. Somerville says that every circumstance concurs in showing that astronomy was cultivated in the highest ages of antiquity.

Josephus attributes the invention of the constellations "to the family of Seth, the son of Adam," and refers for his authority to ancient writers, whose names alone have

survived.   Origen tells us that it was asserted in the
book of Enoch that, in the time of that patriarch, the
constellations were already divided and named.   Volney
informs us that everywhere in antiquity there was a
cherished tradition of an expected conqueror of the serpent, who was to come as a Divine person, born of a woman;
and he asserts that this tradition is reflected, in the
constellations, as well as in all the heathen mythologies
throughout the world.   Dupuis also, and other writers of
the same school, have collected ancient authorities abundantly proving that in all nations the traditions always
prevailed, that this Divine person, born of a woman, was
to suffer in his conflict with the serpent, but was to
triumph over it at last.   He also asserts that this tradition is represented in the constellations; and although
both Volney and Dupuis bring this as an argument
against Christianity, we are at liberty to accept their
facts without adopting their conclusions.

A third circumstance must be taken into account, in
connection with their having come down to us through a
period of nearly six thousand years.   There has been in
all ages a sacredness attached to them which it would be
difficult to account for, unless upon the supposition that
they contain mysterious truths which they were intended
to hand down from generation to generation; and although
the key to these mysteries has for many centuries been
lost, superstition and idolatry have endeavoured to supply its place.   First, idolatry transferred the worship that
was due to the Divine Saviour, to the emblems which
represented Him; and next, astrology prostituted the
signs which prophesied of a coming Saviour to the prognostication of individual destinies.   Both combined, however, have preserved to us, with an accuracy which seems

remarkable, not only the figures which Seth is said to
have drawn in the heavens, but even the hermeneutic
names attached to their constituent stars.

Connecting these three circumstances together, each of
them abundantly proved, and each of them independent
of the others, we find a whole system of prophetic imagery
inscribed upon the heavens in the world's first infancy by
some grand antediluvian patriarch, possessing not only
high scientific knowledge, but such regal authority as to
command the veneration of the whole world, and to pro-
ject its teaching downwards through successive generations
with an impetus and a sanctity that have carried it to our
own time over sixty centuries.   Observe, also, the influence that these have had, even when the key was lost,
over the world's traditions, kindling and keeping alive the
expectation of a coming One, and prophesying of His person
and work.   Conspicuous over the whole, and characteristic of all the rest, shines out the promise of Eden, that
the seed of the woman was to bruise the head of the serpent, and, in the conflict, to be wounded in the heel.
Not only the figures in the constellations, but the very
names of the stars, form the articles of the antediluvian
creed.   Even by the confession of the enemies of Christianity it is acknowledged that the twofold nature of
Christ as God and man is inscribed in unmistakable
characters in the traditions with which these emblems are
identified, and indicated even in the emblems themselves.
But, above all, we have conspicuous the symbols of the
great enemy which the promised seed was to destroy,
chief among which is the serpent.   Sir W. Herschel
complains that the heavens are scribbled all over with
serpents; while other truths regarding him are represented under the form of scorpions, lions, bulls, dragons,

The Promised Seed.

&c., which the Messiah was to overcome. The Church, too, is represented, as in the Old Testament, in the character of a woman, and, as in the New Testament, in the character of fishes—indicating, in the one case, the parentage, and, in the other, the innumerable progeny of the promised seed.

In the absence of a printed literature, it was a magnificent idea to inscribe these doctrines upon the heavens themselves, and link them with the discoveries of astronomic science; so that the heavens might declare the glory of God, and that these precious doctrines might be handed down from father to son, and from sage to sage, without any one daring to make any change. We can only introduce a few specimens of these antediluvian prophecies.

VIRGO (*Eden*).

As before the time of Moses, the year of the Hebrews began, as the civil year of the Jews still begins, with the entrance of the sun into Virgo, we shall have no difficulty in discovering the evangelical meaning of the sign as figured by the prophet.

Most appropriately does the prophet commence his teaching by rehearsing the story and the promise of Eden in a symbol that contains an epitome of the whole creed. We behold a woman fallen, and lying on the ground, grasping in her hand an emblem of the promise, and holding in the other the palm of future victory. The brightest star of the constellation, however, is not in the woman, nor in the palm, but in Spica, the ear of corn, representing the promised seed; and, to mark her original dignity, she is represented with wings.

Each sign of the Zodiac is accompanied with three other constellations called decans, the first of which, connected with Virgo, is the one above, called Coma (the desired, the longed-for), represented by a girl holding an infant in her lap. This had been corrupted by the Alexandrian astronomers, who changed the oriental "Coma" into the Greek "Comē," hair; and, instead of the virgin, with the "longed-for child," they drew it in the form of a wig. Albumazer, however, who lived at the court of the Caliphs of Granada, early in the ninth century says,—"There ariseth in the first decan as the Persians, Chaldeans, and Egyptians, the two Hermes and Ascalius teach, a young woman whose Persian name, translated into Arabic, is ADRENEDEFA, a pure and immaculate virgin, holding in the hand two ears of corn, sitting on a throne nourishing an infant, in the act of feeding him, who has a Hebrew name (the boy, I say), by some nations named IHESU, with the signification IEZA, which we in Greek call Christ." In the time of Elizabeth, also, it seems to have been known under this form, as Shakespeare, in Titus Andronicus, speaks of an arrow being shot up "to the good boy in Virgo's lap."

Taking into account the attitude of the woman with the ear of corn, distinguished by the brightest star, and interpreted by the accompanying constellation of the virgin and child; taking also into account the tradition, which traces it to Seth, corroborated by the calculations of modern science, we need have no hesitation in connecting it with the promise to Adam, that the seed of the woman was to bruise the head of the serpent, and that the serpent was to bruise his heel.

LIBRA (*The Flaming Sword*).

The scene changes—the woman disappears—and in the field of prophetic vision we behold a pair of balances suspended in the heavens. The justice of God stands forth, and man is condemned; he is weighed in the balances, and found wanting, One of the scales is borne down, and the other rises; and the star, ZUBEN AL GENEB, which means "the price that is deficient," records the verdict. The antediluvian theology, as well as the Christian, commences by concluding all men under sin, and having no righteousness of their own by which they can be justified.

SCORPIO (*Death, and he that hath the power of Death*).

The scales are withdrawn, and the vision presents to our view a scorpion, intimating that the wages of sin is death, and that he who hath the power of death is the devil. This vision represents the penalty of sin, and the triumph of Satan, in consequence of the broken law; but, in the first decan above, we have the figure of a man treading on the scorpion's head, and grappling with the serpent, which he is strangling. Here, then, we have the promised seed in the figure Ophiucus, crushing the head of the scorpion, while the scorpion is at the same time wounding him in his heel. The brightest star in Scorpio is ANTARES, which means *wounding*. Surely when Seth traced this figure in the sky, he had in remembrance the curse pronounced against the enemy, and the bruising which the coming Saviour was to suffer in the conflict. When our Lord predicted the overthrow of Satan, and rejoiced that, although he should suffer, his people would be invulnerable, he said,—"I beheld Satan as lightning fall from heaven; behold, I give unto you power to tread

on *serpents* and on *scorpions*, and over all the power of
the enemy, and nothing shall by any means hurt you."
This antediluvian prophecy seems as if it were a pictorial
representation of the conflict.

SAGITTARIUS (*Bethlehem*).

Again the scene changes, and now a strange figure
appears in the sky armed with a bow, and shooting an
arrow at the scorpion. He is possessed of two distinct
natures, and yet is only one person. Here, then, is the
first appearance in the Zodiac of the destroyer of the
power of the enemy, because as yet in the previous signs
we have no representation of Christ. The virgin represented fallen man; the scales represented his trial and
condemnation; the scorpion represented the sentence and
penalty that follows the trial; and now we have appearing in the field the promised seed, who is to bruise the
serpent's head; but our attention is first directed to the
person of Christ in his Divine and human natures, represented by the twofold nature of Sagittarius. In this
sign, although the warrior is introduced as about to destroy
the scorpion, there is no representation of the humiliation
or propitiatory sacrifice of Christ—that is reserved for the
sign that follows.

CAPRICORNUS (*Calvary*).

The archer disappears to give place to another representation of the Promised Messiah. He now appears as
a dying victim, the goat being a sacrificial animal. Here,
again, He appears in a twofold nature; but now it is not
His union with the Godhead, but His union with His
Church-that is represented. It is remarkable also that
in all the representations of this sign, the goat is repre-

SAGITTARIUS.

The Slayer of the Scorpion.

sented as if fainting or dying, while the fish which terminates his body appears lively and in action. Again, the names of the stars give the interpretation of the sign ; and the star AL DABIH, which means the *sacrifice slain,* removes all doubt regarding its true meaning, teaching the antediluvians that the Messiah should suffer and die. Fishes, both in Old and New Testament times, signify multitude, and are frequently applied to those who are converted by the Gospel. "I will make you to become fishers of men," was the promise given to the apostles by our Lord; and among the early Christians the fishes were a well-known emblem of the Church. We shall find in the other constellations that the same interpretation is always attached to them. Here, then, we see the atonement represented by the death of the sacrifice, and the life of the Church represented in its union with Him.

AQUARIUS (*Pentecost*).

Once more the scene is changed, and in virtue of the sacrifice of Christ, the Holy Ghost is exhibited as poured forth upon the Church. This is represented by a water-bearer, who holds a water-pot, from which a stream is flowing; and in order to show its destination, it is represented as entering into a fish called *Piscis australis.* Nothing could be more appropriate than this type of the Spirit poured out in consequence of the death of the sacrificial victim. Entering into the mouth of a fish, it represents the outpouring of the Spirit on the day of Pentecost, and the gift of tongues, with the indwelling of the Spirit in all them that believe. The fish represents the Church both in Capricornus and Aquarius, so that we see in the one the justification of those who are united to Christ by faith, in the other, their sanctification through the Holy Ghost entering into and dwelling in them. The decans of this sign are the Southern fish, which receives the stream, Pegasus, the flying horse, and Cygnus, the flying swan, intimating the carrying of the Gospel of Christ over land and water to all nations, after the pentecostal shower.

PISCES (*The Church*).

We must not dwell too long on this theme, and yet we cannot leave it without noticing the closing sign of this first section of the prophecy, which also connects it with the opening sign of the section which follows. The sign of Aries, the ram, has been in all ages regarded as the first of the series; but its proper figure is not a ram, but a lamb; and in its hand, or rather its forefoot, it holds a ribbon, which is connected with the two fishes of the sign before. The constellation Pisces is represented by two fishes which have been caught, and are united together by a starry band, exhibiting the fruits of the Spirit's power. We have already said that the fishes signify the Church, and here we have them in their twofold relation, first to one another, and then to Christ. Being united to one another, the band that unites them represents the bond of peace and love by which they become one; and the ribbon being extended and carried into the succeeding sign, and placed in the grasp of the Lamb, shows that they are also united to Christ, and that He has the keeping of them in His loving charge. Both of these ideas are represented by the stars OKDA, "the united," and AL-SAMACHA, "the upheld." The decans of this sign, beside the starry band, are Cepheus, a king, who holds out a branch, and Andromeda, a female figure, delivered from the Dragon.

These are but specimens of pages taken from a book four thousand years old, full of gospel teaching, not only of Christ, but of the enemy which He came to destroy, and over whom, although He suffers, He eventually triumphs.

Those who would pursue this interesting study, are referred to "MAZZAROTH; OR, THE CONSTELLATIONS," * a work of great learning, ingenuity, and research, by the late Frances Rolleston of Keswick, to which the author is indebted for the materials here introduced, although he has not altogether adopted her interpretation.

CHAPTER XVII.

THE RIVAL THRONES.

OUR modern theology differs somewhat from the ante-diluvian and apostolic in saying little or nothing of Satan in connection with the work of Christ. Since the days of Anselm, our theory of the Atonement leaves him out altogether; but perhaps, in avoiding one error, we may not altogether have escaped falling into another. How is it that Satan is the accuser of the brethren; or, as a lawyer would put it, what *locus standi* has he in the matter? What interest had he in opposing and chal-

---

* Published by Rivingtons, London. Miss Rolleston, who died at an advanced age, was not only an earnest Christian but a great Oriental-ist, and devoted much of her time to the subject here illustrated. She was much interested in the publication of "The Stars and the Angels," and before her death expressed a wish that in a second edition the author should introduce her favourite subject. This wish he has now much pleasure in fulfilling.

longing the work of Christ? and how came he to have his head bruised in the encounter?

Our own interest in the work of Christ is abundantly plain. By our natural birth we became sons of Adam and inheritors of his fall. We were in the loins of Adam when he ate the forbidden fruit; and as the Count of Paris fell when Louis Philippe was dethroned, we are just what we are and what Adam made us, a royal family dethroned. Supposing, then, that Christ the son of Adam entered procedure for the recovery of Adam's inheritance, Satan had the greatest possible interest in the result. By his craft he had succeeded not only in dethroning his rival Adam, but in subjecting his posterity to his own rule; and would regard with alarm any attempt to recover the lost sovereignty. If Christ should succeed, the crown would be plucked from Satan's brow, and the prince of this world cast out; whereas if, in the conflict which was about to take place, the Son of man should fall, the ancient dominion of Satan would be re-established, and he and his kingdom would stand.

It was by our *natural* birth that we became heirs of Adam; and that, not in a legal point of view only: it was a real and constitutional union, by which all that we are and have is from and through him; our bodies, our intellect, our moral character and dispositions,—all have come to us through him.

Such also are our relations to Christ, although in a less external and corporeal form. Our *spiritual* birth is not a legal or judicial fiction, but a real and constitutional change of nature. A foreign element is introduced, of which there was not a vestige at our natural birth; and this, which is called "the seed of God," comes to us directly through Christ; so that we become *really* united to

Him by receiving into our persons a portion of His Spirit. It is a wonderful change which takes place at conversion, because by the new birth we become sons of God and joint-heirs with Christ, not by any legal fiction or judicial whitewashing, but by Christ's Spirit actually and really dwelling in us and becoming part of us; so that, in fact and in reality, we become "partakers of the Divine nature," * and "members of his body, of his flesh, and of his bones" (Eph. v. 30), which suffered the agony of Gethsemane, was crucified upon Calvary, and thus gave full and legal satisfaction to Divine justice for the sins of all its members (Gal. ii. 20).

But this is not all. This personal union and actual indwelling of the Spirit of Christ communicate a new LIFE, which was not there before, and without which men are but the branches of a dead Adam; and moreover, if it be real and not fictitious, it will produce an entire change of character and dispositions, and will eventuate in resurrection (2 Cor. v. 5; Eph. i. 14). This is the Bible doctrine of salvation by Christ: it is a real, a present, and a certain salvation. None can understand it who have not experienced it; but when it does take place, and when the teaching of the Bible finds its counterpart in personal experience and supernatural change, the man who experiences it feels as if he had awakened from a dream; the Bible seems to have acquired not only new light, but new warmth and life. It fits into his nature with such wonderful *rapport*, like a key into a lock, searching all its chambers, that although, before conversion, it commended itself to His veneration by its native majesty and supernatural surroundings, now, the experimental evidence outshines all the rest; and you

* 2 Pet. i. 4.

will as soon persuade the infant, that his mother's breast is an invention and an imposture, as you will persuade the new-born Christian that the Bible is not the Word of God.

But what has Satan to do with all this?

It is too much the fashion to deny or explain away whatever we do not understand; and to construct our theories upon the principle that no part of them shall belong to the unknown. The best and most legitimate theories, however, are those that, like the map of Africa or Australia, mark off whole regions as unexplored. In the spirit of this caution, let us enter on the inquiry before us.

CHRIST VERSUS ANTICHRIST.

When we are introduced into a court of justice, a very cursory glance is sufficient to enable us to understand the course of the procedure, and the nature of the conflict that is going on; and yet we may not understand the questions which are at issue, or the bearings of the arguments which we hear discussed. Even the clients themselves, who are most interested in them may not be able to fathom the technicalities which are involved; and yet it would be impossible for even the most ignorant observer to confound such a controversy with the struggle between a policeman and a burglar, or a battle fought between two contending armies.

And so, when we stand in presence of the conflict between Christ and Satan, we may not altogether understand the controversy, or the plea, or even the points at issue; but we can easily discern that the antagonism is not the result of purely personal antipathy, nor an encounter which is to decide who is the more capable of inflicting injury and enduring pain; it is evidently a political and dynastic struggle, a process of ejectment according to law, Christ *versus* Antichrist, for the sovereignty of the world. The power of Satan, against which our Lord had to contend, was not his angelic strength, but his magisterial claims; the weapons of his warfare, therefore, were neither carnal nor spiritual, but legal, and the arena of the conflict was not the battlefield, but the bar. Had the question been one of might, there would have been no struggle at all, because to Satan the issue would have been instant destruction from the presence of the Lord; but this was not the case : he evidently had a legal standing which was admitted both by the Father and the Son; and his acknowledged rights had to be dealt with by judicial process, and abrogated according to law. When the Father, therefore, brought forth into the field His antagonist, He also fully recognised the right of Satan to challenge His claims.

Although Jesus, the Son of Mary, was *born* King of the Jews, with lineage and title perfect, yet, His claim to the sovereignty of the *World* had still to be made good. His father David, whose throne he inherited, had only a limited dominion, and his father Adam, whose promised heir He was, had forfeited the crown. It appears, for reasons, some of which we may not understand, to have reverted to the senior race of the world's humanity; and Satan, at this time, appears to have been not only *de facto*, but *de jure* "the Prince of this world."

From the time of Adam downwards (may we not now go higher and say, from the time of Satan downwards?), the principality has always been lodged in the elder son. The subjection of Eve to her husband Adam was not more pronounced than was the subjection of Abel to his elder brother Cain. "Unto thee shall be his desire, and thou

P

shalt rule over him;" not because of any moral or intellectual superiority in Cain, but simply because he was the elder. Monarchy is the instinct of our race, and on the death of Adam, the princedom would have descended to Cain. But, we must also remark, that although the rights of primogeniture are everywhere recognised in Scripture, these rights are almost continually superseded by electing grace. Japhet, the elder, is superseded by Shem; Ishmael, by Isaac; Esau, by Jacob; Reuben, by Judah; Manasseh, by Ephraim; Aaron, by Moses; and so on. The institution itself is maintained, and the firstborn is the rightful heir; but in all these recurring cases, electing grace vindicates its superiority, and it is ordained that "the elder shall serve the younger." Had Adam maintained his integrity, he would also have maintained his title, and Christ would not have recognised Satan as prince of this world (kosmos), but only as the god of this world (aiōn). But because he fell he forfeited his crown, and that crown reverted in the meantime to its original possessor in virtue of his seniority until it was legally recovered by the " Son of Adam."

The purpose for which the Son of Man was come, therefore, was to cancel by deed of law the attainder by which the dominion had been forfeited; and, after that had been done, to re-establish the kingdom in His own hands.

Up to the time of our Lord's baptism, He had not as the seed of the woman, been formally installed into His office as the Messiah of the Church, and the champion of God. From His birth He was both God and Man, the Son of God, and the Son of Man; but He had not yet been anointed with the Holy Ghost and with power. But when the Holy Ghost descended bodily upon His human nature, He became the Christ of God, the *Third* Person of the Trinity dwelt in His humanity, He was filled with the Holy Ghost without measure, and now, for the first time, His human nature wielded an infinity of prophetic power. The difference between the prophetic character of Christ and that of the prophets consisted in this, that they received the Spirit from Him (1 Pet. i. 11), whereas in Him there dwelt all the fulness of the Godhead bodily (Col. ii. 9).

The baptism or anointing of Jesus being his official installation into office, it was appropriately accompanied by the public presentation of his credentials by the Father in person, as well as by the testimony of John the Baptist, who had been raised up exclusively for that purpose. From that moment Satan beheld in Jesus the long-looked-for Seed of the woman, and the claimant of his throne; so that he could truly say, "I know thee who thou art, the Holy One of God."

In the temptation of Christ immediately after His installation into office, we have something more than a mere incident of His holy life: like His death and resurrection, it partook more of an official than of a personal character. Standing in the room, and as the representative of His people, He had to retrieve the disaster of the Fall, not only by enduring the penalty which had been incurred by His predecessor, but by working out a righteousness for them which should challenge the approbation of the Judge, and meet the utmost demands of the accuser. The contest which was now about to open was one upon which not only the sovereignty of the world, but the supererogative glory of God and the everlasting destinies of the Church were suspended.

The temptation of our Lord was an event which was

not only permitted but arranged in the providence of
God. He did not voluntarily enter into temptation, but
was driven of the Spirit into the wilderness for the purpose—not that He resisted the Spirit's movement, for in
all things He was subject to His Father's will; but His
subjection to temptation was not an act of His own free
will, for He could not, without sin, have invited the
tempter. It is evident from all the circumstances, that
the adversary was permitted to dictate the terms of the
encounter; it would almost appear as if there had been a
conference between God and Satan on the subject. "Hast
thou considered my servant Job?" was the challenge
addressed to Satan many centuries before; and it is not
unlikely that, as in the precedent of Job's temptation,
Satan had the choice not only of his own weapons and
the ground on which the battle was to be fought, but of
the very armour, or, rather, want of armour, in which our
Lord was to abide the assault. His demand appears to
have been that the wilderness should be the scene of the
conflict, and that, previously to his entering the field,
hunger should prepare his adversary for the particular
temptation with which he intended to assail him. Our
Lord was evidently made to understand that it was His
Father's will that He should not resist the movements of
Satan, so far at least as merely bodily arrangements were
concerned; so that He permitted the tempter to carry
Him to the pinnacle of the temple in Jerusalem, and then
to the exceeding high mountain, that Satan might have
the opportunities he desired for the purpose of the temptation. One restriction, probably, as in the case of Job,
was imposed upon Satan, that he should "spare his life;"
His further ministry requiring that the end should not
be yet. But this was not the final conflict which was to

decide the victory, for that was reserved for the bloody field of Calvary : but it was to be the first passage of arms in that great contest which was to decide not only the sovereignty of the world, but the everlasting destiny of a multitude which no man can number; and in that conflict every facility and advantage was given to Satan, that he might not be able to boast, that if the circumstances had been less favourable, the issue would have been different. Hitherto he had been victorious over every warrior that had been brought into the field—Adam, Job, Moses, David, and Solomon—all of them mighty men : each of them in succession had been successfully encountered and overthrown; and still the proud boast of this formidable Goliath went forth against the armies of the living God —"Give me a man that I may fight with him." Now, he stands face to face with God's own champion, the man with whom he is to dispute the empire of the world, having obtained all that he demanded as the preliminaries of the conflict.

CHAPTER XVIII.

THE FIRST CONFLICT.

BEHOLD, then, the two champions face to face, and if ever there was silence in heaven, there must have been silence then. A cloud of witnesses in breathless expectation must have been gathered round the arena on which that battle was to be fought, to witness the conflict, and to be ready to minister to the fainting warrior when he sank exhausted, but victorious, on the field.

To make the triumph more complete, everything was

in favour of the enemy. Here was no Eden, with its soft delights, its fruitful orchards, and its lovely bowers. A bleak and howling wilderness, with beasts of prey and haunting demons, had been for forty days the dwelling-place of the lowly Son of Man, who had not where to lay His head.

It might even be said that He came disarmed to the conflict, with nothing but the smooth stones of the Word of God, and the sling of the Spirit, with which He sent them deep into the forehead of His enemy; and He entered the field fasting and hungry, weak and wasted, patient, but expecting whatever God would send Him to sustain His fainting manhood; and then the tempter came.

We have not the slightest reason to suppose that upon this occasion Satan assumed any personal or bodily form. It was not necessary, as in the case of Eve, because our Lord, being invested with prophetic power, could hold converse with spirits, even as the prophets are able to receive direct communications from the Spirit of God.

The first temptation with which our Lord was assailed was in these words, " If thou be the Son of God, command that these stones be made bread ;" and here we cannot but observe three very remarkable peculiarities.

In the first place, here was a knowledge and acknow-ledgment of the person and power of Jesus as Christ, far in advance of anything which had been directly revealed. Satan had, indeed, heard the Father acknowledge Him as His beloved Son, but who told him that Jesus had the power of working miracles ? for Scripture informs us that up to this time He had not as yet wrought any miracles (John ii. 11).

In the second place, we observe how dexterously the

tempter addresses himself to the weaknesses of human nature. Our Lord was hungry; what more reasonable than that He should be fed ? Our Lord was the Son of God, having all power in heaven and on earth; what more proper than that, in the absence of bread, the very stones should be made to minister to his necessities. And if our Lord had been subject to the frailties of humanity, and if the pride of life had had any part in Him, what was to prevent Him from vindicating the majesty of His Sonship by giving this decisive evidence of His power ?

But, thirdly, and most important of all, we must observe the subtlety of the temptation; because it seemed to be in fact no temptation at all, but only a suggestion which might have been adopted and acted on without any sin. Thousands have read the narrative without being able to discover the moral poison which was lodged in the proposal. What harm would there have been, supposing that Jesus had made the stones to become bread ? Where would have been the sin ? Did not our Lord on different occasions feed the multitudes by miracle ? Did He not with five loaves and two small fishes feed more than five thousand of those who were less hungry, and less needful, than He ? If there was no sin in the one miracle, why should there be sin in the other ? Was it because it was bread in the one case that was turned into bread, and only stones in the other ? Our common sense rejects the explanation, for there can be no more sin in making bread from stones, than in making it from nothing. In the case of Elijah, the widow's oil was multiplied, and the meal in the barrel never failed, just as the loaves and the fishes were multiplied as loaves and fishes; but did not our Lord at the marriage of Cana in Galilee change the water into wine, showing that it was not the turning the stones into bread that was the sin? It must have been something else.

Some have supposed that there would have been no sin if He had performed a miracle to do good to others, but that it would have been a sin for Him to work a miracle on His own behalf. " The gift of working miracles (says one divine) belonged to Him as a talent for the use of others, not as a privilege for the ease or gratification of Himself." This, however, cannot be the true explanation, because upon several occasions, He wrought miracles for His own deliverance, when His life was threatened by His enemies. When the men of Nazareth dragged Him to the brow of the hill whereon their city was built, intending to cast Him down headlong, we are told that, passing through the midst of them, He went His way; and on another occasion, when the Jews took up stones to stone Him, He suddenly hid Himself from them, and, passing through the midst of them, went His way.* On both of these occasions our Lord wrought a decided miracle; whether it was by rendering Himself invisible to the Jews around, or by so blinding His enemies that they should not see Him; in either case He used miraculous power to work out His own deliverance, and not the deliverance of others. It must also be observed in this connection, that there was as much an outputting of miraculous power in His subsisting forty days and forty nights without food, as in turning the stones of the wilderness into bread; and although this might have been an argument to silence Satan, it affords no explana-

* We might add a third occasion, on which He miraculously prostrated the company that came to take Him (John xviii. 6), although He did not use the miracle for His deliverance. It was evidently performed to show that He could have escaped if He had been so inclined.

tion of the sinfulness of the temptation. If it had been in itself a sin to turn the stones into bread, it would have been equally a sin to escape by miracle from death before His time.

Others have supposed that the sin would have consisted, not in the act itself, but in doing it at the suggestion of Satan. According to their view, there would have been no harm in Christ's turning the stones into bread if He had done it of His own accord, but it is supposed that if He had done it when the Devil asked Him it would have been sin. This is but a vulgar error, and has no countenance from the Word of God. If the turning of the stones into bread had been a sinless act in itself, the mere circumstance that Satan asked Him to do it would not have changed its nature and made it sin. This would not have been the first time that God acted on Satan's suggestions, neither would it have been the last. The calamities which Satan proposed to inflict upon Job received the consent of God, and who will say that that was sin? A similar request was made in regard to the disciples. "Satan hath desired to have *you*, that he may sift you as wheat;" and it is evident that the permission was granted, for our Lord said to Peter, "I have prayed for *thee* that *thy* faith fail not."

But a still more remarkable instance of our Lord's doing what the devils asked Him, is found in His conduct at Gadara, when a whole legion asked Him to allow them to enter into the herd of swine, and when He gave them leave. This conclusively proves that, if the turning the stones into bread had been otherwise lawful, the mere circumstance that Satan asked Him to do so would not have made it sin.

What, then, was the reason for our Lord's refusal?

How was it that Satan knew that if Christ had yielded
to the temptation, sin would have been committed, and
man's redemption lost?

The explanation is to be found in that which constituted the perfect righteousness of Christ; the entire
conformity of His will to the will of His Father in heaven.
His righteousness consisted, not only in doing nothing
against the will of His Father, but in doing nothing
without it. Other men have wills of their own, and it
is only when they discover that the will of God is
opposed to their will, that they give up their own will,
and do the will of God. But in regard to Christ, so
complete was His obedience, so perfect was His righteousness, that He was continually guided, and directed, and
controlled by the will of his Father who was in heaven.
This implied, of course, that He was in perpetual correspondence; that there was not a moment of His life in
which He was not conscious of His Father's will, nor a
circumstance of providence in which He did not, as it
were, hear the voice saying, "This is the way, walk ye
it, when ye turn to the right hand, and when ye turn to
the left."

This is the habit of mind to which each of us should
aspire, and which many of God's people are conscious of
possessing, at least in some small degree. Their communion with God is so constant and so direct, that the
candle of the Lord is continually shining on their path;
and in every thing that they do they look upward for
guidance, instead of inward for direction. David had
somewhat of this experience when he said, "As the eyes
of servants look unto the hand of their masters, and as
the eyes of a maiden unto the hand of her mistress, so
our eyes wait upon the Lord our God" (Ps. cxxiii. 2);

and the promise that God gives to such a spirit is this, "I will instruct thee, and teach thee in the way which thou shalt go. I will guide thee with mine eye" (Ps. xxxii. 8).

If such be the spirit, more or less, of all believers, how perfect and how constant must have been that conformity and correspondence which existed between the will of Christ and the will of His Father in heaven. Not but that His human nature had a will—a sinless, holy will, distinct from that of His Father; it was that will which determined His actions, for His Father's will never operated except through His own. If He had had no will of His own, there could have been no obedience, because the actions would have been no longer His, but His Father's, but His will was so finely touched, so infinitely responsive to His Father's will, that it never on any occasion acted till it knew that the Father's will was the same. "I came down from heaven (said He); not to do mine own will, but the will of him that sent me;" and in Hebrews x. 9, "Lo, I come to do thy will, O God."

In the garden of Gethsemane his human nature had a will distinct from that of God's. That will shrank from suffering; and when called on to look forward to the cup of God's curse being put into His hand, His nature would not have been human if it had not recoiled; but although it did recoil, and although He prayed in agony that the cup might pass from Him, He was not the less submissive and obedient. "Not my will, but thine be done."

Such, then, was our Lord's life of obedience, that in everything, even to the most minute particular, His eye was directed to His Father's hand. When His Father said "Come," He came. When He said "Go," He went; and when He said "Do this," He did it. There was not a miracle that He performed, not a word that He spoke, not a foot that He lifted, nor a hand that He raised without His Father's will and consent. "My doctrine," said He, "is not mine, but his that sent me. He that speaketh of himself, seeketh his own glory; but he that seeketh his glory that sent him, the same is true, and no unrighteousness is in him."

When Satan, therefore, proposed to Him the performance of this miracle, the turning of the stones into bread, in order to relieve His hunger, and prove that He was the Son of God, he was, in fact, proposing that Christ should do not His Father's will but His own.

The circumstances in which He was placed were very trying. His Father had brought Him into the wilderness, and had made no provision for His sustenance. There was no bread in the wilderness, no means (as yet appearing) by which to satisfy His hunger; but what of that? His Father had brought Him there, and His Father had kept Him there, and His Father alone was the party to whom He was to look. He had no doubt about His Father's faithfulness; no suspicion that He had forgotten him. He knew that His Father could send manna from heaven as He did to Israel of old, or send His angels to minister to Him, as He really did immediately after. But that was God's concern, not his; and, therefore, the idea of doing anything without His Father's will was not to be entertained for a single moment. The doing of it of His *own* will, without the instructions from His *Father*, would have amounted to disobedience, which was impossible.

That this was the light in which Christ viewed the temptation is evident from the reply which He gave. Jesus answered and said unto him, "It is written, Man shall not live by bread alone, but by every word that proceedeth out of the mouth of God." This, as is well known, is a quotation from the law of Moses, in which the Lord is addressing Israel, and reminding them of the dealings by which He had proved His chosen people, to know what was in their heart, whether they would keep His commandments or no. "And he humbled thee, and suffered thee to hunger, and fed thee with manna, which thou knewest not, neither did thy fathers know; that he might make thee know that man doth not live by bread only, but by every word that proceedeth out of the mouth of the Lord doth man live. Thy raiment waxed not old upon thee, neither did thy foot swell, these forty years. Thou shalt also consider in thine heart, that, as a man chasteneth his son, so the Lord thy God chasteneth thee. Therefore thou shalt keep the commandments of the Lord thy God, to walk in his ways, and to fear him." (Deut. viii. 2-6).

The application which our Lord made of the passage was evidently this. His Father had brought Him into the wilderness, as He had brought the children of Israel before, in order to try Him and prove Him; and His purpose was to show that man is not to live by bread alone (for there was none in the wilderness) but by whatever other food the Lord would provide, whether that might be manna, or angels' food ministered by the angels. In any circumstances, his duty was to wait upon God, and do nothing without His guidance and direction.

Our Lord at once detected the unrighteousness of the proposal, and rejected the temptation.

But this was not all; we must notice the manner in which our Lord combated the tempter, and in this also

He manifested His obedience. He answered him by a reference to the Word of God, "It is written." Not only was He subject to the Father in doing that which He knew to be His Father's will, but He here also subjects himself to the authority of God's Holy Scripture.

Our Lord had no doubt committed the whole of the law to memory, and perhaps written out a copy according to the commandment (Deut. xvii. 18); and now He shows us the use to be made of it, not only for the purpose of leaving us an example that we might follow his steps, but as a substantial part of his mediatorial work; so that although He was a son yet learned He obedience, not only to the *will* but to the *word* of God; and this homage which He paid to the authority of Scripture, was as if He had said, " It is to the Bible that I am to look for direction in all my duties; it and it alone is a lamp unto my feet, and a light unto my path; and as God has said in His word, man shall not live by bread alone, I shall not dare to live upon anything which does not proceed out of the mouth of God."

So ended the first temptation, the first encounter of a long and weary war: but, as usual in such cases, the first struggle of the conflict was decisive of the victory. The Son of Man came forth from the trial, not only unwounded, but unsullied, and not only unsullied, but unapproachable by the very shadow of a sin. How must the tempter have been amazed! He had never seen anything like this before.

It would be doing Satan great injustice to suppose that he intended or prepared for more than a single temptation. He evidently staked the issue of the contest on a single fall, and made no provision for defeat. The first was a most subtle and carefully-planned temptation, the most brilliant effort of Satanic genius; the second was beneath contempt. Carrying our Lord to Jerusalem, and perching Him upon the very pinnacle of the temple, he bade Him cast Himself down from thence to prove that He was the Son of God. A garbled quotation of Scripture is clumsily introduced, evidently in imitation of our Lord's reply, and showing that it was but the desperate resource of an unsuccessful enterprise—which also failed.

There remained but one hope, and that hope was compromise. Was it not possible that both should reign? The proposal might seem to be desperate, yet it must be tried. Carrying our Lord up to an exceeding high mountain, and causing to pass before Him in prophetic vision all the kingdoms of the world in a moment of time, he offers to resign his throne. The price which he asks in return for His being spared all further humiliation and suffering is, that He will do homage for the crown. "All this power will I give thee, and the glory of them, for that is delivered unto me; and to whomsoever I will I give it. If thou therefore wilt worship me, all shall be thine."

We must not look on this offer as a fictitious compromise or as a gigantic lie. Throughout the temptation there does not appear to have been any attempt to deceive our Lord. The assertion that the kingdoms of the world and the glory of them had been delivered to him, appears, for anything that we know, to have been literally true; and if he had not the power of transferring the crown, he had, at least, the power of resigning it, and this was what he now proposed to do. That which had been delivered to Satan was offered by Satan to be surrendered

to Christ,—" ALL shall be thine." Satan could not suppose that Christ would purchase a title which had no
existence, or do homage to a fictitious prince for a fictitious
crown. It was a veritable rival and a real antagonist
that was before Him, and the imperial interests for which
these high powers were contending were not words but
things. The offer which was then made, therefore, was
not an attempted delusion, as is generally supposed, although it was a snare; because the royal power and
authority which he assumed and asserted as the prince of
this world were not denied. We are prevented from
understanding the plausibility of this temptation by an
erroneous idea of his personality. We think of him as
the personification of evil; but he was not so. He was
a great personage, and his rank and dignity as prince of
the kings of the earth, was yet undisturbed. He still
wore the crown which was shortly to sit on another
brow, so that doing homage to him was no more than
the mightiest potentates on earth had all along been
accustomed to do. Satan no doubt viewed this proposal
from his own stand-point as the solution of a question
of disputed sovereignty. The strength of his position
rested, not on might, but on claims of law. *Might* he
really had none, in presence of the acknowledged Son
of God; but he had TITLE, and that title he was now
prepared to compromise, if not to resign, and thus to
end the controversy. He knew that he need not attempt
another temptation; and, therefore, reserving to himself
nothing but his feudal superiority, he offers to surrender
the throne. In one point of view if Jesus had been any
other than He was, it would have been a tempting
offer to the Son of Man. All the privations of a lowly
and lonely ministry, all the persecutions of malignant

enemies, all the horrors of Gethsemane and Calvary were before His eyes, and here was an offer in which it was proposed to Him to escape them all, and mount the throne of the world at a bound.

With all his wisdom, Satan did not see the utter impracticability of his proposal : he thought only of himself as the accuser at the bar; he thought nothing of offended justice on the throne. The cross to him was but a weapon of offence, with which he might avenge himself upon his adversary if his proposal should be rejected; and although it stared him in the face, that in the homage he demanded, there was a sin so gross that it could not be given, he was blinded by his own despair. The events of the day had virtually ruined his cause, and blasted his hopes, and he grasped at a shadow to prevent his fall. But it was in vain: "Get thee behind me, Satan," was the indignant reply, "for it is written, thou shalt worship the Lord thy God, and him only shalt thou serve."

Even though no sinful compliance had been appended such as that which met so instant and scornful a rejection, there were high reasons of state why even a voluntary surrender of the throne should not be accepted by Christ. The princedom of this world, like His many other crowns, were to be won and worn, not by the gift of Satan, but by the might of His own obedience unto death; and the spoils of the vanquished must adorn the triumph of the conqueror.

CHAPTER XIX.

SALVATION ACCORDING TO LAW.

SUCH was the close of the first campaign of that great war; but although it was decisive, it was not the last: Satan departed from Jesus only for a season; and when the hour and power of darkness arrived, and when He was delivered into the hands of sinners, with it came also that fearful conflict, in which, tortured in body, agonised in soul, and deserted by His Father, He had to abide the assaults of His cruel and revengeful foe, who, with all his legions, was let loose against Him. Scripture has drawn a veil over this last and most dreadful struggle, and we must not attempt to raise it. The three long hours of darkness and silence cover an unfathomable ocean of woe, and it is only as He emerges from the agony that we feel relieved by hearing that shout of victory as it escapes from His dying lips, "It is finished," and He dies.

He died, and in dying completed the overthrow of our great adversary; whose claims, power, and authority were forthwith abolished, for at that moment the "prince of this world was cast out" (John xii. 31); by His death He "blotted out the handwriting of ordinances that was against us, which was contrary to us, and took it out of the way, nailing it to His cross," so that the accuser of the brethren was silenced. "Having spoiled principalities and powers, He made a show of them openly, triumphing over them in it" (Col. ii. 14, 15); and "through death He destroyed him that had the power of death, that is the devil" (Heb. ii. 14).

And why must Jesus die ?   Could not God forgive our
sins and take us to heaven, without laying our iniquity on
His Son? Could He not close the account of our transgres-
sions without carrying the balance anywhere ?   It would
appear not ; for there are some things that men can do,
that God cannot do, and this is one of them ; not because
law is above God, but because God IS to Himself law.

The author remembers the pleasure with which in early
life he read " Combe's Constitution of Man," and the profound conviction with which the reading was accompanied,
that Combe's philosophy might be right, and yet Combe
himself be wrong.   His argument was intended to prove
that there can be no lawless mercy with God; and that if
man is to be saved *in any case*, it must be by some means
by which the inexorable demands of law shall be fully met
and satisfied : and he justifies God's government by showing that He has different administrations of law, each of
which vindicates the inviolability of its own jurisdiction,
without suspending or violating the laws of the others. The
PHYSICAL laws, he says, are inviolable, and inflict their own
penalties as inexorably as if there were no social and no
moral administrations above them. They will do execution
alike upon the greatest saint and the greatest sinner. The
SOCIAL laws, in like manner, are inexorable, and vindicate
their own authority; the man who neglects his business, or
is surly to his customers, will lose his trade even though
he taught a Sabbath school, and devoted himself to works
of charity and usefulness.   The MORAL laws, too, are
equally inflexible, so that the immoral man must be
miserable, even though he were lodged in a palace, and
commanded the resources of an empire.   According to
Mr. Combe a man may be prosperous in one administration and ruined in another, smiled upon in one adminis-

tration and frowned upon in another, beautiful in one administration and deformed in another. What a magnificent idea! how simple is its solution of a thousand difficulties, and how boundless the region which it opens up for exploration!

We feel strongly disposed to concede to Mr. Combe the entire principle which he demands, not only in regard to the coördinate jurisdiction of God's different administrations, but even the absolute inviolability of law. Even in regard to the physical laws, we can now (thanks to Mr. Combe) afford to rest our defence of miracles, not on the violability of law, but on the possible action of a higher coördinate administration. But waiving at present the question of miracles, we accept Mr. Combe's principle as applicable especially to the moral administration, whose laws are *at least* as inexorable as the physical laws, and from that we infer the absolute necessity of an atonement for the salvation of man.

All God's works are according to law; it is His method, and the more we study it, the more do we see its absolute necessity as a covenant between God and creation, without which there could be no independent action among the creatures, far less any responsibility. It is God who makes the gunpowder explode according to law in the assassin's pistol, or who makes the poison operate according to law in the body of his victim : and if He did not do so, —if, in every case, He introduced His own moral perceptions and sovereign will, so as to determine whether or not He would modify or suspend the law of His own administration, the act would be the act no longer of the creature, but of God.

Belief in law is an instinct of our nature, but it is stronger in some men than in others. In some it is so weak that they seek an explanation of all extraordinary phenomena in the sovereign will of the Deity: in others it is so strong as to assert its absolute inviolability, which no evidence could contradict. They are quite prepared to admit the goodness, mercy, and justice of God; but they feel that these must act, not in violation of, but according to law.* Such a mind was Hume's; and there can be little doubt that, in his celebrated argument against miracles, he drew his inspiration from a deep-seated and intuitive conviction of the inviolability of law; and that when he elaborated it into a logical shape, it must have been to his own mind the least satisfactory form into which he could put it. His convictions rested on the assurance of what is the deepest of all intuitions, which even he could not destroy, "Let God be true, and every man a liar;" but he preferred to that a halting logic, which had to go begging for its major proposition, because he had to remember that he at least professed to be an Atheist.

Why then did Christ die? We answer, because God's moral government is even more sacred and unbending than His physical; and if in the physical administration we expect no lawless mercy with God, in His moral government it is still more impossible. So long as Divine justice follows with inexorable punishment every violation of the moral law, and so long as that punishment is adjusted with infinite accuracy, according to the nature and amount of the transgression, God's justice is vindicated notwithstanding the existence of *any* amount of sin. The one being exactly the equivalent of the other, nothing remains on the hands of God to defile the spotless purity of His administration.

Supposing, then, that God were to pardon sin, allowing

* See Appendix C.

the demands of love to neutralise the demands of justice,
how is the equilibrium to be restored? Here is the sin,
where is its equivalent? The balance must be carried somewhere; and if there be no equivalent of punishment,—no
place where the outstanding balance may be carried, it
must inevitably remain on the hands of God.

We are apt to misunderstand the obligations of a judge,
by considering the duties of those who are not judges. In
the ordinary dealings of men, they never fail to make the
distinction. If a man be not a judge he may forgive as
much as he chooses, because he is not responsible for the
administration of justice; but if he be a judge, what he
has to do is to administer law; and if in any case he, as a
judge, does not award the penalty which the law requires,
to that amount he himself is guilty. The unavenged
crime for which the criminal is set free, remains in the
hands of the judge, quite as much as if he punished an
innocent man for a crime of which he was not guilty. In
so far as we are not judges, it is well for us to have mercy,
because God has not delegated to us the avenging of crime.
Our brother who injured us did not offend our justice, but
God's, and therefore He says, "Vengeance is mine, I will
repay, saith the Lord." God, and God only, is judge, and
for that reason He is the more pledged to the punishment;
the administration of justice being his special and official
function. Passing into the hands of God, as judge, it will
meet with the same infinitely accurate amount of penalty
that distinguishes his physical administration. This is a
duty for which man is utterly incompetent.

How, then, can man be saved? Man has sinned, and God,
being judge, must not only punish the sinner, but must
award the punishment with infinite exactitude, according
to the infinite perfection of His justice. If man is to be

XIX.—SALVATION ACCORDING TO LAW.   239

saved, it must be according to law, and by means which are consistent with the most perfect justice. Such is the declaration of Scripture, and it finds an echo in the natural conscience, as that which alone would be suited to the character of God. We feel, no doubt, that mercy is more lovely than justice ; but we also feel that it is not so absolutely indispensable; and unless it can be exercised in consistence with justice, its exercise would cease to be a virtue, and would partake very much of the character of a crime. Unless God can be just at the same time that He justifies the ungodly, man's salvation would be altogether impossible.

The Scriptures represent the atoning death of Christ as a solution of the difficulty, and as the means by which justice is satisfied, and the sinner saved. The general principle upon which this scheme of redemption is based is perfectly intelligible, and when applied to mercantile transactions is perfectly satisfactory. But there is a difference between mercantile justice and criminal justice which does suggest a difficulty, and raises the question whether this atonement be really a satisfaction of justice, or whether it be not opposed to that instinctive sense of right and wrong with which God has endowed our natural conscience, and which we must suppose to be in harmony with His own character. If one man owes a certain sum of money, and another man pays it for him, justice is satisfied, and the debtor is entitled to receive a discharge in full. But crime cannot be dealt with in this manner, for reasons which are too obvious to require an argument. It would be no satisfaction to justice if an innocent man were to be put to death in order to enable the judge to set a murderer free; and therefore the theory of mere SUBSTITUTION is not enough to explain the efficacy of the atonement, on the supposition that it is according to law.

Some theologians have attempted to meet this difficulty by saying that, although such a transaction would
be a violation of justice on the part of man, it is not so
on the part of God, because He is a Sovereign as well as
a Judge. But this does not meet the case, because it
confounds the functions of the judge with those of the
sovereign. If the sovereign could do justice in saving a
criminal by putting an innocent man to death, he could
do justice quite as well, if not better, by pardoning the
criminal without inflicting death upon a substitute.

But the Scriptures do not represent the efficacy of the
atonement as a *mere* substitution, although in our theological systems the idea of substitution is generally placed in
the foreground. In Scripture the grand idea presented is
not so much substitution, as *union;* and for every passage
in which substitution is presented as the theory of salvation, there are ten which represent it under the idea of a
union. In fact, without union there could be no substitution according to law.

There is a story told of a lady who was given up by
her physicians; and when the fond husband asked them
if there was really nothing that could by possibility save
her life, they replied that she was dying for want of
blood, but, if that could be supplied, it was possible that
she might live. The husband in a moment bared his arm,
and bade them take from his veins whatever quantity
was necessary for the purpose. We are told that the
communication was formed, the blood was transfused from
the strong body of the husband, and made to flow gently
into the veins of his wife. The consequence was that she
revived and lived. Here there was no miracle—no violation of the physical laws. The lady should have died but
for the transfusion, and, in that case, the laws of nature

would have been satisfied; but these laws were equally satisfied when the blood flowed into her body, and she revived.

In this incident we have an illustration of the mode of salvation by Christ, in which the law is satisfied, and the sinner saved.   There is, indeed, in the atonement a *substitution*, because, in reality, the just suffers for the unjust, and the innocent Jesus becomes the substitute of the guilty sinner. But there must be more than substitution; there must also be union, for without union there could be no substitution according to law.   In the case of the lady, union without substitution would have been useless, because the mere forming of the communication, without the transfusion of the blood, would not have been enough: the husband must be weakened that the wife might be strengthened, and the blood which was gained by the one must be lost by the other.   But, on the other hand, substitution without union would have been equally impossible, because the death of the husband would have been as contrary to law as the recovery of the wife, unless the transfusion had taken place by means of the union.

It is thus in all God's administrations: there can be no salvation without substitution, and there can be no substitution without union.   A life-buoy will not sustain a shipwrecked sailor unless he be united to it; but if the union has been formed, they become as one, and the life-buoy will sink exactly to the same extent that the sailor is lifted up.   The life buoy becomes the substitute of the sailor; but the substitution cannot take place according to law, unless there be union.   The floating of the sailor, unless he had been attached to the life-buoy, would have been a violation of the laws of nature, and the sinking of the life-buoy without the sailor being united to it, instead of being a satisfaction to the law, would have been a double impossibility.

The objection which has been raised to the doctrine of the atonement, as opposed to our instinctive sense of justice, is founded on a misapprehension of its nature; and the moment that we introduce the idea of union, the objection ceases to have force. In so far as there is no union there can be no substitution according to law, or consistent with justice; and if the Scripture had represented the atonement as a substitution without union, it might not have been very easy to reply to the objection. But Scripture does not represent the Gospel as a substitution without union: there is union; and unless it can be shown that the union is not such as to satisfy law—that is to say, unless it can be shown that it is not a real and personal, but only a theoretical and ideal union—the objection cannot be held to have any force. Now, the Scripture asserts that the union between the Saviour and the saved is not only a real and personal union, but a union so complete that it is described as being not so much a *union* as a *unity*. The unity which exists between Christ and His people is spoken of in the most absolute terms. He is the vine, they are the branches;* He is the head, they are the members of His body, of His flesh, and of His bones;† they are one with Him, He being in them, and they in Him.‡ Such references might be multiplied to any extent, because the Scripture is full of them, both in type and doctrine.

So far from this union being merely metaphorical and fictitious, it is as real and as personal as that which subsists between the spirit and the body or the man himself.

* John xv. 5. † 1 Cor. vi. 15 ; xii. 27 ; Eph. v. 30.
‡ John xv. 4 ; 1 Cor. vi. 17.

The Spirit of Christ actually enters into and dwells in the body of the man at and after his conversion, changing his character and influencing his motives, so that he becomes a temple of the Holy Ghost. "What! know ye not that your body is the temple of the Holy Ghost which is in you?" (1 Cor. vi. 19). "Now, if any man have not the Spirit of Christ, he is none of his" (Rom. viii. 9). Of course this is a mystery, but it is a mystery well known to every one who has undergone the change, although it may be perfectly unintelligible to others. "The natural man receiveth not the things of the Spirit of God: neither can he know them, because they are spiritually discerned" (1 Cor. ii. 14).

If this, then, be the nature of the atonement, and if this union be real and personal, and not merely legal or metaphorical, the death of Christ must necessarily be a complete satisfaction to justice, not in theory only, but in fact. When the head was crucified, the members must be reckoned as having died; when the head rose from the dead, the members could no longer be held as prisoners; and when Christ ascended to heaven, every member of His body was entitled to regard it as his home. If the head be in heaven, the members may for a time be on earth; but they cannot remain there, far less can they ever be in hell.

Taking for granted, then, that the Scripture representation is true—and it would be foolish to make Scripture responsible for a theory which it does not assert—the death and resurrection of Christ render the salvation of his people not a possibility only, but a necessity according to law. Either the connection must be severed, or Christ's people must be admittted to heaven: if He be the head and they be the members, where He is, there must they be also.

When Noah went into the ark, no miracle was needed for his salvation. He and the ark were dealt with as a unity, because it bore his weight, and he was lifted up by its buoyancy; *it* was subjected to the storm without, *he* was sheltered in its chambers within. The *effect* might be said to be substitution, but the *cause* was union. If that union had not existed, that is to say, if he had not been in the ark, and if *he* had floated and the *ark* had sunk, such a result, instead of being a satisfaction to law, would have been a double miracle. In like manner, if there were no union between Christ and His people, his death and their salvation, instead of being a satisfaction to justice, would be a double outrage.

If it be objected that there is not, and cannot be, such a real and personal union between Christ and His people as to constitute identity, and thus satisfy law, we are entitled to reply, "Vain man would be wise, though man be born like a wild ass's colt." The former objection was competent, because God has given us a conscience, and He appeals to that conscience for a vindication of the justice of his administration. We have, therefore, every reason to expect that the justice which he administers should not be inconsistent with that instinctive sense of justice which He transcribed from his own moral nature upon ours. But when we step beyond that province, and enter on the region of *facts* and *possibilities*, presuming to determine what can and what cannot be, we have clearly gone beyond our depth, and have no ground to stand upon.

Even the first objection was a perilous one, because it questioned the truth of what God affirmed; and although the argument itself might be correct in principle, the conclusion happened to be wrong; and if any man ventures to reject the Gospel on the ground that substitution does not satisfy his ethical sensibilities, his soul will not the less be lost because he had not rightly understood the theory upon which the Gospel is founded. He has no right to expect that God will work a miracle to save him from the consequences of his mistake. When He sends a gracious message of mercy to mankind, all that we have to do is to believe and obey; if we reject His overtures, we do so on our own responsibility.

But to come to this question of possibilities, we ask, How can we know what is possible and what is impossible in a matter so deep as the mystery of Christ's person, and so unknown as the constitution of our own being? There are elements introduced in connection with the union between Christ and His people which we do not and cannot understand, and whose bearings we can know only in so far as they are revealed. The person of Christ is an unsearchable deep, but there are facts regarding it which we do know, and which are sufficient to cover all the difficulties. We know that by means of His humanity it became possible for Him to suffer and to die; and we also know that, because of His divinity, His person was possessed of an existence which is superior to time, so that He could truly say, "Before Abraham was, I AM." It would be presumptuous for us to speculate on the influence which this eternity of being had upon the relations which He sustained to those who are saved, or attempt to explain how it is consistent with law that the efficacy of the blood shed on Calvary reached backwards to Abel and all the Old Testament saints, and forward to the latest convert who shall lay his burden on the great Burden-bearer. If Christ had been a mere man, this, of course, would have been impossible; but because He is God as well as man, the argument enters a region where we cannot follow it, and faith is content to receive simply that which is revealed. There is, in some way or another, such a union between the Saviour and the saved, as is sufficient to account for the sufferings of Christ on the one hand, and for the justification of the sinner on the other.

Perhaps this may suggest to those who may be trusting to the general mercy of God, that mercy to any one not united to Christ is an utter impossibility. Out of Christ there is no mercy, and can be no mercy, else Christ died in vain. There would have been no necessity whatever for an atonement in such a case, because if God could be merciful to *any one* out of Christ, he might have been merciful to *all*. Those, therefore, who are trusting to the general mercy of God, and are conscious that they are not united to Christ, must be labouring under a very dangerous mistake. There can be no lawless mercy with God, and this would be a violation of law which we have no right to expect. Both Mr. Combe and Mr. Hume tell us that it is impossible—so impossible that it is actually incapable of proof; and even though an angel from heaven were to tell us that God forgave the sinner without punishing his sin, we must not believe him. Our sins, in order to be forgiven, must be conveyed somewhere; the only place to which they can be conveyed is the person of Christ, and the only means of conveyance is union. If they are not so disposed of, and yet remain unpunished, they would stain the justice and the throne of God, which is impossible.

Here, too, we have an explanation of that which otherwise would be inexplicable—the line drawn between the

saved and the unsaved.   An eternal heaven and an
eternal hell, with no intermediate state between them, are
tremendous contrasts.   But in a world containing such an
infinite variety of moral character, shaded off by an almost
infinite variety of degrees, it would be impossible to draw
a well-marked line of demarcation between the righteous
and the wicked.   Commencing with the very best and most
exemplary of the human race, we go down, by the most
delicate gradations, to the very lowest and most degraded
of our species.   But who will undertake to say how good
a man must be before he can be sure that he will be received into heaven, or how wicked a man must be before
he is certain to be cast into hell?   Where is it possible
to draw the line?   There is no conceivable point where,
if the line were drawn, justice would not be outraged.
The difference between the worst of those who should be
saved, and the best of those who should be lost, would be
so slight, and the distinction so delicate, that no human
mind could appreciate it.   It cannot be that the infinite
justice of God, which in His physical administration, is
so perfect, and measures out its penalties to the very
millionth part of a grain, can be so grossly rough and
inconsiderate in the higher and nobler sphere.   The
supposition is so monstrous, that it would be a libel, not
upon God only, but upon the most incompetent judge
that ever sat upon the bench, to suppose that he could
measure out justice after such a fashion.

But this is not the Bible doctrine of salvation, and
therefore it cannot be responsible for the absurdity.   The
line which it draws between the saved and the unsaved is
a reasonable and intelligible line, approved not only by
every principle of philosophy, but by common sense.
The line which it draws is as grand and as broad as that

which separates life and death, between which there is a
gulf as deep as that which separates between heaven and
hell. According to the Bible, a man is saved, not because
he is better than others, but because he is IN Christ, and
because Christ is IN him; and a man is lost, not because
he is worse than others, but because he is not IN Christ,
and because Christ does not dwell IN him. Man being
a sinner, must die, not by the sentence of a judge only,
but by the operation of a law, and when he dies he
descends into hell, because there is no other place to
which he can go, *unless some one interfere to save him.*
Every sin that a man commits is a moral poison that
further corrupts his moral nature, and ensures his death,
upon the same principle that the physical laws inexorably
inflict their own penalty, without regard to moral character. Why is cancer incurable, and why does the person
who is poisoned die? Simply because it is a law. And
so do the moral laws ensure that "the soul that sinneth,
it shall die," and all that is needed to ensure that soul's
destruction is that it should be LET ALONE. Whatever
men may think of the severity or the unmercifulness of
this moral administration, no one can say that it is not
awfully intelligible, and dreadfully consistent.

But why should it be called unmerciful? We do not
speak of the physical laws so. The child of a profligate
man inherits a body full of weakness and suffering. Does
God work a miracle to save him? Ask Mr. Combe. He
does not; and yet we do not say that God's physical
administration is unmerciful, because the law inexorably
inflicts its own punishment. It is true that in the higher
administrations we should expect a more loving regimen
than in the lower and less important; but no man can
complain that, in introducing this element of mercy,

there should be the same infinity of justice, and the same inviolability of law. The plan and mode of salvation revealed in the Bible may contain many unknown and mysterious elements, but this one grand feature which it presents of its having been framed in the interests of holiness, and recognising the inviolability of law, commends it to the veneration of mankind. "God so loved the world, that he gave his only-begotten Son, that whosoever believeth in Him should not perish, but have eternal life." That God COULD give up His Son to suffering and shame for the sake of His ruined creatures, but COULD NOT, by any means, pardon them by a violation of law, does not convey to us the idea of a remorseless tyrant, or an insensate God, but rather that of a Being who commands at once our highest admiration and adoring love.

According to the Bible, then, it is easy to understand why a man is lost; it is because he is not IN CHRIST, and all that is necessary to ensure his ruin, is that he should be LET ALONE. Like a man who is wrecked, and floating on a plank in the wide ocean, he perishes, simply because he is not rescued from his danger, and because no life-boat comes that way to save him. No one would accuse God of injustice, in allowing the physical laws to take their course, supposing the shipwrecked mariner to be allowed to perish; but in this higher administration God *did* provide a life-boat in His Son, for perishing sinners, and bade the mariners go out to every creature and intreat them to come in. Eighteen hundred years have passed, and these unfaithful and unmerciful mariners, although they had the life-boat in their hands, have *not* gone out to save the lost; and the consequence is that, whereas ALL might have had the Gospel offered to them, if the

R

mariners had done their duty, thousands have never heard
the joyful sound. But what shall we say of those to whom
the Gospel has been preached, and the offer made, but
who, because they did not believe, would not accept it,
and are LET ALONE? They may, indeed, be virtuous, and
moral, and benevolent, but because they are not IN
CHRIST, they are not saved. Whose fault is this?

At the same time, it must be observed, that, in order
to satisfy the requirements of law, the union between the
sinner and Christ must be a real and personal union, not
theoretical only, nor fictitious. There is no possibility of
over-reaching the laws of God by any legal equivocation.
The union must be a union like that of the husband and
wife in regard to property, or the head and hand in regard
to crime. Justice will not be fooled into mercy by a pretended union which exists only in fancy, and has no reality
in fact. The union must be such, that justice and law
cannot distinguish the parties, the one from the other, so
that when it has struck the one, it has struck the other,
and when it has got the blood of the one, it has got the
blood of the other—in short, there can be no salvation,
except to those who are *bona fide* in Christ, and Christ
in them.

But, whenever this union has really been formed, when
the Holy Ghost really dwells in the body of the Christian,
so that it becomes a temple of the Holy Ghost, when the
union is such that he is a member of Christ's body, " of
His flesh and of His bones," then the man has become
really and truly a new creature, with new feelings, new
desires, new sympathies, and new dispositions. The
Spirit of Christ dwelling in him, shows itself in giving
him the dispositions of Christ, so that the " family like-

ness" becomes conspicuous to all. His views and his affections are heavenly, and he does that which is pure, and honest, and lovely, and holy, not because he so inclines, nor because it is beautiful, nor because it is profitable, nor because it is safe, but because his Father God desires it, and that alone is paramount. This union with Christ, and this indwelling of the Holy Ghost, is not fictitious, but real and practical, and pregnant with every heavenly consequence. When this is the case, the very operation of law necessitates salvation; in fact, anything else would be more than a miracle, it would be a violation of law.

And, then, in regard to those who are lost: with what astonishment will they discover that it is the *physical* laws, and their own *physical constitution*, that combined to ensure their eternal misery? Their spirits are immortal in their own nature, and in spite of themselves; and when these spirits are cast out from their dead bodies, houseless and naked into the deep, even though there were no hell, this alone would ensure their misery. In the physical administration we are told that there is no lawless mercy with God, and that He would not suspend the laws of nature to save the lives of a thousand saints. It may be so; but if that be the fate of the green tree, what will become of the dry? God cannot be expected to work a miracle for those who rejected His mercy, and trampled on the blood of His well-beloved Son. The time was, when He entreated them, but they would not hear; the time will come when they will entreat Him, but it will be too late. "Because I have called, and ye refused; I have stretched out my hand, and no man regarded; but ye have set at nought all my counsel, and would none of my reproof: I also will laugh at your calamity; I will mock

when your fear cometh ; when your fear cometh as desolation, and your destruction cometh as a whirlwind ;
when distress and anguish cometh upon you, then shall
they call upon me, but I will not answer ; they shall seek
me early, but they shall not find me ; therefore shall they
eat of the fruit of their own way, and be filled with their
own devices."

CHAPTER XX.

THE REVELATION OF ANTICHRIST.

THE revelation of antichrist, previous to the second
coming of Christ, is intimately connected with our
present subject; because it is presented to us as something more than merely an apostacy; it is Satan himself
distinctly and personally coming into view, and engaging
in one last and desperate attempt to overthrow the kingdom of God in the world.   This is what might be called
an incarnation of Satan, but, more properly speaking, a
possession, Satan himself being revealed and taking
possession of the "Man of Sin," who is either a single
individual or a succession of men, by whom this great
enterprise is to be conducted.   In all the demoniacal
possessions recorded in the New Testament, the possessing
spirit was some inferior demon, not Satan himself; and
therefore the demoniac presented a result not superior
but inferior to other men.   It was as if the spirits of the
savage hunters of the mammoth or the cave-bear had
come forth to hunt the miserable Israelite among the tombs
of Gadara.   But in this final assault, Satan himself is to
come forth in person, and to exercise an influence in the

affairs of the world such as he had never done before;
because although, in the temptations in Eden and in the
wilderness of Judea, he himself came forward personally
as the agent of his wickedness, we do not find that he
ever took possession of a human body as the instrument
of his purposes.   Whether this abstention was voluntary
or not we cannot tell : it would almost appear from the
words of the apostle that it was not.   " Now ye know
what withholdeth that he might be revealed in his time.
For the mystery of iniquity doth already work : only he
who now letteth will let, until he be taken out of the way.
And then shall that Wicked be revealed" (2 Thess. ii.
6-8).

It is evident from this, as well as from other passages,
that Antichrist or the Wicked One was Satan himself : it
was a person in existence at the time of the apostles, the
same words being applied to him that are applied to
Christ at His second coming, which was to be the " revelation " of Christ, and the " coming " of Christ.   It may
be observed, however, that these words, " *apokalupsis* "
and " *parousia* " do not imply movement : *apokalupsis*
means " uncovering," and *parousia* means " presence,"
but both of them imply previous existence.   The advent
may or may not be seen, but the actual presence will be
manifest.

The one passage which seems to make a distinction
between the " Man of Sin " and Satan, is not inconsistent
with, but rather confirmatory, of this view.   " Even him
whose coming (*parousia*) is after the working of Satan,
with all powers and signs and lying wonders" (2 Thess.
ii. 9).   The expression "after the working of" (*kat
energeian*) is a phrase used only by Paul, and occurs six
times; in his epistles to the Ephesians (i. 19 ; iii. 7 ;

iv. 16); Philippians (iii. 21); Colossians (i. 29); and Thessalonians (in the present passage) ; and in every one of them it expresses, not resemblance, but identity.   In all the other passages it is the Spirit of God working either in Christ, Ephes. i. 19 ; or in the apostle, Ephes. iii. 7, and Col. i. 29 ; or in the whole Church, Ephes. iv. 16 ; or in the mortal body, when it is made a spiritual body, Phil. iii. 21 ; and, therefore, it must have the same meaning here, Satan himself working in, or energising, the body of the Man of Sin, " with all powers and signs and lying wonders."

Such an incarnation as this would be very different indeed from the demoniacal possessions recorded in Scripture, in which there was neither guile nor wisdom, but only indolent infirmity or blind ferocity displayed.   We are informed that, in addition to the cunning and policy which so distinguish the devices of Satan, there will be added a personal administration, fortified " with all power, and signs, and lying wonders, and with all deceivableness of unrighteousness," " in so much that, if it were possible, they shall deceive the very elect."   Under such circumstances, nothing is more likely than that the world would go after him.   Satan's efforts have all been directed to the anticipation of this ; and for centuries he has been labouring to mislead mankind in regard to himself.   His first great effort is to make men believe that there is no such person in existence ; that the idea of Satan and Satanic influence is a vulgar superstition, which will disappear as soon as science and civilisation have gained the supremacy.   But, when he does not succeed in this, his next effort is directed to the creation of popular superstition in regard to his appearance and character, investing them with all the horrors and terrors of fiendish deformity and malevolence ; so that when he is revealed, and presents himself in the character of an angel of light, the nations will refuse to believe in his identity, and will hail him as their king and god.   How easy will it be for him, with his six thousand years' experience, to exercise a kingcraft more cunning and less scrupulous than even that of Machiavelli ! and, with the aid of his legions, and the principalities, and powers, all under his sway, it would be a miracle if he did not succeed.   Civilisation and literature, science, and the arts, with every fashionable accomplishment, would be cultivated under the reign of a universal empire under which everything would be tolerated except evangelical Christianity, and the Bible, which would then be denounced as the most dangerous of books.

Has the Man of Sin been already revealed or has he yet to appear ?   Upon this point there is by no means a unanimous opinion among Bible students.   Some believe that the Romish apostacy fulfils all the predictions which we find recorded concerning him : others are of opinion that they do not, and therefore they expect that there is before us a season of great trial and tribulation, which is to be terminated by the coming of Christ to judgment.   They think that instead of Christianity spreading over the world it will gradually decline until the faith shall have disappeared from the earth, and then Christ will come.   The passage from which these sad forebodings are drawn is 2 Thess. ii. 8, " And then shall that Wicked be revealed, whom the Lord shall consume with the Spirit of his mouth, and shall destroy with the brightness of his coming."   But were the original words more correctly translated, it might, with equal propriety, be quoted on the other side, " whom the Lord shall consume with the Spirit of his mouth, and bring to nought by the manifestation of his presence." The word translated " consume " means literally to " use up," as in Gal. v. 15, and might well be applied to the effect produced upon popery by the Bible, and the reason why the Bible has not a more wasting effect upon Popery is that Bible Christians exhibit too little the presence of their Master. If the Papal system be really the Antichrist predicted, there is nothing more likely to use it up and abolish it than the Spirit of God's mouth, and the manifestation of His presence in His people.

The interpretation of prophecy, however, forms no part of our theme, and, so far as our subject is concerned, it matters little whether the Man of Sin be Popery or not. If not, and if Antichrist has yet to be revealed, the second coming of Christ is indefinitely postponed; because in that case it is as true of us now as it was of the Thessalonians at the time of Paul, that we need not be soon shaken in mind or troubled, as that the day of Christ is at hand," for that day shall not come till the Man of Sin be revealed.

If, on the other hand, the great apostacy has already taken place, and if we are to look on the Papal system as the revelation of Antichrist, it may be that the second coming is at the very door. If this be the right interpretation we must acknowledge that Romanism is the masterpiece of Satan's genius, and that its authors were possessed of more than human sagacity derived from an experience of more than forty centuries of the weakness and wickedness of the human heart.

These authors and architects of the Papal system were something more than inspired; they were actually "possessed " not by inferior demons, but by the prince of this world himself, not for blind gratification, but for the exercise of consummate skill. This is implied in the *kat energeian* of 2 Thess. ii. 9; and, if so, there is nothing impossible in their having displayed their supernatural power in signs and lying wonders; and with all deceivableness of unrighteousness, which we have perhaps too hastily ascribed to collusion and imposture.

We present these thoughts as mere alternatives, without offering any confident opinion regarding them, further than this, that in this third dynastic assault upon the kingdom of God in order to secure the princedom of this world for himself, Satan comes forth in person and not by the agency of his angels. In the first he spoke directly to Eve in the organism of the serpent, because he had no internal access to her understanding, for as yet " he had nothing in " her. In the second it was not necessary to clothe himself in any organism in order to converse with Christ, because the Son of Man was endued with prophetic powers, and was capable of holding converse with spirits. But in this third assault he appears upon the stage as the Man of Sin, the Antichrist, the Wicked One, the Son of Perdition, whether he be already come, or whether he has yet to be revealed.

Everything connected with this second coming of Christ seems to be purposely shadowy and dim, and is itself shrouded and involved in other events of a kindred character, from which they cannot be disentangled until the time of their fulfilment has arrived. It is evidently God's purpose that the time should not be known. " Of that day and hour knoweth no man; no, not the angels of heaven, but my Father only."

But although we have no revelation to guide us, in regard to the second coming, it is not so with the Millen-

nium which bears the same relation to the world's history
that the Sabbath bears to the other days of the week.
The very idea of a Sabbatic rest of a thousand years
suggests that it should occupy the seventh millennium.
" Six days shalt thou labour and do all thy work, but the
seventh is the Sabbath of the Lord thy God, in it thou
shalt not do any work."

According to our received chronology, our Lord was
born on the four thousandth year of the world; and if
the creation of the sun on the fourth day was typical of
the birth of the Sun of Righteousness, we should not regard the figure as inappropriate. After the birth of
Christ, therefore, other two thousand years would be
necessary to complete the world's week of labour, and in
that case we should expect that after the year 2000 the
Millennium should commence. To speak more accurately,
however, it would be the year 1996, because it has been
ascertained that there is an error in our chronology of
four years, our Lord having been born four years before the
Christian era. The six thousand years of the world's toil and
unrest, therefore, would be completed in the year 1996.

It is a remarkable circumstance, and one that lends
confirmation to this idea, that the two great apocalyptic
numbers 666 and 1260 bring us exactly to the same
date, provided that we take, not the birth of Christ, but
the destruction of Jerusalem as the starting point, which
took place in the year 70, thus—

Error in our chronology, ...	4
Destruction of Jerusalem, ...	70
Number of the name of the Beast, .	666
The forty and two months, . . .	1260
	2000

Interpreters of prophecy have erred in counting these numbers from the birth of Christ, which would bring us only to the year 1926, which would leave the world's preparation day incomplete, and they have endeavoured to find some event in the year 666 which would signalise it as the birth of Popery; but in both of these there is an error. The birth of Christ although it is *the* great era of history is not a prophetic era at all. The death of Christ might have been an era, and the descent of the Holy Ghost might have been an era, being the commencement of the new covenant and the New Testament Church, which the birth of Christ was not. But neither of them was a prophetic era. Jerusalem alone is the true index or gnomon of prophecy. Jeremiah's seventy years counted from the destruction of Jerusalem by the Chaldeans till its restoration by the returned captives. Daniel's prophecy, too, counted from the going forth of the edict to rebuild Jerusalem onwards to the destruction of "the city and the sanctuary," and where Daniel's specific prophecy ends, there John's specific prophecy begins. The destruction of Jerusalem, therefore, is the starting point from which we must count prophetic numbers.

Although the New Testament began on the day of Pentecost the Levitical economy did not take end till nearly forty years later. In the time of the Apostles it was "ready to vanish away;" but it did not vanish away till the Temple disappeared, and then it vanished. Up to that time the Jewish Christians circumcised their children, and thereby pledged them to the keeping of the whole law, Gal. v. 3; and, unless we keep this in mind, we shall entirely misunderstand a number of passages in the New Testament. But when Jerusalem and its temple were destroyed, the foundation of the Levitical system was taken away, and it could not be restored again without a new revelation. This is acknowledged by every Jew.

There is no single year in which it could be said that Popery was born, or that Antichrist arose. Already in the time of the Apostles, the mystery of iniquity had begun to work, and even then it gave indications of the channel in which it was to flow. It took centuries to develop itself, and the inclination to return to the weak and beggarly elements of external observances was as much then as it is now the weakness and the sin of our carnal nature. If Popery was born at all, it was born in Eden, when Adam and Eve tried to hide themselves among the trees of the garden, by putting them as a screen between them and the presence of an unreconciled God. Ritualism and Sacerdotalism are the very spirit of Antichrist.

CHAPTER XXI.

THE RESURRECTION ACCORDING TO LAW.

THE glory and beauty of the work of Christ in the salvation of man consisted in this, that from beginning to end it was all according to law. Infinite love proposed the object to be aimed at, but it required infinite wisdom to devise the means, because it had to be accomplished in a manner consistent with that perfect order and symmetry which characterise all God's administrations.

There would have been no wisdom needed, and therefore little glory displayed in man's salvation, if infinite power had at once stepped forth and done all that was required, independent of law. Such a salvation would not have been worthy of God, and would have called forth no great adoring wonder and admiration from his intelligent creatures.   We therefore expect that the resurrection, which is the concluding stage of the great salvation, will be not only prepared for, but consummated according to law, and that the adaptation of means to an end will be as conspicuous in this, as in any of the preceding parts of the work of redemption.

It was for this that the person of Christ was so wonderfully prepared in its twofold nature, and it was for this that the Captain of our salvation was made perfect through suffering.   It is not necessary that we should be able to comprehend this adaptation, and, indeed, it would be strange if we were; but the fact that there is such adaptation is proof that law was paramount, not only in the moral, but in the physical administration of the work of Christ.

We have seen that the original constitution of man provided that the "natural body" should be developed into the "spiritual body" (which is the angelic), provided that nothing interfered to interrupt the normal course of its progression.   We have also seen that in the case, first of Satan, and then of Adam and his descendants, this progression was interrupted by sin; so that our natural bodies, having lost their original powers of development, are incapable of rising higher, and therefore decay and die, like the bodies of the lower animals.

The work of Christ had for its object the recovery of man from this degradation and ruin, and his elevation from the natural into the spiritual state.   In short, the object of Christ's mission was to retrieve the disaster of the fall, and to accomplish in His people that development which would have taken place if Adam had never sinned.

For this purpose it was necessary, not only that Christ should be possessed of a human nature, so as to be capable of being united with humanity, but that He should also be possessed of the Divine nature, that He might have an inexhaustible supply of life and power to be communicated through His humanity. This adaptation of the person of Christ to the work which had to be done indicates the exercise of infinite wisdom, as well as of infinite power, and suggests not only the supremacy, but the glory of law. It is not to be expected that we should be able to understand the order and process by which every requirement is met and every obstacle overcome in this covenanted work of salvation : it is enough to know that it is ordered in all things and sure, and that God is satisfied. We may, therefore, be certain that, whatever be the process or the means employed, the end will be accomplished; and that, at the resurrection, our bodies will be " fashioned like unto His glorious body, according to the working whereby He is able even to subdue all things unto Himself."

Upon a subject to us so interesting, the Scripture supplies us with not a little most valuable information, although it does not altogether correspond with opinions which are popularly entertained on the subject. The doctrine of the resurrection is presented in Scripture as one of magnificent importance, involving all our hopes of future glory; whereas in modern times it is by many viewed simply as an interesting fact, that the body is ultimately to share the blessedness enjoyed by the spirit after death. The general impression is, that the spirit after death is admitted into heaven, and immediately experiences the full enjoyment of celestial blessedness. For this reason, the question of a future resurrection of the body is viewed as of comparatively little importance; for, although it is acknowledged that the blessedness of the saints will not be complete until that event takes place, it is scarcely ever felt as if the want of it would be a matter very greatly to be deplored.   How different is the estimate which Paul forms on the subject!   "If the dead rise not at all," says he, "why are they then baptised for the dead?   And why stand we in jeopardy every hour?   I protest by your rejoicing which I have in Christ Jesus our Lord, I die daily.   If after the manner of men I have fought with beasts at Ephesus, what advantageth it me if the dead rise not? let us eat and drink; for to-morrow we die" (1 Cor. xv. 29-32).   The difference may be accounted for by the different ways in which the doctrine is regarded.   Christ and His apostles, as well as the Pharisees and the Sadducees, regarded the doctrine of the resurrection as involving the entire question of a future state.   If there be a resurrection, then there is a future state; but if there be no resurrection, in that case there is no future state.   Whatever be the reason, it is evident that no difficulty was felt on either side in regard to the rising of the body.   The Sadducees did not raise the question; and when our Lord silenced them by His celebrated argument, he never even alluded to it. He quoted the words of Jehovah: "I am the God of Abraham, and the God of Isaac, and the God of Jacob;" and He adds, "God is not the God of the dead, but of the living."   This answer, it is said, "put the Sadducees to silence," showing that they felt that, when the doctrine of a future state was proved, the resurrection of the body necessarily followed.   The Swedenborgians — who say that the resurrection is already past, or rather that the resurrection is nothing more than the rising of the spirit

from the body when it dies—argue, with apparent plausibility, that, as our Lord does not assert anything more
than the fact that Abraham, Isaac, and Jacob are still
living, and makes no allusion to any future resurrection,
He does not assert the resurrection of the body at all.
This evidently cannot be the true explanation, because
the resurrection of our Lord (which is repeatedly identified
in its nature* with our resurrection) did not take place
when His spirit left the body, but on the third day, when
He came out of the sepulchre alive. The true explanation is to be found in the necessity of the spirit being
lodged in a body in order fully to enjoy existence, and the
utter incompleteness of a future state without a resurrection. It is quite true that our Lord's argument was
principally directed to the proof of the spirit's existence
after death, a doctrine which the Sadducees denied; but
it proved more than that, for if God was not ashamed to
call Himself their God, he became thereby pledged to their
resurrection.

The doctrine held by the pious Jews was this, that
although life was forfeited by sin, and the spirit was
deprived of its tabernacle, yet the spirits of the just were
not destroyed at death, but returned to God to await the
resurrection. This resurrection, which was to be the evidence of the pardon of their sin, and was to restore to
them the full enjoyment of their existence, was to be
accomplished by the promised Messiah, who was, for
this reason, called the Hope of Israel, Acts xxvi. 6;
iii. 21.

It is interesting to observe how anxiously Paul pleads
for the resurrection on these grounds. Without a resurrection there could be no justification : " If Christ be not

* 1 Cor. vi. 14; xv. 20; 1 Thess. iv. 14.

raised, your faith is vain; ye are yet in your sins " (1 Cor. xv. 17). He regarded the resurrection of Christ as the very citadel of the Gospel, and if that was lost, all was lost : " Then they also which are fallen asleep in Christ are perished " (ver. 18).

But it may be asked, If the spirits of believers are received by Christ at death, what greater happiness could they enjoy ? We answer, that the happiness which believers enjoy in Christ, besides being merely of a passive and sabbatic character, is imperfect in its kind, although it is perfect in degree. The human being consists of body, soul, and spirit ; and so long as any of these is wanting, he is an imperfect creature, and unable to fulfil or enjoy the full end and design of his creation. The lodging of the spirit in heaven, although it provides enjoyment and repose, is not of such a kind as to produce individual action, such as would result from its being normally united to a body of its own. For this reason we cannot but notice that the spirits of the saints although delightfully conscious of their presence with Christ, are represented as " entering into rest." It appears, therefore, that the resurrection occupied a much more important place in the hopes of the Church during the apostolic age than it does now.

There are at least three different forms in which the process of resurrection is presented to us in Scripture. In the person of Christ the resurrection took place three days after death ; and the body in which He rose was identical with that in which He suffered. He showed His disciples the prints of the nails in His hands and feet ; and we are informed that the body which was laid in the sepulchre was not to be found when the women came to embalm it. This was one form of the process of resurrection, and, so far as we know, it appears to be unique. The marks of crucifixion appear to have been preserved for a special purpose, and would not justify the fear or expectation that in other individuals any scars or mutilations inflicted by their enemies on the natural body shall be allowed to mar the beauty of the glorified saints. A second form of resurrection is presented in the persons of those who shall be alive and remain at the second coming of Christ. So far as they are concerned, there will be no death; and, as in the case of our Lord, and perhaps also in the case of Elijah the resurrection body will be identical with the natural—the change taking place "in a moment, in the twinkling of an eye," and the materials of the spiritual body being furnished by the natural body, from which it is to be developed.

But there is a third form, and it is that which will be experienced by those who shall have died before the second coming of Christ. These will form the vast majority of the resurrection saints; and in regard to them the question arises, "With what bodies do the come?" because after their death, the elements composing the bodies in which they died may have been dispersed towards the four winds of heaven, or used for the composition of other bodies.

We must remark, however, that Scripture, in speaking of the resurrection, refers more to the persons than to the bodies of believers as being raised; whereas it is generally understood as referring to the bodies rather than to the persons. It is unfortunate that our English word resurrection contains the idea of rising *again*. This idea is not contained in the Greek substantive *anastasis*, or in the verb *egeirō*. It is true that the prefix *ana* often means "again," but in this word *anastasis* it does not mean "again" but "up." The word *egeirō*, which also occurs frequently in this connection, has very much the same meaning " to raise *up*," and cannot mean to raise *again*. Some may, perhaps, think that this is an unimportant criticism, because, if the dead be raised up, it is of little importance whether we add the word "again" or not; for it is implied under the circumstances. But the criticism is somewhat important; because if we understand, in connection with our preceding remarks, that it is the person rather than the body that is raised up, we may say that the dead rise up, without attaching much importance to the idea of their bodies rising *again;* as if it were necessary that the same materials should rise that had been laid down.

The question, " With what bodies do they come ? " appears to have been agitated also in apostolic times, and was answered by Paul in his First Epistle to the Corinthians (chap. xv. 35) : " But some man will say, How are the dead raised, and with what bodies do they come ? Thou fool, that which thou sowest is not quickened, except it die : and that which thou sowest, thou sowest *not that body that shall be,* but bare grain, it may chance of wheat, or of some other grain." Here the question is answered so plainly, that it is strange that it should ever have been repeated. "That which thou sowest, thou sowest NOT that body which shall be." The body, therefore, with which the dead rise, is not necessarily any more the body that was laid in the grave than is the stalk of wheat which is ripened in autumn the same as the grain of wheat from which it germinated in spring.

This is the chief portion of the reply, but it is not the whole : it answers only the second question, " With what body do they come?" The first question, "How are the dead raised?" is of a more general character, and invites an illustration taken from nature, which, although it may not explain the doctrine, will at least help to illustrate it. This St. Paul proceeds to give by means of the figure of the seed, which in several particulars presents appropriate analogies.

In the first place the seed is a part of the plant which is generated *in the plant;* and which, when it has arrived at maturity, is capable of being separated *from the plant* without losing its vitality.

In the second place, it contains within itself all the characteristic qualities of the plant on which it grew, and is capable of producing another plant of the very same kind whenever it shall be placed in circumstances favourable to its germination. And,

In the third place, germination cannot take place until the seed has been shed from the parent stalk, and buried in the ground.

It is in these three particulars that the germination of a seed is emblematic of the resurrection, and the question arises, What is it that the seed represents? The plant that springs from the seed is evidently the representative of the resurrection body; but what is it that forms, as it were, the seed from which it springs? When viewed in the light of the corresponding passage (John xii. 24), the seed, or "bare grain," represents the person who dies. Thus, Jesus speaks of Himself when He says, "Verily, verily, I say unto you, Except a corn of wheat fall into the ground and die, it abideth alone : but if it die, it bringeth forth much fruit." It is true, that this is an entirely different application of the figure from that which is made by Paul, but the subject is essentially the same.

It might be objected, that if the seed really died, it could not germinate; but this is evidently refining too much. Modern science has shown that the seed consists of two parts, one of which dies in order to provide nourishment for the other. The little germ that exists in every seed swells with the moisture of the ground in which it is sown, and the perisperm, or cotyledon, which surrounds it, is simply a storehouse of nourishment to enable it to grow, until it has sent its root downwards and its plumule upwards, to draw its support from the soil and the atmosphere. The perisperm must die in order to accomplish this; because, until it has been reduced to a soluble, and then a liquid state, it cannot pass into the tissues of the plant. The seed, therefore, does die in one of its parts, though not in the other, and for that very reason is an accurate representative of mortal man. His spirit, like the germ, does not die; but the body, like the perisperm, does die before the spirit can assume its germinating powers in order to produce the spiritual body. In the case of our Lord, as well as in that of those who are alive and remain at His coming, the mortal body, like the perisperm, supplies the material from which the spirit and soul have to elaborate their glorious tenement; but in the case of all the others, the mere convenience of having the materials at hand will not be important; and the dust which is scattered to the winds need not be gathered again, because the identity of the future body is not dependent upon its being composed of the very same particles which constituted the former body at the time of decease.

The remaining verses of this wonderful passage, down to the 50th, are devoted to the illustration of the difference between the natural and the spiritual body. Ver. 38, "But God giveth it a body as it hath pleased him, and to every seed his own body." In this verse we are to notice,—

1. That, while the changes that take place in the seed are produced by the operation of the natural laws, Paul ascribes both the laws and the changes to the will and the hand of God. This suggests to us that the principle thus indicated is applicable also to the resurrection. The dead are raised up by the power of God; but He works by means and according to law. And,

2. Every seed produces its own body—that is to say, there is a correspondence between the nature of the seed and the nature of the plant that rises from it, not only in regard to the species, but also in regard to the individual. Not only will the resurrection body be a human body, it will also be *our* body—not perhaps composed of the same materials, but it will be a true continuation of our own body—the continuity depending on the identity of soul and spirit in both, and the identity of the type and form of body which that soul and spirit are capable of producing, because it is the soul and spirit, or at least the soul that gives form and life to the body.

In the 39th verse the apostle illustrates this principle a little more in detail—"All flesh is not the same flesh : but there is one flesh of men, another flesh of beasts, and another of birds." The idea contained here is still an appeal to the operation of natural laws, but for a different purpose. Every seed produces its own body, but there are different kinds of seeds. From man is produced man, from beasts are produced beasts, and from birds are produced birds; and it altogether depends on what the seed is, and what the result will be. The apostle has in view the grand conclusion towards which

he is drawing the reader in verse 49, where he asserts
the great fact that the body which shall rise will be a
spiritual body, whereas the body that is sown is a natural
one. In the case of wheat, the plant and the seed are
alike; in the case of the believer, there is a change,
and it is to account for this change that he proceeds in
his argument.

Ver. 40. " There are also celestial bodies, and bodies
terrestrial: but the glory of the celestial is one, and the
glory of the terrestrial is another." The English reader
is very apt to misunderstand this verse, as if it were
more intimately connected with the succeeding verse than
it really is. "Celestial bodies" (*somata epourania*) do
not mean such bodies as the sun, moon, and stars, for the
Greek word is never used in such a sense. What is
meant is, the bodies of people in the heavens; and the
glory that belongs to them is here said to be different
from the glory that belongs to the "bodies that are on
earth." The apostle is still drawing nearer to his
conclusion, because the difference between the bodies of
men and the bodies of beasts was not so appropriate an
illustration of the change as the difference between the
bodies of men and the bodies of angels. It is not so
much a difference of structure as a difference of glory.

Ver. 41. "There is one glory of the sun, and another
glory of the moon, and another glory of the stars: for
star differeth from star in glory." Here the idea of the
previous verse is followed up and enlarged. Not only
does the resurrection body differ from the natural body
in its kind of glory, there will also be a difference in the
amount of glory in the resurrection saints.

The verses that follow are simply an application of the
argument; but it ceases to be merely argumentative, for

the apostle appears to have caught fire from his theme, and his exulting spirit expatiates upon the glory that is to follow, and towards which his soul was seeking. He says, "So also is the resurrection of the dead; it is sown in corruption, it is raised in incorruption : it is sown in dishonour, it is raised in glory : it is sown in weakness, it is raised in power : it is sown a natural body, it is raised a spiritual body." This last contrast, which expresses what might be called the scientific distinction between the two bodies, introduces another, and altogether different view of his subject; and it is one for which he had been gradually preparing his readers. "There is a natural body, and there is a spiritual body;" that is to say,—Whatever might have been the fate of Adam and his children, and whether a resurrection had been provided for them or not; even, indeed, though Adam had not existed at all,—as there is a flesh of beasts and a flesh of birds, so there is a natural body and a spiritual body; and it is to these two classes respectively that we do now, and shall hereafter belong. We have at present a natural body, and one, on that account, allied to the lower animals; but at the resurrection we shall have a spiritual body, glorious and incorruptible, like that of the holy angels.

We have already remarked, that the translation of this passage, in the authorised version fails to exhibit the correspondence between the 44th and 45th verses. The word "natural" in the 44th verse, and the word "soul" in the 45th, would never suggest to the English reader, that in Greek these two words are radically the same : yet so it is. "There is a *psychical* (or *soul*) body, and there is a *spiritual* body : and so it is written, The first Adam was made a living *psuche* (or *soul*), the last Adam was made a quickening *spirit.*" What, then, is meant by a "*psychical body*"? In the first place, it is evident that being an adjective, formed from the substantive *psuche,* it may be most literally, though not very elegantly, translated a "*soul body,*" as distinguished from a "*spirit body;*" and a little farther light may be thrown upon it by examining the only other passages of the New Testament in which the word occurs—viz., 1 Cor. ii. 14; James iii. 15; Jude 19. In one of these it is translated, as it is here, by the word "natural;" but in the other two it is translated by the word "sensual." There is another English word, "animal," derived from the Latin *anima* (the soul), which expresses, with considerable accuracy, the meaning of the Greek word *psuchikos;* and if we unite these two translations we shall have a very valuable key to the meaning of all these passages; thus—

There is a *sensual or animal* body, and there is a spiritual body, 1 Cor. xv. 44.

The *sensual or animal* man receiveth not the things of the Spirit of God, 1 Cor. ii. 14.

This wisdom descendeth not from above, but is earthly, *sensual or animal,* devilish, James iii. 15.

These be they who separate themselves, *sensual or animal,* having not the Spirit, Jude 19.

We might also show very clearly the connection between the 44th and the 45th verses, by translating both words as animal:—44. "There is an animal body, and there is a spiritual body. 45. And so it is written, The first Adam was made a living animal, the last Adam was made a life-giving spirit. 46. Howbeit that was not first which is spiritual, but that which is animal; and afterwards that which is spiritual."

The contrast which is here so much insisted on between the soul and the spirit, as characteristic of the two natures which are respectively animal and angelic, directs our attention necessarily to the difference between the soul and the spirit in the human person, and a hasty judgment would, perhaps, lead us to suppose that at the resurrection the soul shall be wanting inasmuch as the "sensual" will disappear. This idea, however, will not bear a close examination. The body, the soul, and the spirit, will still be there, but the spirit will predominate over the soul. That the soul will still be present in the resurrection body is rendered exceedingly probable from such passages as these, "His soul was not left in hell, neither his flesh did see corruption," Acts ii. 31 ; "Fear not them which kill the body, but are not able to kill the soul; but rather fear him which is able to destroy both soul and body in hell" (Matt. x. 28). We might even draw an argument from the statement regarding the two Adams, the first being a living soul, the last a quickening spirit; for inasmuch as the first Adam, though the soul predominated, had also a spirit; so, the second Adam, though the spirit predominated, must also have a soul.

This introduction of Adam and Christ in their covenant relations, brings up the last element of the theory of the resurrection. In the case of the angels who never sinned and never died, the animal body naturally became transformed into a spiritual body, which, according to the constitution of the angelic nature, was its last and most perfect development. But when Adam fell, his animal body lost its power of development ; and it became necessary that an external power should interfere, to restore the constitution to its original condition. The last Adam was not only a living spirit, he was a life-giving spirit; and it is through the power communicated by him that the resurrection takes place. "He that raised up the Lord Jesus, shall raise up us also by Jesus" (2 Cor. iv. 14).

In a former chapter (VIII.) we have had occasion to speak of the soul and spirit in their relation to the body; the physiology of the resurrection requires us to look more carefully into the functions which they perform in the animal economy. When light shines upon a living plant, the light, which is one of the inorganic forms of force, is absorbed by the plant, and is changed into another form of force, different from any of its inorganic forms, and is capable of producing effects which neither light, heat, nor electricity, as such, is capable of producing; it has assumed an organic form, and is capable of producing organic changes. Thus, if there be water and carbonic acid present, this organic form of force can not only separate the oxygen from the water and the carbonic acid, but can also unite the carbon of the latter with the hydrogen of the former, and use up, at the same time, as much of the oxygen as is needed to form wood, or starch, or sugar, according to the necessities of the plant, or the part of the plant in which it is operating.

It must also be remarked that the inorganic forms of force (for convenience we shall call them inorganic forces) cannot be changed into organic forces, except where there is already organic life. For example, light may be changed into organic force when it falls upon a living plant, and in this new form can produce wood or resin, or any other vegetable substance wherever it may be needed, provided the materials are present from which they can be formed; but if light fall upon a piece of dead wood, or a piece of vegetable substance in which life is extinct, the light may be changed into some of the other inorganic forms of force, but it can never rise into any of the organic forms. Water and carbonic acid may be formed in any quantities, or they may be decomposed in any quantities; but wood, gum, or any vegetable substance can only be produced where there is already vegetable life.

We now turn to the animal kingdom, and find the same principles at work. The blood conveys the nourishment to every part of the body, but it depends on the presence of life in each part whether it will produce any organic change or not. Wherever there is life, some organic change will be produced; at one place the blood will deposit skin, at another flesh, at another cartilage, and at another bone. In each of these parts there is the life-power, but the kind and quality are different in each. The life-power which determines the formation of bone, must be different from that which determines the formation of flesh; so that throughout the whole body there is as great a diversity of life-power as there is diversity of material.

We must next observe that these exquisitely diversified life-powers are not independent existences, but connected and harmonious agencies, forming one grand and symmetrical whole, the counterpart and cause of the material body. The body without these is dead, and the organic forces—if we be permitted to speak of them as intelligent agents—even supposing them to act, would not know what to do, unless the *anima*, or soul, continue to energise the body, causing all its functions to proceed harmoniously.

But let us look a little closer at this *anima*, or soul,

which so wonderfully gives direction to the organic forces. In every individual it has a type or pattern, according to which it controls its labourers, and models its materials. The *anima* of a bird produces from the egg a bird : this is its type of working, from which it is incapable of deviating. The *anima* of a dog, on the other hand, produces a dog, and nothing else.

This, however, is not all; not only is there a *specific* type in each, there is also an *individual* type, according to which every individual has its own particular form. The materials of which a man is made are constantly undergoing change. The hair, the nails, and the skin, the fluids, the flesh, and the bones, are all undergoing a process of continual renovation, constantly throwing off the old matter, and constantly receiving deposits of the new. The Falls of Niagara are not more changeful in their material than is the body of every living man. Every hour is producing a change in the materials of our bodies, although in some parts the change is more rapid than in others; and it may be truly said that every part of our body is but a slow cascade, receiving fresh matter in one place, and throwing off old matter in another; and yet, notwithstanding this continual change of material, the form always remains the same. Like the Falls of Niagara, the matter changes, but the form and fashion in every particular continue unchanged. There is the same eye, the same nose, the same mouth, the same colour, the same height, and the same general form. What is it, then, that constitutes the identity of the individual? Is it the visible matter that is without? No! it is the unseen psyche or soul within.

To illustrate the bearing of these truths on the doctrine of the resurrection, we shall consider the case of a man who, either by disease or famine, is reduced to a mere skeleton—his eyes are sunk, his cheeks hollow, and his bones protrude from underneath the skin. We shall first suppose that this man recovers his former health, and that by careful nursing for a few months, his strength and fulness return, so that those who now look on his bright eye and powerful frame would not suppose that he had ever been sick. The question naturally presents itself, Is this man's body which we now see the same as the body he had before he became ill? When he was in his lowest state of emaciation, his friends could not have known him; and had he been weighed, it would have been found that he had lost many pounds in weight. *Now*, he is as heavy as he was before, and we perceive no change in his appearance, notwithstanding all that he has suffered. In one sense it is the same body as before, but in another it is not the same. There is the same appearance, the same form, the same colour, the same peculiarity of features; but as regards the materials, they are not the same; besides the regular change that is always taking place in the body, there are all the fresh materials which have been added during recovery. If even the bones, the flesh, and the liquids, which remained at the time of emaciation, have been continually changing, so that not even they are the same, when we take into account the increase in weight which has taken place, and which is attributable, of course, to the nourishment which he has received, we are forced to the conclusion, that the materials of his body are not, to any great extent, the same. Nothing can be more certain than that the flesh which was lost in disease, is gone for ever, and that the flesh that is now present has been acquired from the food received during his recovery.

But we shall next suppose that the man does not recover; he dies, and his emaciated body is laid in the grave—the dust returning to its kindred dust. Another question suggests itself, When this man rises at the resurrection, with what body shall he come? If in the resurrection morn, he arises, not as when he died, spent and emaciated, but as when he was in health, strong and robust, what are the materials of which his body is composed? If it be asserted that the body which rises at the resurrection is the same as that laid in the grave, or rather as that which he had in health before the sickness of which he died; then it does seem strange that the materials which were wasted from his body before he died, should be available for the resurrection, though they would not have been available for his recovery; in other words, that the flesh which he lost in sickness, would be really lost if the man recovered, but that if he died it would not be lost, but, on the contrary, though it had been carried by the four winds of heaven, and dispersed over all the earth, every particle would be watched over by a superintending Providence, and at the resurrection reunited, so as to make up the healthy body, of which it once formed a part.

When viewed in this light, it is evident that the real identity of our bodies does not depend so much upon the identity of the materials of which they are composed, as the identity of the soul or psyche, which gives them their form. If we acknowledge this principle in health and in sickness, why should we not acknowledge it also in regard to the resurrection? Let us revert, for illustration, to our old idea of a cataract, in which the waters are continually changing, though the cataract itself remains unchanged; and we shall suppose that by some great convulsion of nature the waters of the Niagara, instead of pouring down over the ridge, should find an outlet to the ocean by some other channel, the rocky shelf, over which they were wont to leap, would be left bare and dry, and the great Niagara would be dead. But let us next suppose that, by another convulsion of nature, the waters return to their former channel, after an interval, say, of a thousand years,—the rocky precipice over which they once plunged is the very same as it was before,—every projecting rock, every torn gulley, is still there; and when at length the waters reach the edge, and again commence their song of thunder, every minute feature that the traveller used to mark in the living landscape would re-appear, and the great Niagara would be alive again—the very same Niagara that it was before.

Even so may we suppose that, when by the power of the Holy Ghost, which raised up Christ from the dead, the human soul and spirit shall be enabled to re-organise a body formed after the same fashion as that which the soul had been previously accustomed to organise, the identity of that body will not consist in the identity of the materials of which it shall be composed (for such an identity never existed), but in the identity of the soul and spirit which will fashion them, and the identity of the type upon which they shall be fashioned.

CHAPTER XXII.

THE CONCLUSION.

LET us now briefly sum up the more general conclusions at which we have arrived, so that when they are brought together we may be the better enabled to form an estimate of their consistency with Scripture and with one another, their comparative probability, and their general correspondence with all that we know of the works and the ways of God.

In the first place, we have discovered a remarkable and most suggestive difference between the physical constitution of the angels and the physical constitution of the unclean spirits. The one we have found to be in every respect identical with that of the resurrection bodies of Christ and His saints; the other we have found to be in every respect identical with the disembodied spirits of men. The very same test which our Lord invited to prove that His body was material, and consisted of flesh and bones, as it appeared to the disciples, was also applied to the bodies of the angels. They were "handled and seen;" and if this were not sufficient, as Jesus ate the piece of broiled fish and honeycomb, in order to remove the possibility of doubt, the angels ate unleavened cakes, with butter, milk, and veal, in the presence of Abraham, to convince us that they are not spirits, but have flesh and bones as we have.

We have further found that there is really nothing in

T

Scripture which in the slightest degree countenances the
idea that they are not really and truly human beings like
ourselves. They are actually *called* men; and although
they are sometimes called also angels, we have found that
there is nothing in that word which would imply that
they are not men, inasmuch as men also are frequently
called angels. The only difference which we can discover
between the two is, that we are of the earth, while they
are from heaven; and that we are still in our natural
bodies, while they are possessed of spiritual bodies.
The powers and actions of these celestial men are certainly greater than those of terrestrial men, but they are
not greater than those exhibited by the body of Jesus
after He rose from the dead. We have, besides, additional
confirmation of the identity of the two natures in the
statement made by Christ Himself, that the resurrection
saints will be " equal to the angels."

Here, then, are facts, facts which cannot be disputed;
what is the explanation? Our hypothesis is, that the
angels had originally natural bodies, which have been
developed into spiritual bodies, not by miraculous agency,
but by the action of natural laws, according to the original
constitution of their nature. As Adam was created with
a natural body (1 Cor. xv. 45), immortal, and in the image
of God, so we conceive the angels to have been created
with natural bodies, which afterwards were developed into
spiritual bodies instead of dying. This is corroborated, if
not proved, by Paul's assertion, that there are celestial
bodies as well as terrestrial (ver. 40); spiritual bodies as
well as natural (ver. 44); and that the spiritual body is
not first, but must be preceded by the natural body (ver.
46). If this hypothesis be not legitimate, we ask wherein
it is defective. We do not present it as more than a

hypothesis, because we are not able to prove it. The angels may have been each a separate creation, ten thousand times ten thousand Adams, with spiritual bodies instead of natural. It may have been so; but this, it must be remembered, is quite as much a hypothesis as the other, and is as incapable of proof.

In the second place, we have found that Satan and his angels belonged to the same species as the angels of heaven, but kept not their first estate: whatever difference, therefore, is found between them is to be attributed to their fall. If our first hypothesis be correct, that is to say, if the angels were created with natural bodies, then Satan and his angels were also created with natural bodies; but if our hypothesis be not correct, then the devils were created at first with spiritual bodies. But we have also found that, by some means or in some manner, a change has taken place upon them, and they are no longer possessed of spiritual bodies, or bodies of any kind. Unlike the resurrection body of Christ, or the spiritual bodies of angels, they could not be handled and seen, so as to prove that they were not spirits, but had flesh and bones, as Christ had. Neither do we find that at any time they were able to eat, or were entertained as the angels unawares. On the contrary they are called spirits, and are never called men. They perform all the actions which a spirit might be supposed to be capable of performing, but which an angel could not. They enter into the bodies of men, they influence their actions, they speak with their tongues, and thousands of them are capable of occupying the same body. Such things the angels never do. These are facts, and they cannot be disputed; what is the explanation? Our hypothesis is, that the devils were created with natural bodies, in which they sinned and died; and being cast out at death as naked and houseless spirits, they await the resurrection and the judgment. How else can we account for the change? and if our hypothesis be not legitimate, we ask in what is it defective, and where shall we find another?

In the third place, we have found that Satan is the recognised prince of the devils, identical in nature, but superior in authority and power; and that there are intermediate principalities and powers, rulers of the darkness of this world, and rulers of the subordinate agents called "the spirit which now worketh in the children of disobedience" (Eph. ii. 2). He and they must have been originally possessed of bodies like the angels, either natural or spiritual. These are the facts; what is the explanation? Our hypothesis is, that Satan's authority was patriarchal, he having been the first created of his race, and they his descendants. His superiority might be accounted for by his having come directly from the creating hand of God, and their inferiority may be accounted for by the gradual degeneracy of their natural constitution in consequence of sin. We do not say that this has been proved; we only offer it as a hypothesis. It may have been that each of the devils was an independent creation, and that each had an independent fall. We also admit that the superiority and authority of Satan over the other unclean spirits may have been not original, but by conquest. At the same time it is necessary to observe that this also is nothing more than a hypothesis, and rests on no better proof than our own. We are content, therefore, to leave it to the reader to form a judgment for himself as to which is most in conformity with all the analogies which we see around us.

In the fourth place we have found that Satan is called the "Prince of this world," and that the earth is the boundary, not only of his dominion, but of his residence and walk. His angels are called "the power of the air;" whereas the holy angels are spoken of as not of this world, but as sent to this world from heaven. We have also found that, although the devils are never spoken of as men, they are identified with men in their moral history, and correspond in nature and constitution with the disembodied spirits of men. They are represented as inhabiting the same prison, awaiting the same resurrection, about to stand at the same judgment-seat, and eventually to share the same punishment of everlasting fire, which we are told was originally prepared for the devil and his angels.

How is it that angels and devils, sprung from the same origin, and diverging so remarkably, should, nevertheless, find each an analogue in man? Our hypothesis is, that while the physical constitution of the angels with their spiritual bodies, is identical with that which Adam would have possessed if he had never sinned, the physical constitution of the devils is identical with that which Adam would have possessed if there had been no Saviour. Our hypothesis suggests that all the revealed facts might be accounted for by supposing that the devils belonged originally to this world; that they were its first human inhabitants; and that they lived and sinned, and died and became extinct, before Adam was created : we suggest that Adam's fall was but a second chapter of this world's history, and the continuation of a previous apostacy, whose punishment it was doomed to share. If, therefore, it shall really be found that there are human remains belonging to an age previous to the creation of our own first parents, these remains are sufficiently accounted for by our hypothesis, if they cannot be accounted for by any other. At the same time, we wish it to be understood that we present this only as a hypothesis which we cannot prove, but which we offer for examination, and more thorough scrutiny. We admit that Satan and his angels may have been created upon some other planet, and been transferred to our world at the creation of Adam, to become its prince when he fell; but it must be remembered that this, too, is no more than a hypothesis, and is as destitute of proof as our own. We also admit that there may be other reasons, which we do not know, why Satan and his angels should be confined in the same prison, await the same resurrection, and stand at the same judgment-seat with man; and there may be some other reason why men should be cast into the same eternal fire that was prepared for the devil and his angels: but our hypothesis upon this point has the advantage of having no rival, because no other has hitherto been suggested.

In the fifth place, we have found that, in some way or another, Satan was connected with, and interested in, the fall of the human race by Adam, and their recovery by Christ. He was permitted to tempt our first parents when they fell, as well as our Lord Jesus Christ when He came to recover us from the disaster of the fall. His success in Eden was not only a triumph, but a victory, else his defeat upon Calvary would have been merely a disappointment, and not the bruising of his head. His recognised standing as the accuser of the brethren, and the challenger of their righteousness, assigns to him a forensic character, which needs to be accounted for consistently with God's holiness and justice. His authority and power, as the Prince of this world, whatever that title implied, was acknowledged by Christ; but it also appears that the work of Christ involved His deposition; so that, as Prince of this world, he should be " cast out," and his power over death " destroyed." Our hypothesis is, that Satan's rights as Prince of this world were founded on his patriarchal authority; that they were undisputed till the creation of Adam; but that, when he was created, the rights of primogeniture yielded to the superior majesty of sinless innocence in the younger race. When Adam fell, the foundation of that superiority would be destroyed, and the crown would revert to the older dynasty, and then Satan would again become not only *de facto*, but *de jure*, the Prince of this world, with the Adamic race added as new subjects to his kingdom. When Christ came, therefore, to dispute his title, it was Satan's interest to challenge his work; and hence the temptation in the wilderness. Our hypothesis, if it does not account for the facts, is at least in entire accordance with them; and as no other consistent hypothesis has been attempted since before the days of Anselm, it is at least entitled to examination. The subject cannot yet be exhausted, and, therefore, further scrutiny will bring forth corroboration or disproof; in either case, the result will be beneficial, provided the investigation be conducted with that candour which loyalty to truth demands.

APPENDIX.

APPENDIX (A.)

SUPPOSED ANTEDILUVIAN SCRIPTURES.

WE have stated in the text (chap. ii.) that it is a rule in
history that the nearer the historian lived to the events
which he records, the more trustworthy is his narrative.
It is so in profane history; for up to the time of the first
historian in each country, the events that occurred before
him fade away backwards into mythical romance. If it
be not so also in sacred history, the only exception must
be this very Book of Genesis, which we hold to be no
exception at all. From the Exodus under Moses till
Paul's imprisonment at Rome, when "only Luke was
with him," embracing a period of about fifteen hundred
years, the narratives are contemporary histories, written
by the men who saw and heard of the events which they
record.

The Book of Genesis embraces a period of twenty-
three * centuries, which is a great deal more than that
of all the rest of the Bible narrative put together; and
it would be an exception to all history, whether sacred or
profane, if a trustworthy record should be written for the

---

* This computation is founded on the Hebrew text, which gives the
lowest estimate. Many scholars prefer the chronology of the Septua-
gint, which enlarges the patriarchal period by upwards of eighteen
additional centuries.

first time, two thousand years after the events which it describes had taken place. *A priori*, therefore, we should expect that there were records in existence when Genesis was written, and that they were in Moses' hands when he compiled his history. We should require very satisfactory evidence to the contrary to induce us to entertain even a doubt. The very character of the narratives is decisive upon the point; because the want of symmetry is very apparent, and, in some of the narratives, the details-and circumstantialities are such as to make it impossible (except by miracle) that they should have been preserved beyond the generation in which they occurred.

Even though there had been no prophets before Moses, and, therefore, no inspired documents in his possession, we should not wonder, if, in guaranteeing (by inspiration) that which was not inspired, he nevertheless refrained from altering the narratives so far as to destroy their fragmentary character, and disguise the differences in their style. Even for hermeneutic purposes he might regard such treatment as inexpedient and unsafe. But since we do know that there were prophets before Moses, and supposing these documents to be inspired, it was most accordant with that reverence which Scripture shows for Scripture, that he should preserve, as much as possible, the *ipsissima verba* of the sacred records.

Without presuming to speak very confidently on a subject where confidence would be presumption, the following experiment (and it is nothing more) is offered with a view to show how much has been allowed to remain of the original character of these documents so as to afford a clue to their probable origin. Those words and expressions which are supposed to afford the clue, are printed in prominent type to draw attention to them.

No. I. *Suggested as having been written by Noah.*
APOCALYPSE OF CREATION.

IN the beginning God created the heaven and the earth. And the earth was without form, and void; and darkness was upon the face of the deep, and the Spirit of God moved upon the face of the waters. And God said, Let there be light: and there was light. And God saw the light, that it was good: and God divided the light from the darkness. And God call.d the light Day, and the darkness he called Night. And the evening and the morning were the first day.

And God said, Let there be a firmament in the midst of the waters, and let it divide the waters from the waters. And God made the firmament, and divided the waters which were under the firmament from the waters which were above the firmament: and it was so. And God called the firmament Heaven. And the evening and the morning were the second day.

And God said, Let the waters under the heaven be gathered together unto one place, and let the dry land appear: and it was so. And God called the dry land Earth; and the gathering together of the waters called he Seas: and God saw that it was good. And God said, Let the earth bring forth grass, the herb yielding seed, and the fruit tree yielding fruit after his kind, whose seed is in itself, upon the earth: and it was so. And the earth brought forth grass, and herb yielding seed after his kind, and the tree yielding fruit, whose seed was in itself, after his kind: and God saw that it was good. And the evening and the morning were the third day.

And God said, Let there be lights in the firmament of the heaven to divide the day from the night; and let them be for signs, and for seasons, and for days, and years: And let them be for lights in the firmament of the heaven to give light upon the earth: and it was so. And God made two great lights; the greater light to rule the day, and the lesser light to rule the night: he made the stars also. And God set them in the firmament of the heaven to give light upon the earth, and to rule over the day and over the night, and to divide the light from the darkness: and God saw that it was good. And the evening and the morning were the fourth day.

And God said, Let the waters bring forth abundantly the *moving creature that hath*

life, and fowl that may fly above the earth in the open firmament of heaven. And God created great whales, and *every living creature that moveth, which* the waters brought forth abundantly, *after their kind, and every winged fowl after his kind:* and God saw that it was good. And God blessed them, saying, *Be fruitful, and multiply,* and fill the waters in the seas, and let fowl multiply in the earth. And the evening and the morning were the fifth day.

And God said, Let the earth bring forth the living creature after his kind, *cattle, and creeping thing, and beast of the earth, after his kind:* and it was so. And God made the *beast of the earth after his kind, and cattle after their kind, and every thing that creepeth upon the earth* after his kind: and God saw that it was good. And God said, Let us make man *in our image, after our likeness:* and let them have dominion over the fish of the sea, and over the fowl of the air, and *over the cattle, and over all the earth, and over every creeping thing that creepeth upon the earth.* So God created man in his own image, *in the image of God created he him; male and female created he them.* And God blessed them, and God said unto them, *Be fruitful, and multiply, and replenish the earth,* and subdue it: *and have dominion over the fish of the sea, and over the fowl of the air, and over every living thing that moveth upon* the earth. And God said, Behold, I have given you every herb bearing seed, which is upon the face of all the earth, and every tree, in the which is the fruit of a tree yielding seed; to you it shall be for meat. And to every beast of the earth, and to every fowl of the air, and to every thing that creepeth upon the earth, wherein there is life, I have given every green herb for meat: and it was so. And God saw every thing that he had made, and, behold, it was very good. And the evening and the morning were the sixth day.

Thus the heavens and the earth were finished, and all the host of them. And on the seventh day God ended his work which he had made; and he rested on the seventh day from all his work which he had made. And God blessed the seventh day, and sanctified it: because that in it he had rested from all his work which God created and made.

The reasons why this is supposed to have been written by Noah are, *first,* No personal recollection was needed to enable one prophet more than another to be the seer. *Second,* The name of God here used is the same as that used by Noah, whose words are quoted in No. 6 (Gen. ix. 27.) *Third,* In style and expression it has an extraordinary resemblance .to Nos. 5 and 6, and to no other. Compare the words printed in *Italic.*

No. II. *Suggested as having been*

THE BOOK OF THE PROPHET ADAM.

THESE are the generations of the heavens and of the earth when they were created, in the day that Jehovah God made the earth and the heavens. And every plant of the field before it was in the earth, and every herb of the field before it grew: for Jehovah God had not caused it to rain upon the earth, and there was not a man to till the ground. But there went up a mist from the earth, and watered the whole face of the ground. And Jehovah God formed man of the dust of the ground, and breathed into his nostrils the breath of life; and man became a living soul. And Jehovah God planted a garden eastward in Eden; and there he put the man whom he had formed. And out of the ground made Jehovah God to grow every tree that is pleasant to the sight, and good for food; the tree of life also in the midst of the garden, and the tree of knowledge of good and evil. And a river went out of Eden to water the garden; and from thence it was parted, and became into four heads. The name of the first is Pison: that is it which compasseth the whole land of Havilah, where there is gold; And the gold of that land is good; there is bdellium and the onyx stone. And the name of the second river is Gihon: the same is it that compasseth the whole land of Ethiopia. And the name of the third river is Hiddekel: that is it which goeth toward the east of Assyria. And the fourth river is Euphrates. And Jehovah God took the man, and put him into the garden of Eden to dress it and to keep it. And Jehovah God commanded the man, saying, Of every tree of the garden thou mayest freely eat: But of the tree of the knowledge of good and evil, thou shalt not eat of it: for in the day that thou eatest thereof thou shalt surely die.

And Jehovah God said, It is not good that the man should be alone; I will make him an help meet for him. And out of the ground Jehovah God formed every beast of the field, and every fowl of the air; and brought them unto Adam to see what he would call them: and whatsoever Adam called every living creature, that was the name thereof. And Adam gave names to all cattle, and to the fowl of the air, and to every beast of the field; but for Adam there was not found an help meet for him.

And Jehovah God caused a deep sleep to fall upon Adam, and he slept: and he took one of his ribs, and closed up the flesh instead thereof; And the rib which the Jehovah God had taken from man, made he a woman, and brought her unto the man. And Adam said, This is now bone of my bones, and flesh of my flesh: she shall be called Woman, because she was taken out of Man. Therefore shall a man leave his father and his mother, and shall cleave unto his wife: and they shall be one flesh. And they were both naked, the man and his wife, and were not ashamed. Now the serpent was more subtil than any beast of the field which Jehovah God had made. And he said unto the woman, Yea, hath God said, Ye shall not eat of every tree of the garden? And the woman said unto the serpent, We may eat of the fruit of the trees of the garden: But of the fruit of the tree which is in the midst of the garden, God hath said, Ye shall not eat of it, neither shall ye touch it, lest ye die. And the serpent said unto the woman, Ye shall not surely die: For God doth know that in the day ye eat thereof, then your eyes shall be opened, and ye shall be as gods, knowing good and evil. And when the woman saw that the tree was good for food, and that it was pleasant to the eyes, and a tree to be desired to make one wise, she took of the fruit thereof, and did eat, and gave also unto her husband with her; and he did eat. And the eyes of them both were opened, and they knew that they were naked; and they sewed fig leaves together, and made themselves aprons. And they heard the voice of Jehovah God walking in the garden in the cool of the day; and Adam and his wife hid themselves from the presence of Jehovah God amongst the trees of the garden. And Jehovah God called unto Adam, and said unto him, Where art thou? And he said, I heard thy voice in the garden, and I was afraid, because I was naked; and I hid myself. And he said, Who told thee that thou wast naked? Hast thou eaten of the tree, whereof I commanded thee that thou shouldest not eat? And the man said, The woman whom thou gavest to be with me, she gave me of the tree, and I did eat. And Jehovah God said unto the woman, What is this that thou hast done? And the woman said, The serpent beguiled me, and I did eat. And Jehovah God said unto the serpent, Because thou hast done this, thou art cursed above all cattle, and above every beast of the field; upon thy belly shalt thou go, and dust shalt thou eat all the days of thy life: And I will put enmity between thee and the woman, and between thy seed and her seed; it shall bruise thy head, and thou shalt bruise his heel. Unto the woman he said, I will greatly multiply thy sorrow and thy conception; in sorrow thou shalt bring forth children; and thy desire shall be to thy husband, and he shall rule over thee. And unto Adam he said, Because thou hast hearkened unto the voice of thy wife, and hast eaten of the tree, of which I commanded thee, saying, Thou shalt not eat of it: cursed is the ground for thy sake; in sorrow shalt thou eat of it all the days of thy life; Thorns also and thistles shall it bring forth to thee; and thou shalt eat the herb of the field; In the sweat of thy face shalt thou eat bread, till thou return unto the ground; for out of it wast thou taken: for dust thou art, and unto dust shalt thou return.

And Adam called his wife's name Eve; because she was the mother of all living. Unto Adam also and to his wife did Jehovah God make coats of skin, and clothed them.

And Jehovah God said, Behold, the man is become as one of us, to know good and evil: and now, lest he put forth his hand, and take also of the tree of life, and eat, and live for ever: Therefore Jehovah God sent him forth from the garden of Eden, to till the ground from whence he was taken. So he drove out the man: and he placed at the east of the garden of Eden Cherubims, and a flaming sword which turned every way, to keep the way of the tree of life.

That this is a monograph is evident from its contents and title. Its close indicates the time when it was written, and its probable author. No prophet was so well qualified to write it as Adam; and if Adam wrote any of the books this must have been the one.

No. III. *Suggested as having been the concluding portion of*
THE BOOK OF THE PROPHET SETH.

And Adam knew Eve his wife: and she conceived, and bare Cain, and said, I have gotten a man from Jehovah And she again bare his brother Abel. And Abel was a keeper of sheep, but Cain was a tiller of the ground.

And in process of time it came to pass, that Cain brought of the fruit of the ground an offering unto Jehovah. And Abel, he also brought of the firstlings of his flock and of the fat thereof. And Jehovah had respect unto Abel and to his offering: but unto Cain and to his offering he had not respect. And Cain was very wroth, and his countenance fell. And Jehovah said unto Cain, Why art thou wroth? and why is thy countenance fallen? If thou doest well, shalt thou not be accepted? and if thou doest not well, sin lieth at the door. And unto thee shall be his desire, and thou shalt rule over him.

And Cain talked with Abel his brother: and it came to pass, when they were in the field, that Cain rose up against Abel his brother, and slew him. And Jehovah said unto Cain, Where is Abel thy brother? And he said, I know not: Am I my brother's keeper? And he said, What hast thou done? the voice of thy brother's blood crieth unto me from the ground. And now art thou cursed from the earth, which hath opened her mouth to receive thy brother's blood from thy hand; When thou tillest the ground, it shall not henceforth yield unto thee her strength; a fugitive and a vagabond shalt thou be in the earth. And Cain said unto Jehovah, My punishment is greater than I can bear. Behold, thou hast driven me out this day from the face of the earth; and from thy face shall I be hid; and I shall be a fugitive and a vaga-

bond in the earth; and it shall come to pass, that every one that findeth me shall slay me. And Jehovah said unto him, Therefore whosoever slayeth Cain, vengeance shall be taken on him sevenfold. And Jehovah set a mark upon Cain, lest any finding him should kill him.

And Cain went out from the presence of Jehovah, and dwelt in the land of Nod, on the east of Eden. And Cain knew his wife; and she conceived, and bare Enoch: and he builded a city, and called the name of the city, after the name of his son, Enoch. And unto Enoch was born Irad: and Irad begat Mehujael. and Mehujael begat Methusael: and Methusael begat Lamech.

And Lamech took unto him two wives: the name of the one was Adah, and the name of the other Zillah. And Adah bare Jabal: he was the father of such as dwell in tents, and of such as have cattle.   And his brother's name was Jubal: he was the father of all such as handle the harp and organ. And Zillah, she also bare Tubal-cain, an instructer of every artificer in brass and iron: and the sister of Tubal-cain was Naamah. And Lamech said unto his wives, Adah and Zillah, Hear my voice; ye wives of Lamech, hearken unto my speech: for I have slain a man to my wounding, and a young man to my hurt. If Cain shall be avenged sevenfold, truly Lamech seventy and sevenfold.

And Adam knew his wife again; and she bare a son, and called his name Seth: For God, said she, hath appointed me another seed instead of Abel, whom Cain slew. And to Seth, to him also there was born a son; and he called his name Enos: then began men to call upon the name of Jehovah.

The monographic character of this portion is not so evident as of the others. If Seth was a prophet, this is the only book which could be attributed to him. The title, and probably the commencement, are awanting. The close indicates the probable author.

No. IV. *A Fragment of*
THE BOOK OF ENOCH.
(*Preserved by the Apostle Jude.*)

Behold **Jehovah** cometh with myriads of his saints to execute judgment upon all, and to convince all that are ungodly among them, of all their ungodly deeds which they have ungodly committed, and of all their hard speeches which ungodly sinners have spoken against him.

No. V. *Suggested as having been*
THE FIRST BOOK OF THE PROPHET NOAH.

THIS is the book of the generations of Adam. In the day that God created man, *in the likeness of God made he him; male and female created he them; and blessed them,* and called their name Adam, in the day when they were created. And Adam lived an hundred and thirty years, and begat a son in his own likeness, after his image; and called his name Seth: And the days of Adam after he had begotten Seth were eight hundred years: and he begat sons and daughters: And all the days that Adam lived were nine hundred and thirty years: and he died.

And Seth lived an hundred and five years, and begat Enos: And Seth lived after he begat Enos eight hundred and seven years, and begat sons and daughters: And all the days of Seth were nine hundred and twelve years: and he died.

And Enos lived ninety years, and begat Cainan; And Enos lived after he begat Cainan eight hundred and fifteen years, and begat sons and daughters: And all the days of Enos were nine hundred and five years: and he died.

And Cainan lived seventy years, and begat Mahalaleel: And Cainan lived after he begat Mahalaleel eight hundred and forty years, and begat sons and daughters: And all the days of Cainan were nine hundred and ten years: and he died.

And Mahalaleel lived sixty and five years, and begat Jared: And Mahalaleel lived after he begat Jared eight hundred and thirty years, and begat sons and daughters:

And all the days of Mahalaleel were eight hundred ninety and five years: and he died.

And Jared lived an hundred sixty and two years, and he begat Enoch: And Jared lived after he begat Enoch eight hundred years, and begat sons and daughters: And all the days of Jared were nine hundred sixty and two years: and he died.

And Enoch lived sixty and five years, and begat Methuselah: And *Enoch walked with God* after he begat Methuselah three hundred years, and begat sons and daughters: And all the days of Enoch were three hundred sixty and five years: And *Enoch walked with God*: and he was not; for God took him.

And Methuselah lived an hundred eighty and seven years, and begat Lamech. And Methuselah lived after he begat Lamech seven hundred eighty and two years, and begat sons and daughters: And all the days of Methuselah were nine hundred sixty and nine years: and he died.

And Lamech lived an hundred eighty and two years, and begat a son: And he called his name Noah, saying, This same shall comfort us concerning our work and toil of our hands, because of the ground which the LORD hath cursed. And Lamech lived after he begat Noah five hundred ninety and five years, and begat sons and daughters: And all the days of Lamech were seven hundred seventy and seven years: and he died.

And Noah was five hundred years old: and Noah begat Shem, Ham, and Japheth.

That this is a monograph is evident from its title. Its close indicates the time when it was written, and its probable author. The words printed in *Italic* are the expressions which suggest a similarity of the style to that of Nos. 1 and 6.

No. VI. *Suggested as having been*

THE SECOND BOOK OF THE PROPHET NOAH.

THESE are the generations of Noah: Noah was a just man and perfect in his generations, and *Noah walked with God*. And Noah begat three sons, Shem, Ham, and Japheth.

The earth also was corrupt before God, and the earth was filled with violence. And God looked upon the earth, and, behold, it was corrupt; for all flesh had corrupted his way upon the earth.

[And God saw that the wickedness of man was great in the earth, and that every imagination of the thoughts of his heart was only evil continually.]

And God said unto Noah, The end of all flesh is come before me; for the earth is filled with violence through them; and, behold, I will destroy them with the earth. Make thee an ark of gopher wood; rooms shalt thou make in the ark, and shalt pitch it within and without with pitch. And this is the fashion which thou shalt make it of: The length of the ark shall be three hundred cubits, and the breadth of it fifty cubits, and the height of it thirty cubits. A window shalt thou make to the ark, and in a cubit shalt thou finish it above; and the door of the ark shalt thou set in the side thereof; with lower, second, and third stories shalt thou make it. And, behold, I, even I, do bring a flood of waters upon the earth, to destroy all flesh, wherein is the breath of life, from under heaven; and every thing that is in the earth shall die. But with thee will I establish my covenant; and thou shalt come into the ark, thou, and thy sons, and thy wife, and thy sons' wives with thee. And of every living thing of all flesh, two of every sort shalt thou bring into the ark, to keep them alive with thee; they shall be male and female. Of *fowls after their kind, and of cattle after their kind, of every creeping thing of the earth after his kind*, two of every sort shall come unto thee, to keep them alive. And take thou unto thee of all food that is eaten, and thou shalt gather it to thee: and it shall be for food for thee, and for them.

Thus did Noah; according to all that God commanded him, so did he.

. . . . . .

There went in two and two unto Noah into the ark, the male and the female, as God had commanded Noah.

And it came to pass after seven days, that the waters of the flood were upon the earth.

· In the six hundredth year of Noah's life, in the second month, the seventeenth day of the month, the same day were all the fountains of the great deep broken up, and the windows of heaven were opened.

And the rain was upon the earth forty days and forty nights. In the selfsame day entered Noah, and Shem, and Ham, and Japheth, the sons of Noah, and Noah's wife, and the three wives of his sons with them, into the ark; They, and *every beast after his kind, and all the cattle after their kind, and every creeping thing that creepeth upon the earth after his kind, and every fowl after his kind*, every bird of every sort. And they went in unto Noah into the ark, two and two of all flesh, wherein is the breath of life. And they that went in, went in male and female of all flesh, as God had commanded him: and Jehovah shut him in.

And the flood was forty days upon the earth; and the waters increased, and bare up the ark, and it was lift up above the earth. And the waters prevailed, and were increased greatly upon the earth; and the ark went upon the face of the waters. And the waters prevailed exceedingly upon the earth; and all the high hills, that were under the whole heaven, were covered. Fifteen cubits upward did the waters prevail; and the mountains were covered. And all flesh died *that moved upon the earth, both of fowl, and of cattle, and of beast, and of every creeping thing that creepeth upon the earth*, and every man: All in whose nostrils was the breath of life, of all that was in the dry land, died. And every living substance was destroyed which was upon the face of the ground, both man, and cattle, *and the creeping things, and the fowl of the heaven;* and they were destroyed from the earth: and Noah only remained alive, and they that were with him in the ark. And the waters prevailed upon the earth an hundred and fifty days.

And God remembered Noah, and every living thing, and all the cattle that was with him in the ark: and God made a wind to pass over the earth, and the waters asswaged; The fountains also of the deep and the windows of heaven were stopped, and the rain from heaven was restrained; And the waters returned from off the earth continually: and after the end of the hundred and fifty days the waters were abated. And the ark resteth in the seventh month, on the seventeenth day of the month, upon the mountains of Ararat. And the waters decreased continually until the tenth month: in the tenth month, on the first day of the month, were the tops of the mountains seen.

And it came to pass at the end of forty days, that Noah opened the window of the ark which he had made: And he sent forth a raven, which went forth to and fro, until the waters were dried up from off the earth. Also he sent forth a dove from him, to see if the waters were abated from off the face of the ground; But the dove found no rest for the sole of her foot, and she returned unto him into the ark, for the waters were on the face of the whole earth: then he put forth his hand, and took her, and pulled her in unto him into the ark. And he stayed yet other seven days: and again he sent forth the dove out of the ark; And the dove came in to him in the evening; and, lo, in her mouth was an olive leaf pluckt off: so Noah knew that the waters were abated from off the earth. And he stayed yet other seven days; and sent forth the dove; which returned not again unto him any more.

And it came to pass in the six hundredth and first year, in the first month, the first day of the month, the waters were dried up from off the earth: and Noah removed the covering of the ark, and looked, and, behold, the face of the ground was dry. And in the second month, on the seven and twentieth day of the month, was the earth dried.

And God spake unto Noah, saying, Go forth of the ark, thou, and thy wife, and thy sons, and thy sons' wives with thee. Bring forth with thee every living thing that is with thee, of all flesh, both *of fowl, and of cattle, and of every creeping thing that creepeth upon the earth;* that they may breed abundantly in the earth, and *be fruitful, and multiply upon the earth.* And Noah went forth, and his sons, and his wife, and his sons' wives with him: Every beast, every *creeping thing, and every fowl, and whatsoever creepeth upon the earth, after their kinds,* went forth out of the ark.

And God blessed Noah and his sons, and said unto them, *Be fruitful, and multiply, and replenish the earth.* And the fear of you and the dread of you shall be upon every beast of the earth, and upon every fowl of the air, upon all that moveth upon the earth, and upon all the fishes of the sea; into your hand are they delivered. Every moving thing that liveth shall be meat for you; even as the green herb have I given you all things. But flesh with the life thereof, which is the blood thereof, shall ye not eat. And surely your blood of your lives will I require; at the hand of every beast will I require it, and at the hand of man; at the hand of every man's brother will I require the life of man. Whoso sheddeth man's blood, by man shall his blood be shed: *for in the image of God made he man.* And you, *be ye fruitful,*

and multiply; bring forth abundantly in the earth, and multiply therein.

And God spake unto Noah, and to his sons with him, saying, And I, behold, I establish my covenant with you, and with your seed after you; And with every living creature that is with you, *of the fowl, of the cattle, and of every beast of the earth with you;* from all that go out of the ark, to every beast of the earth. And I will establish my covenant with you; neither shall all flesh be cut off any more by the waters of a flood; neither shall there any more be a flood to destroy the earth.

And God said, This is the token of the covenant which I make between me and you and every living creature that is with you, for perpetual generations: I do set my bow in the cloud, and it shall be for a token of a covenant between me and the earth. And it shall come to pass, when I bring a cloud over the earth, that the bow shall be seen in the cloud: And I will remember my covenant, which is between me and you and every living creature of all flesh; and the waters shall no more become a flood to destroy all flesh. And the bow shall be in the cloud; and I will look upon it, that I may remember the everlasting covenant between God and every living creature of all flesh that is upon the earth. And God said unto Noah, This is the token of the covenant, which I have established, between me and all flesh that is upon the earth.

And the sons of Noah, that went forth of the ark, were Shem, and Ham, and Japheth: and Ham is the father of Canaan. These are the three sons of Noah: and of them was the whole earth overspread.

And Noah began to be an husbandman, and he planted a vineyard: And he drank of the wine, and was drunken; and he was uncovered within his tent. And Ham, the father of Canaan, saw the nakedness of his father, and told his two brethren without. And Shem and Japheth took a garment, and laid it upon both their shoulders, and went backward, and covered the nakedness of their father; and their faces were backward, and they saw not their father's nakedness. And Noah awoke from his wine, and knew what his younger son had done unto him. And he said, Cursed be Canaan; a servant of servants shall he be unto his brethren. And he said, Blessed be the LORD GOD of Shem; and Canaan shall be his servant. God shall enlarge Japheth, and he shall dwell in the tents of Shem; and Canaan shall be his servant.

That this is a monograph is evident from the title; its close is ascertained only by the change which takes place in the name of God—the monograph which follows, instead of *God,* uses the name *Jehovah.* Noah was a prophet, and was certainly the most likely to be the author of this book—no other could be so competent.

No. VII. *Supposed to be Extracts from*

THE BOOK OF THE PROPHET SHEM.

And it came to pass, when men began to multiply on the face of the earth, and daughters were born unto them, that the sons of God saw the daughters of men that they were fair; and they took them wives of all which they chose. And Jehovah said, My spirit shall not always strive with man, for that he also is flesh: yet his days shall be an hundred and twenty years.

There were giants in the earth in those days: and also after that, when the sons of God came in unto the daughters of men, and they bare children to them, the same became mighty men which were of old, men of renown.

And it repented Jehovah that he had made man on the earth, and it grieved him at his heart. And Jehovah said, I will destroy man whom I have created from the face of the earth; both man, and beast, and the creeping thing, and the fowls of the air; for it repenteth me that I have made them. But Noah found grace in the eyes of Jehovah.

And Jehovah said unto Noah, Come thou and all thy house into the ark; for thee have I seen righteous before me in this generation. Of every clean beast thou shalt take to thee by sevens, the male and his female: and of beasts that are not clean by two, the male and his female. Of fowls also of the air by sevens, the male and the female; to keep seed alive upon the face of all the earth. For yet seven days, and I will cause it to rain upon the earth forty days and forty nights; and every living substance that I have made will I destroy from off the face of the earth.

And Noah did according unto all that Jehovah commanded him. And Noah was six hundred years old when the flood of waters was upon the earth. And Noah went in, and his sons, and his wife, and his sons' wives with him, into the ark, because of the waters of the flood. Of clean beasts, and of beasts that are not clean, and of fowls, and of every thing that creepeth upon the earth.

And Noah builded an altar unto Jehovah; and took of every clean beast, and of every clean fowl, and offered burnt offerings on the altar. And Jehovah smelled a sweet savour; and Jehovah said in his heart, I will not again curse the ground any more for man's sake; for the imagination of man's heart is evil from his youth; neither will I again smite any more every thing living, as I have done. While the earth remaineth, seedtime and harvest, and cold and heat, and summer and winter, and day and night shall not cease.

And Noah lived after the flood three hundred and fifty years. And all the days of Noah were nine hundred and fifty years: and he died.

And the whole earth was of one language, and of one speech. And it came to pass, as they journeyed from the east, that they found a plain in the land of Shinar; and they dwelt there. And they said one to another, Go to, let us make brick, and burn them throughly. And they had brick for stone, and slime had they for morter. And they said, Go to, let us build us a city and a tower, whose top may reach unto heaven; and let us make us a name, lest we be scattered abroad upon the face of the whole earth.

And Jehovah came down to see the city and the tower, which the children of men builded. And Jehovah said, Behold, the people is one, and they have all one language; and this they begin to do: and now nothing will be restrained from them, which they have imagined to do. Go to, let us go down, and there confound their language, that they may not understand one another's speech.

So Jehovah scattered them abroad from thence upon the face of all the earth: and they left off to build the city. Therefore is the name of it called Babel; because Jehovah did there confound the language of all the earth: and from thence did Jehovah scatter them abroad upon the face of all the earth.

That this is not a continuation of the preceding, is evident from the decided change of style; and if Noah was the author of only one of them, it must have been of the former. After Noah, Shem is the most likely to have been the author. Moses appears to have used only a portion of this book to supplement the other.

APPENDIX (B.)

THE FIRST FOUR DAYS OF CREATION.

IN searching out the early history of our world, as revealed by Scripture and science combined, our subject branches out in two very different directions, the astronomical, and the anthropological. In studying astronomy, our text-book may be said to be, "Nature, with annotations from Scripture;" in studying anthropology, our text-book is "Scripture, with annotations from nature." Although the subject be single, therefore, the branches are so different, that it has been deemed desirable to make a separation, and so remove the astronomical, which is least important, to the Appendix. At the same time, it will be observed that both subjects are viewed from the same stand-point, and that in both, regard is paid to the supremacy of law. In the ANTHROPOLOGICAL department it has been shown that what might be called the phenomena of Scripture, may, to a large extent, be explained by the phenomena of nature, dispensing with a great deal of that mystery and myth in which they have so long been enveloped. In the ASTRONOMICAL department the same principle has been followed; and, if in our anticipations of the future, we ought to be guided by our experience of the past, we may expect that the unknown will be found to bear a far greater resemblance to the known than was ever suspected; and that there is a unity and characteristic simplicity extending over all God's works of creation, which every discovery tends to demonstrate, dissipating at every step some cloud of mystery with which it had previously been surrounded.

In the following pages there is no pretension to original observation or discovery, their purpose being rather to collate and harmonise that which has already been observed and discovered. Such an employment is both legitimate and useful, more especially if its object be to eliminate the mysterious, and reduce the multiplicity of the unknown.

DARKNESS ON THE FACE OF THE DEEP.

The most important astronomic discovery of the present century is the FUEL of the Sun. Others may be more brilliant, and some of them much more astonishing; but none of them throws such a flood of light upon the natural history of the heavens as this. Of all the mysteries of astronomy, the Sun was at once the most prominent and the most perplexing. The moon and the stars might be beautiful objects of contemplation, and might be greatly admired; but the sun was a potential agency of light and heat, far beyond anything which was known to exist elsewhere, and altogether mysterious and incomprehensible. From every square yard of its surface there comes forth a heat equal to that of a blast surface consuming a ton of coal every ten minutes, and this tremendous expenditure of force is not a merely temporary incident, but has been going on not only for hundreds, but for thousands, if not for millions of years. The philosophers were puzzled, because they could not conceive how it was possible that it should be a case of simple combustion; for even though the whole body of the sun had been a storehouse of fuel it must have burned itself out long ago, and choked itself up with the ashes. The intensity of the light also was a difficulty which electricity alone seemed capable of solving; and, therefore, it was supposed that the sun must be a great electric lamp hung up in the heavens; although, whence the electricity came they could not even conjecture. Now that the mystery has been solved, we are as much astonished at its simplicity as at its grandeur. It has been discovered that the sun could no more supply us with light and heat without a constant supply of fuel, than a lamp could burn without oil, or a fire without wood or coals. But, instead of the supply being within, it has been found to lie on the outside, while the products of combustion are swallowed up in its capacious interior as they are generated.

No doubt it requires an enormous quantity of fuel to keep up such a gigantic furnace, but this also has been discovered, or rather recognised, in an immense reservoir of meteoric matter which is revolving round the sun, and extending outwards to a great distance, its outskirts reaching even towards our own orbit. It is this reservoir which supplies the meteoric stones which occasionally fall (the stones sometimes weighing several tons); and it is this same reservoir that is seen in tropical climates after sunset and before sunrise, as a conical glow called the Zodiacal light, rising over the position of the sun.

It has been calculated that a fall of about sixty feet deep of meteoric fuel annually is required to produce the actual amount of light and heat generated in the sun; and, of course, this must add to its diameter, about a hundred and twenty feet every year. Now, although this increase is a trifle compared with the sun's diameter, yet, as its age is counted not by years but by millenniums, it follows, that it is constantly growing in size, and that its growth has been going on ever since it was kindled some fifty millions of years ago.

But the sun is only one of many millions of stars, each of which resembles it in its composition and constitution ; and, as each of them is (like our sun) living on the fuel with which it is surrounded, and growing in bulk as it grows in age, we discover that the whole heavens are in a state of continual change; and that every member of that great celestial family has an age and a history of its own. We must keep in mind also that these stars do not live always—they are not immortal. Our own earth was itself once a miniature sun, but the meteoric fuel upon which it fed has long since been exhausted, its flame has been extinguished, and its surface cooled. The moon and the planets also are all of them extinct suns, having been kindled, and grown, and decayed, while the sun was yet in its infancy; a member of a long-lived family, but certainly not immortal.

In what state was our sun then, say some fifty millions of years ago? The answer is—It had not then been born, and the materials of which it is composed were simply meteoric stones, and other matter, scattered far apart throughout the region now occupied by the solar system.

But this is not all : as there was once a time when the sun had not begun to grow, so there will arrive a time when, the meteoric fuel exhausted, the growth will be complete, and the flame extinguished. It will then cool down into a dark and solid ball, presenting all the appearance of a planet instead of that of a sun.

Such, indeed, has been the history of our own earth, which bears indubitable evidence of having been once a miniature sun. The materials of which our earth is

composed are exactly the same as the meteoric matter
which we find falling from the heavens, and it has now
been established, almost to demonstration, that the
interior of the earth has been, and still is, a mass of
molten lava, which, were it stripped of the thin crust
which now covers it, would glow with a brilliancy so
intense that the eye could not look upon it. In the
geological strata of which the outer crust of our earth is
composed, we read a history of millions of years after
our world had began to cool : we have now to add to
these, millions of previous years, when that molten mass
was still growing up into a world in the form of a little
sun.

And now that we have got the key to the mechanism,
or rather, the natural history of the heavens, we find
ourselves introduced into a new kingdom of nature, the
members of which, like those of the vegetable and
animal kingdoms, have each a birth and a growth, with
a decay and death, accordant with the type of the
families to which they respectively belong. We now
look up into the starry heavens, and see there the great
first family of God ; and whereas they formerly appeared
to us as if they had come directly from the hands of
the Creator, and as if they would continue to shine in
the firmament for ever, we now discover that, like ourselves, they have a natural history of their own, and that
the members of that giant race are all of different ages,
having been kindled at widely different times, have
arrived at different stages of maturity, and, when they
have fulfilled their course, will decay and die, leaving
their remains floating as dead worlds in the wide waste
of heaven.

On entering a forest we see the trees on every side in

all their various stages of growth, from the little seedling
that has just raised its head above the ground, to the
majestic oak that has braved a hundred winters, or even
the lifeless trunk, and mould of rotten leaves, that lie
upon the ground.   We know that they were not created
so : and although we cannot wait to watch the completion
of the course of any individual, we can read its history,
both past and future, by studying its various companions
which we see around it, without needing to witness the
actual change.   So may we study in the heavens the
various stages of star-life by observing, in the different
members of its grand community, the birth, the growth,
and the death of stars.   In the sun we behold a
specimen of their infancy and growth ; in Jupiter and
Saturn their youth, in the earth their full maturity, and
in the Moon their inevitable decay and death.   Analogy
would even carry us further, because the Sun is but an
infant world in the process of formation, but as it
belongs to a long-lived species, it is older even in its
infancy than the decrepid moon; while in the shooting-
star we find an analogue of the infusory animals and
cell-plants of the vegetable kingdom, for in a few seconds
we behold its sudden ignition and extinction, a stellar
monad, composed of the same materials, kindled by the
same means, moving according to the same laws, and
submitting to the same inexorable destiny that awaits
them all.   " Yea, all of them shall wax old like a garment, and as a vesture . . . they shall be changed."

But besides this meteoric matter of which the sun
and stars are composed, we must next direct our attention to another substance, of a totally different character,
which we find existing in great abundance in our system
—viz., oxygen gas. By means of spectrum analysis, it has

been found that all the heavenly bodies are composed of almost the same elementary substances. In one respect, however, the materials of our planet differ very much from the meteoric matter of which it was originally formed. The substances found on our earth are almost entirely saturated with oxygen, whereas the same substances floating in the sky are not so; that is to say, the meteorites, generally speaking, before they fall, are combustible, whereas the same substances found on earth, generally speaking, are not combustible, having been already burned. Nearly one-half of our world is composed of oxygen gas united to meteoric substances; and the question arises, Where did the oxygen come from? Oxygen, in its gaseous form, occupies a large space, whereas, when it is united with combustible substances, and condensed into a solid form, it occupies little room; so that the oxygen which is locked up in our planet, if it were set free, would expand into a gigantic sphere, whose diameter would extend beyond the orbit of Neptunè.

It has long been known that there exists throughout space a thin elastic atmosphere called ether, by means of which the vibrations of light pass from one part of the heavens to another. No conjecture has yet been formed by scientific men regarding its chemical qualities. It may, or it may not, be identical with our own atmosphere. If it be not identical with our atmosphere, the mystery of the oxygen of our planet must continue to be a mystery still; but if, on the other hand, it be identical with our atmosphere, then the mystery of our planet is solved along with other mysteries of the same kind.

We should have discovered the probable identity of our atmosphere with the ether of the universe, had it not been for the misinterpreted testimony of the moon. If we had known that the celestial bodies possess the power of attracting the ether towards them, many enigmas would have been solved, and a basis constructed upon which an entirely new series of investigations would have preceded ; but 'the testimony of the moon seemed to give an instant and peremptory denial to such an assumption, because, if the ether of the solar system had been of the nature of our atmosphere, it would have been attracted by gravitation to the moon's surface, and would have formed an envelope similar to that which surrounds the earth. But as no such atmosphere exists around the moon, it has been too hastily concluded that the ether of the solar system differs in its nature from our atmosphere, and that those planets which have atmospheres have received them by special creation, and not by attracting them from the surrounding ether.

But this supposed absence of an atmosphere from the moon is a fallacy which will be explained in a succeeding chapter. We need not enter upon the subject now : all that is necessary at present is to set aside, in the meantime, the testimony of the moon, and to examine whether we have not reason to believe upon other grounds, that the solar system has an atmosphere, and that all the planets attract towards themselves envelopes composed of that atmosphere proportioned to their mass.

In the first place, if there be no atmosphere in the Solar System, we know of no property possessed by our own atmosphere which would prevent it from vanishing into space by its own elasticity. *In the second place,* the materials of our earth show that the meteoric matter which has gone to form our planet has all been oxidised. It has already been explained that the difference between the meteoric substances which fall from the heavens, and those which form the materials of our planet, is, that the latter are oxidised, while the former are not. Supposing, then, that the earth's substance was formed by an accumulation of these meteorites, there is bound up with it an amount of pure oxygen, the presence of which has to be accounted for, and, unless it has been supplied by miracle, it must have been got from the surrounding ether as it was consumed.

There are other proofs of the presence of oxygen in the ether, which will be noticed when we come to examine the constitution of the sun; but we have shown sufficient reason at present to conclude that, when God at first called into being the materials of the universe, these consisted not only of the meteoric materials of which we have spoken, but also of a thin ether, whatever might be its character, in which they floated throughout space. These two in conjunction contained the germs of the future creation.

Our minds are thus directed backwards to the time when these stars had not yet been kindled : when the meteorites scattered throughout the universe had not yet begun to gravitate towards each other, and when the atmosphere in which they were to burn had not yet been robbed of even an atom of its oxygen. At that time the materials of which the earth is now composed lay scattered far and wide over an immense region of the heavens, and the enormous amount of oxygen required to transform these metallic and metalloidal substances into earth and water, must have occupied a space immensely greater than that occupied by the entire solar system. The earth at that time, therefore, was without form and void, and there was then no firmament dividing between the materials of which the earth was to be created and those from which were to be formed the other heavenly bodies which are above the firmament.   The great clock of the universe had come from the hands of its Maker wound up in silence and in darkness, and only awaited the command of Deity to commence its movements.

Those who are accustomed to regard gravitation and chemical affinity as essential properties of matter, will find some difficulty in accounting for all the phenomena connected with them upon such a hypothesis.   They ought to bear in mind that gravitation invests every particle of matter with a consciousness of, and a sympathy with, every other particle in the universe.   Chemical affinity, in like manner, invests every particle of matter with likings and dislikings to every other.   Whence this omniscience and infinite propriety of conduct?   Is it essential to, and inherent in matter?   If we say that it is so, we merely attribute to it qualities which belong to Deity, without supplying any explanation of the fact.   Is it not more reasonable and quite as consistent with all that philosophy teaches us to say, in the language of Scripture, that "the Spirit of God brooded over the face of the deep."   Having first formed, as it were, the lifeless materials of the universe, He breathed upon its universal presence, and immediately it became a living thing.

This second creation of immaterial force in correlation to its subject matter meets us at every stage and turn. The human spirit, animating the human body, is merely the culminating point of a duality, which, running down through animal and vegetable organism, finds its base in the body and spirit of inorganic life.   It was not enough, therefore, that the Logos should provide the matter and create the idea of space; the Pneuma also must provide the force and create the idea of time.

THE CREATION OF LIGHT ACCORDING TO LAW.

It has long been supposed that the work of the first day of creation was the miraculous production of the substance of light, which was afterwards concentrated and lodged in the sun and in the stars. This is an idea which is not only inconsistent with the discoveries of science, but is altogether unnecessary to the interpretation of the text. There is no such thing as the substance of light, because light is only one form out of many in which kinetic force is developed, and, therefore, the creation of light as a substance would mean the creation of heat, sound, electricity, magnetism, and all those other forms which force is capable of assuming.

We have already endeavoured to trace backwards the processes which we find now going on in the universe around us, and if we are right, supposing that presently existing substances are the results of processes such as those which we have indicated, we have no choice but to believe that there was a time when these processes had not yet commenced, when the stars which are at present burning had not yet been kindled, and when the fuel which has been used up was still in the same state as that which is still unspent. The inference is so plain and inevitable, that it ceases to be a speculation or a theory, that, at the beginning, there were no suns, no stars, no worlds, as yet formed, but only the meteoric substances of which they were to be made, together with the ether or atmosphere in which these substances floated. We arrive at this result with the same certainty with which we know the original state of a mining district in which we see coal-pits and steam-engines, with little hills of black debris gathered round them. These may have taken years or centuries to attain their present state; but we know and feel assured that originally the pits and mounds were not there, and that the minerals that have been carted away, or that are lying in useless heaps, were once reposing in their native strata below the ground, undisturbed by human hands. We can in imagination even picture to ourselves the green fields and smooth pastures that once were there, and, if at the same time, we endeavoured to describe the beginning of the change, when the virgin sod was cut to sink the first shaft, and the little heap of earth marked the place of the first venture, no one could say that it was a presumptuous or a fanciful theory.

In like manner, when we survey in the heavens, the gradual growth of stars, and observe the raw materials of which they are composed, we do not state a theory, but a fact, when we affirm, that there was once a time when there were no suns and no stars, but only the materials of which these were to be composed, scattered over the boundless fields of space, and at immense distances from one another.

It is true that, at that time, there was no created eye either of man or angel to witness the changes which then began to take place, and yet, looking back with nothing to guide us except the laws of nature which we see operating around us, we can determine with the greatest certainty what those changes must have been, gravitation and chemical affinity being the grand moving powers of creation, and the very same then that they are now. We know, therefore, how these powers would act, and we know also that the very first effect which would be produced would be combustion and the production of light.

Phosphorus and iron are both of them meteoric and simple substances, and both are alike in this, that they are combustible—that is to say, they both unite with oxygen, and give off heat during their combustion.

But phosphorus and iron differ very widely from one another in regard to the heat which is necessary for their combustion. Phosphorus will take fire when it is simply warmed, whereas iron requires a heat of great intensity, before it bursts into a flame. Now, these two substances are representative of two great classes of meteoric fuel which require our attentive consideration, because they are widely different from one another. The phosphorus represents the shooting stars, and the iron represents the meteoric stones. The phosphorus class is still comparatively abundant in the orbit in which the earth revolves; the meteoric stones are fortunately rare, and appear not to extend beyond our own orbit. The phosphorus class of meteorites, on the contrary, seems to extend beyond even the orbit of Neptune, and flows in streams, whose orbits, like those of the comets, are very eccentric, and have every variety of inclination. These showers are so combustible, that they take fire immediately on coming into contact with our atmosphere; but they never reach the earth in a state in which we can examine them, being dissipated in the atmosphere as they fall.

But this is not the class of substances which forms the chief part of the fuel of the sun, or which was principally used in the formation of our own world; it is the other class —the metallic and metalloidal class, or *quasi* metallic, which forms the great mass of our planet's substance, and which constitutes the great reservoir from which the sun is supplied.   This class, which we generally speak of under the name of "meteoric stones," has been almost entirely cleared away from our orbit, and it is well that it is so; because if they were of as frequent occurrence as the other, neither life nor property would be safe from their destructive power.   They do, however, fall occasionally; and although they are so hot when they fall, that they would burn the hands of any one attempting to lift them, they arrive at our earth very little, if at all changed from the state in which for millions of ages they have been floating in free space.   But these same meteoric stones, if, instead of falling to the earth, they fell into the sun, would be first melted, and then boiled into metallic gas, by its intense heat.

Let us examine then how, under the laws of gravitation and chemical affinity, these meteoric substances would act when spread out at immense distances from one another over the unmeasured fields of space in the darkness of primeval night.

The wide separation of these substances from one another, and their general but irregular distribution throughout the universe, would prevent any decided gravitation in any one direction; but unless their positions and magnitudes were so adjusted as to secure a perfect equilibrium (which is impossible), the moment that they were invested with the attribute of gravitation, their positions would begin to change, however slow their movement might be.   It is possible that a thousand years might elapse before the nearest of these masses came together, and perhaps another thousand years before they gathered into heaps, but not the less certainly would both of these changes take place; and as, by every successive change, the equilibrium would become the less perfect, the power of gravitation would be the more effective in gathering little worlds of meteoric fuel together, and in attracting the surrounding meteorites towards them.

But besides the gradual increase of these little worlds of accumulated meteorites, there would at the same time be a corresponding increase of the density of the ether or atmosphere around them, which would also gravitate towards the increasing mass. Its density, of course, could not be great, but still it would be sufficient to offer some slight resistance to the meteorites as they fell, and to supply the oxygen for their combustion when the fall was sufficient to warm them.

All this would be merely a question of time. It might be that accumulations the size of Mont Blanc would, or would not, be sufficiently large to attract an atmosphere fit to consume phosphorus or potassium. But whatever might be the size and amount required, that amount would sooner or later accumulate, and then a conflagration would take place, and then for the first time there would be light. A mass of phosphorus or potassium drawn towards one of these accumulated gatherings would sweep in through the thin atmosphere around it, and, striking it, would take fire, and, by its combustion, ignite also other similar combustibles that had previously fallen. Then, for the first time there would be a grand illumination, because, although the heat would not be sufficient to burn the meteoric iron and other more refractory substances, the whole of the more combustible materials which had previously fallen would certainly take fire, and be consumed before the conflagration became extinct.

Those who observed the meteoric shower of 1867,

must have remarked the great height at which some of the meteors appeared. The atmosphere has been generally supposed to extend only about eighty miles upwards, and at that height it is so exceedingly rare as to give no visible evidence of its presence, but some of these meteors took fire at nearly double that height, proving not only how very combustible this class of meteoric substances is, but also how very little density of atmosphere is necessary for their combustion. If these phosphoric meteorites took fire at that great height, and in that extremely rare atmosphere, and if meteoric stones are not even melted by their fall through the whole extent of our atmosphere, nor even by their percussion when they reach the ground, we have a very remarkable illustration of the great difference between the two classes of meteoric substances, and the two kinds of illumination to which they respectively give rise.

It must be observed, however, that these conflagrations, being the result of combustion only, and being incapable of utilising the meteoric stones, would not be capable of maintaining a constant and permanent star, until they had acquired a magnitude sufficient to dominate the surrounding meteoric matter, and impose upon it an orbital movement in furnishing a supply. Then, and then only, would there be a continuous stream of meteoric fuel; and when the heat produced by the fall, as well as by the combustion, had attained a power sufficient to liquify and boil the metals, we should then have the true astral economy in action, such as we see it in the sun and the stars. But although these preliminary conflagrations would not be permanent, they would be numerous, and, above all, they would be early; and when the first of them shed its light upon the darkness, which till that moment

X

had never been broken, there would soon be others
of the same kind, which would wake up the dawn of
creation millions of years before there was a planet or a
sun.

In connection with these initiatory conflagrations, there
could be no real commencement of orbital motion. There
would be, no doubt, a rush from the surrounding ether to
supply the place of the oxygen which was consumed; but
before a vortex could be established in any one direction,
the conflagration would have ceased, and the atmospheric
movement exhausted.   No converging shower of solids,
however great or however long continued, could ever
generate a vortex, unless they actually touched and rolled
upon one another; but as soon as a decided and permanent
atmospheric movement towards a centre had set in, sooner
or later it will take a spiral direction, and the vortical
movement would continually increase in power. So when
a star has attained such a magnitude as to enable it to
keep up a continual combustion, the rush of the surrounding oxygen towards the centre could not always continue
to be in straight lines; and as soon as the deflection had
taken place in any one direction, the pressure from behind
would increase it, and a vortex in that direction would be
established.   There can be no permanent combustion in
the heavens without a vortex being formed in the surrounding ether; and although the meteoric matter around
could not be subject to that law, and would at first be
attracted and move towards the attracting body in straight
lines, it would gradually be swept in, and carried along
by the atmospheric current, reaching the central luminary
in spiral lines.   It may be, and it is most probable, that
other causes operate to produce the revolution of the
celestial bodies, as we observe them in the heavens; but

that this cause also produces a similar effect, there can be no doubt—indeed, we might say, that nothing but a miracle could prevent it.

It is a remarkable and interesting fact, illustrative of the difference between the first and the following days of creation, that in the distant nebulæ, discovered by the telescope, we find both of these kinds of conflagration going on.   In those which are called resolvable nebulæ, the light of which is identical with that of the sun and the stars, we have evidence of chromospheric envelopes like that of the sun, possessing the power of modifying the light which passes through them, so as to produce the dark lines of their spectrum; and these could only exist where stars are in actual process of formation.   But there are other nebulæ whose light reaches us without having passed through any such medium, and which cannot, therefore, be the light of actual stars, but only of incandescent gases, the centres of whose combustion are not surrounded with chromospheres.   There are some new discoveries awaiting us in regard to hydrogen and nitrogen, whose presence in the sun and other stars has not yet been accounted for, and it is remarkable that in these irresolvable nebulæ, it is chiefly hydrogen and nitrogen whose presence is revealed.   It is not unlikely that hydrogen, especially, has allotropic properties which enable it to descend upon the sun in a solid and incombustible form;*

* One eminent practical chemist, now dead, once stated to the author that there was a mystery connected with hydrogen which he had never been able to penetrate. The phenomena which he described indicated its existence in an allotropic state where its presence was not even suspected ; and Graham discovered that it exists in the heavens in a solid state, in combination with the meteoric metals. The presence of water in our own world, and the spectrum analysis

because upon no other principle can we account for its presence in those rose-coloured flames that are seen bursting out from the sun during a solar eclipse, which indicate its sudden transformation into the gaseous and combustible state. But whatever be the explanation of their presence in the irresolvable nebulæ, the light which they throw out is that of gaseous combustion, and not of solar rays; in other words, it is the light of the first and not of the fourth day of creation.

It is also a remarkable fact, in connection with these irresolvable nebulæ, that they are subject to changes of the most extraordinary kind, extending over regions, the gigantic dimensions of which are beyond all calculation. But this is exactly what we should expect if they are of the nature which we have supposed. If they are, as we suppose, merely temporary conflagrations of the more combustible materials collected, it may be, during hundreds of years; and if, after they have burned themselves out, they leave the little asteroid cold, to collect another supply for another and future conflagration, nothing is more probable than that, when one of these collections has taken fire, it should hasten the ignition of some other in its neighbourhood, which was also ripe for ignition. The two would act upon a third, and the three upon ten, and the ten upon a hundred, till, sweeping along the heavens, they would kindle into a blaze, which would spread over millions of millions of miles in the dark profound, forming fantastic figures of illuminated patterns, to fade away in a few years into comparative darkness, or to change their shape into other forms.

of the red flames of the sun, show that hydrogen must exist in the heavens in considerable quantities in a solid state, for it never could have reached the earth or the sun as a gas.

THE CREATION OF THE FIRMAMENT ACCORDING TO LAW.

The creation of light would necessarily be followed by the creation of the firmament, that is to say, the gathering together of the meteoric masses into centres of conflagration would produce a separation of the materials of one star from those of another, leaving a firmament between them. The creation of light was the work of the first day; the creation of the firmament was the work of the second. It is evident, however, that although the collection of the meteoric masses into centres was the commencement of the creation of the firmament, this second day's work had special reference to the completion of the planetary bodies, and of our planet in particular, so that its definition from all the surrounding substance of the universe would be accomplished. Not only so, but in order to complete the work of the second day, there must be deposited upon each of them an outer envelope of water, so that the firmament really divided the waters from the waters. In this manner the second day took up the work after the creation of light, and prepared it for the work of the third day, which was the creation of dry land.

That this is the right interpretation of the second day's work is evident from a comparison of the 14th with the 20th verse. We find that the firmament there spoken of is not only the atmosphere in which the fowls are said to fly, but also the heavens in which the sun and moon are placed. In other words, it is the open space which stretches between star and star.

The generally received interpretation of the second day's work is that the firmament was the atmosphere that surrounds the earth, and that the waters which are above the firmament mean the clouds and aqueous vapours which supply the rain. There are many reasons why we should reject this interpretation. *First*, and most conclusive is the fact, that there could be no clouds nor aqueous vapour where there was no atmosphere; if, therefore, the creation of the firmament was the creation of the atmosphere, there could be no waters above, from which the waters beneath were to be separated. *Second*, In reality, the atmosphere does not separate the aqueous vapour from the earth; on the contrary, the aqueous vapour is most abundant in the atmosphere nearest to the earth's surface, so that there could be no waters whatever of that kind *above* the atmosphere, from which the waters beneath the firmament were to be separated. *Third*, The firmament is represented as being *in the midst* of the waters, so that we have no reason to suppose the waters above the firmament to be different in kind from the waters under the firmament. And *Fourth*, As the sun and moon are said to be *in* the firmament, the only interpretation which would be consistent with such statements is that the creation of the firmament was the separation of the stars one from another. The meteoric matter of which they were formed was originally undivided, and spread out to a great distance from the centre of each conflagration, but on the second day, the definition of the earth was complete, and the waters which were beneath the firmament were then separated from all similar waters above. Upon the second day our earth became a defined world, separated from all others by the firmament around, and covered over with a shallow but universal sea.

Let us now turn to the teaching of modern science, and observe how this might be accomplished. The work of the first day was the creation of light by the ignition of meteoric matter, long before any permanent star had been kindled capable of inflaming the meteoric metals. That could take place only when one of these centres had attained such a size and such a heat as would be sufficient to melt, and then to boil, the metals which were to become its fuel. When we come to speak of the sun, we shall find that it is not the combustion of the metals which fall into it, but the heat generated by their fall, that gives intensity to its rays; and this source of power could only exist where the attraction was very great. The work of the second day, therefore, consisted in the formation of our own and similar worlds, by their becoming first little suns, each with its own store of fuel, and, when that fuel was exhausted, cooling down into planets.*

It is interesting to contemplate the changes which are involved in this early history of our world; and as we now know not only the physical laws which produced them, but the materials upon which these laws operated, we have no difficulty in tracing their progress, aided by the

* It has long been a favourite theory among astronomers that the universe was created in a gaseous or nebulous state, and that the various systems have been produced by condensation, each great system throwing off ring after ring to produce planets, and ending by the formation of a central sun, the heat being produced by condensation. We know of no substances which could be so condensed, and we know of no laws which could produce such a result. Heat can be produced only by mechanical force or chemical action : there was no mechanical force to produce condensation, and chemical action means combustion. That the planets must be produced from zones is very evident, but it is the inner, not the outer zones, as is generally supposed, which are first detached. There is much that is yet unknown, but we may be certain of this, that action must begin with the great centres, and can only *widen* with their growth.

illustrations which are to be found in the heavens, of corresponding eras in the history of other worlds. In the sun, we have an illustration of our world's history while it was growing up into its present magnitude, and in the variable stars, we have an illustration of that transition period, when, its fuel beginning to fail, it was not able to maintain an equal and continuous flame.

So long as the supply of fuel was abundant, the whole globe would be wrapped round with an exterior photosphere of flame; but when it gradually became exhausted, the flame would contract, until, coming close upon the liquid globe of incandescent lava, which had all the while been growing under the conflagration, it would then be insufficient to wrap the whole sphere in a continuous blaze. The failure of the flame would first take place at the poles, and probably for many a year, the earth would be girdled by a scarf of flame around the equatorial regions, where the ring of meteorites would still be continuing to pour down its fuel. This luminous girdle would slowly and gradually contract, as the meteoric supply continued to fail, giving indications at the same time of an inequality of power, until the ring of meteorites, breaking in its weakest part, would leave a portion of the girdle dark as it swept around. This would give to our planet the appearance of a variable star, the meteoric shower revolving round the earth with its accompanying flame.

This interval between the partial failure of meteoric fuel and the total extinction of the flame, must in the case of every star be accompanied with a periodic variation of its luminosity. In some cases the ring of meteorites may be so concentric as to produce a diurnal rotation of the flame, but in other cases, as in our own periodic showers, the tornado may be more eccentric, and then the period will be much longer.

At length, however, even this intermittent flame must cease; and, although for a long time, the remnants of the great meteoric zone would be still sending down boulders and meteors in considerable abundance, they would not be sufficient to produce anything but a fitful succession, at considerable intervals, of vast sheets of flame, keeping up a powerful incandescence of the lava. During all this time, however, the earth would be surrounded with an atmosphere attracted towards it by gravitation, exactly the same, or nearly the same, both in quantity and composition, as the atmosphere which at present surrounds our earth, but it would be swallowed up by a vastly more extended atmosphere of aqueous vapour, several thousand miles in height. Hydrogen has been observed not only in the sun, but in the stars, and when it is oxidised, water or aqueous vapour is the result. In the formation of the earth, therefore, the hydrogen which was burned would not be able to escape into the ether beyond, because, as soon as it reached the upper regions of the atmosphere, it would be condensed by the cold, and would immediately fall in rain, or rather in snow, downward, till it was again converted into steam. It would not be difficult to calculate the *weight* of our aqueous atmosphere at that period, because we have in our present ocean the actual amount of water which was then suspended in it. The heat of the newly-formed planet would be sufficient to maintain it at first in a state of vapour, even with a pressure of 15,000 lbs. upon every square inch of surface. And although we might not be able to calculate its *height*, because that would be continually decreasing, and would depend upon the temperature, we have in the planet

Jupiter, and especially Saturn, an actual example of an aqueous atmosphere larger than the planet itself. As the surface cooled, however, it would not be long before water was deposited at the surface; and although for several centuries it would not be deep, still, with such a superincumbent pressure, the shallow ocean would be resting on a red-hot bed. The lava beneath being soft, would lie conformably with the water, so that the entire planet would be covered by a shallow sea.

The end of the second day, therefore, which witnessed the creation of a firmament in the midst of the waters, dividing the waters which were under the firmament from those which were above the firmament, would leave the earth covered with a universal ocean, and surrounded with an atmosphere so dense and so deep, that the sun's rays would not be able to reach its red-hot waters.

THE CREATION OF DRY LAND ACCORDING TO LAW.

The dawn of the third day of creation would find the earth covered with a shallow, shoreless sea, lying over a soft integument of red-hot lava, under the pressure of a thousand atmospheres. "And God said, Let the waters under the firmament be gathered together into one place, and let the dry land appear, and it was so. And God called the dry land earth, and the gathering together of the waters called he seas, and God saw that it was good. And God said, Let the earth bring forth grass, the herb yielding seed, and the fruit-tree yielding fruit after his kind, whose seed is in itself upon the earth, and it was so. And the earth brought forth grass, and herb yielding seed after his kind, and the tree yielding fruit, whose seed was in itself after his kind, and God saw that it was good. And the evening and the morning were the third day." This is a passage which needs no interpreter; all that we have to do is to trace its progress as revealed by science.

Astronomers have been enabled not only to measure, but to weigh the various members of the solar system; and the results at which they have arrived are somewhat remarkable. Mercury, which is the smallest of all the planets, is also in proportion the heaviest, and Jupiter and Saturn, which are the largest, are, at the same time, the lightest belonging to our system. Mercury is as heavy as lead, Saturn is as light as if it had been made of pine.

Jupiter and Saturn differ from the moon in this, that the moon shows us its real surface, whereas what we see of Jupiter or Saturn is not the real body of either, but only the outer surface of their cloudy atmospheres. How deep those atmospheres may be, and how small the solid planets within, we have no means of knowing except by weight. Archimedes ascertained how much gold was in the crown by weighing it, because he knew the specific gravity of gold; and if we could only know the specific gravity of the solid nucleus of Saturn, we could at once tell how much of what is visible to us is atmosphere. But this specific gravity we did not know till lately, when spectrum analysis presented to us the unexpected discovery, that not only our own system, but even the most distant stars, are all composed of nearly the same materials as our own planet. This is a most important acquisition to our knowledge, because it furnishes us with the elements by which we can measure not only the outer disk, but the inner nucleus of each of the members of the solar system, not excepting even the sun itself.

. By this new measurement we ascertain that the real body of the sun is not one-half of its apparent diameter, and that Jupiter and Saturn have each a gigantic atmosphere, eighteen or twenty thousand miles deep, before we reach the real surface of the planet. We have in these planets, therefore, although upon a larger scale, a tolerably accurate representation of the state of our own world on the third day of creation. It would be impossible for either Jupiter or Saturn to attract from the surrounding ether an atmosphere of such proportions by means of gravitation only, and it can only be accounted for, by supposing that their future oceans are suspended in the form of aqueous vapour by the excessive heat, which prevents their condensation. It has been calculated by Mr. Bond that the light reflected by Jupiter is fourteen times brighter than that reflected by the moon, and some astronomers have tried to account for this by supposing that Jupiter shines partly by his own light as well as by that which he reflects; but we must remember that the atmosphere of Jupiter, being largely composed of steam, must be sharply defined in the plane of its condensation, or rather, of its freezing, and that the hot vapour will shoot upwards through the descending cold till, reaching the exterior, it is transformed into snow, and immediately begins to fall. The difference between the colour of snow and the colour of basalt is the difference between the light reflected by Jupiter and the light reflected by the moon.

Saturn is too distant to enable us to discover any atmospheric action on its surface, but the belts of Jupiter and the movements of its atmosphere, as of-

clouds in violent commotion, indicate the ascent of great
masses of vapour to its outer regions, and their hasty
condensation by the cold.   It is very probable, too, that
Saturn is yet too hot to allow of any permanent deposit
of water on its surface; but as for Jupiter, considering its enormous atmosphere, it is probable that it is
covered by a shallow sea resting on a red-hot sphere of
lava.

The moon, which is the world nearest to our planet,
exhibits the changes which took place at a corresponding
stage of its existence when passing from the fluid to the
solid state.   There was this difference, however, which
must be taken into consideration; being only the fiftieth
part of the size of our earth, it would probably have
only the fiftieth part of our ocean, and of course only
the fiftieth part of our aqueous atmosphere.   The
deposition of water upon its surface, therefore, must
have taken place only when the surface had cooled
sufficiently to make it as hard as stone, although the
pressure of its atmosphere would still be sufficient to
produce condensation at a temperature far above that of
the boiling-point on our earth.   We have, therefore, on
the moon's surface the marks of nearly the last meteorites that fell while the surface was still soft, and before
the deposition of water had been able to take place.
On this account it was able to retain its original crust
unbroken, notwithstanding the continual shrinking of the
interior lava.   The circumstances of our world at this
stage must, in some respects, have been very different.
The descent of the last meteorites must have taken
place not only while the crust was soft, but also when it
was covered with water; the convulsions, therefore,
which accompanied these falls must have been of an

entirely different character from those which took place on the moon.

It may be, also, that this tended to produce another difference, which has led to the most important results. It would appear that the present surface of the moon has never been changed since the time when the crust began to solidify; our world, on the contrary, has not even yet ceased to grow smaller. This difference may be in part explained by the difference of size. The moon being smaller, and covered with a smaller atmosphere, would cool more rapidly, and, as it cooled, would form a crust upon its surface sufficiently rigid to support itself, leaving the internal lava to shrink in size without producing any change upon the exterior form. Our world, on the contrary, has not been able to preserve its crust unbroken, partly because of its greater magnitude, and probably, also, because of the early formation of water on its surface. The arch would be too flat and too thin in proportion to support itself, and therefore the crust would be continually fractured and contorted, in the vain attempt to lie easily on a bed which was always becoming less.

If the apparent magnitude of the moon shows its size at the time when it began to cool, and if our earth was of the same density at the same stage of its formation, it must have been nearly double its present size. But even though we should allow for the greater compression of the materials of our earth by its greater gravitation, we have still an immense difference between its present bulk, and that which it originally had when it began to cool.

Under the pressure of an ocean-burdened atmosphere, water would be deposited in considerable quantities upon the surface, even while it was still red-hot, and would cover the entire globe, because the soft skin of lava would lie parallel to the water above it, and the tidal wave would also be one of lava.   The atmosphere being composed almost entirely of steam, would become a powerful conductor of the heat, and the lower stratum, which would be intensely hot, would ascend in huge columns to the upper regions, carrying with it immense quantities of heat, and leaving room for the descending columns which had come down from the regions of intense cold. The highest stratum would be the birthplace of snow, the lowest stratum would be of the same temperature as the red-hot lava upon which it was resting.   Such a process must have issued in the rapid cooling of the surface, the cooling of the surface would be followed by the lowering of the temperature of the interior mass, and the cooling of the interior mass would be accompanied with a corresponding diminution of its bulk.

So long as the outer skin was soft and plastic, the shrinking of the earth in size would produce no change in its form; but when the skin had become a crust which could not be compressed, it would begin to throw up wrinkles upon its surface, like the skin of a shrivelled apple, forming an inequality in the depth of water, and at length the ridges would rise above the surface, and thus the dry land would for the first time appear.

We have now no difficulty in following in imagination the transition stages by which our earth has reached its present state.   The gradual loss of temperature would be accompanied by the condensation of the aqueous vapour into water, so that, as the atmosphere contracted, the water would increase.* The cooling of the earth itself would be accompanied with a diminution of its size, and mountain ranges would be thrown up in all directions, to relieve the lateral pressure on the thickening integument, their height increasing with the thickness of the crust. The time would come, however, when, instead of *bending*, these wrinkles would *break*, sometimes above and sometimes below the water, and then would commence those explosions, earthquakes, and volcanoes with which we are still familiar, when the ocean poured down its waters upon the incandescent lava. The process of cooling must necessarily have been slow, and the decrease in size must have been very gradual; but when we consider the countless ages that are recorded in the geological strata of the earth, measured not by years, but by thousands of years, during which the earth was parting with its heat, we see that the total amount of shrinking must have been very great, and quite sufficient to account for all the contortions and displacements which the geologist discovers throughout all the world's strata.

Such is the story which science tells in correspondence with the work of the third day of creation. Every inequality in the outer shell would make a bed for the deeper reaches of the ocean, and raise the mountain ranges out of its waters. Continents would rise and continents would sink in the onward work of the world's changes; at one time raising the temperature of the

---

* The saltness of the sea indicates its enormous antiquity. When first deposited it must have been quite fresh—the pure oxide of hydrogen. Since that time every little stream has been sending down its contribution of saline impurities washed from the soil; the evaporation of the ocean giving back the water, but retaining the salt. If the comparative saltness of the ocean has in any way affected the marine formations, it may yet supply us with a new chronology of the strata.

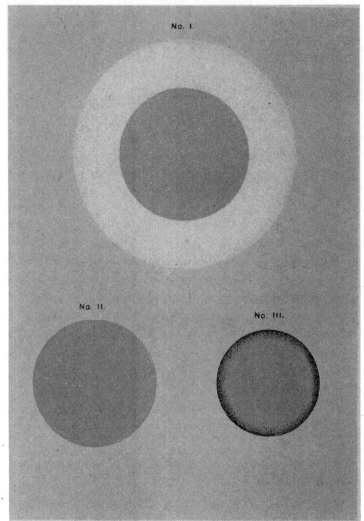

No. I.—Comparative size of the Earth before the deposition of the Ocean, supposing it to have the specific gravity of Saturn.

No. II.—Comparative size of the Earth after the deposition of the Ocean, supposing it to have the specific gravity of the Moon.

No. III.—Comparative size of the Earth, shewing its present amount of shrinkage.

THE PLANETS.

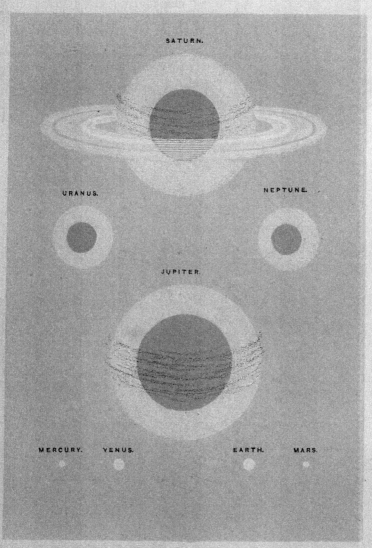

THE PLANETS.

With their specific gravity, indicating the probable extent of their
atmospheres.

southern hemisphere by lifting up the land in the south, or sending-the warm ocean streams southward; at other times raising the temperature of the northern hemisphere by producing a corresponding change in the north. As some of these cosmical changes would be sudden catastrophes produced by causes gradually accumulating, deluges of greater or less extent would be of frequent occurrence.

It is interesting to remark that the creation of the vegetable kingdom took place on the same day with the creation of dry land, and that, until there was dry land, there was neither animal nor vegetable life. This seems entirely in accordance with all that we learn from natural science. There could be no animal life without vegetation; but, as soon as there was a rock uncovered by the sea sufficient to give welcome to a lichen, vegetation would commence, and animal life would immediately become possible.

But the same means, by which we obtain a retrospect of the past, enables us also to discover the inevitable future; and, if we may read in the operation of the natural laws, illustrated by the present appearance of the Sun, Jupiter, and Saturn, the changes of the past, we may also read, in the operation of the same natural laws, illustrated by the present appearance of the Moon, the closing chapter of the world's history. Every century the earth is losing its internal heat,—slowly, no doubt, but surely; and the time *must* come when, even to the very centre, it will be entirely cold. At present, if we could peel off from the earth its outer skin even to the fortieth part of its diameter, we should have a ball of liquid fire that would shine like a star; and, a little further down, we should find a heat far greater than that of any furnace

Y

which we could kindle on its surface. It has been supposed that the interior cannot be so hot, because there is
no lava tide; but it must be remembered that the
pressure of the outer crust is enormous, sufficient not only
to diminish liquifaction, but to repress, as well as retard,
any motion till the cause has passed. Even the ocean
does not immediately answer to the attraction of the
moon, the tidal wave always in some localities for hours
lagging behind. How long this heat will take to pass
outward through the crust, and be dissipated, may be a
question very difficult to answer; but this we know, it is
only a question of time; sooner or later it is a consummation
which *must* arrive. But before that time the crust must
thicken, and is even now thickening and hardening; so
that, at a period long before that of which we are speaking, the outer crust will no longer lie on the bed of lava
on which it at present rests; but, arching itself all round,
will become a rigid shell, self-supporting; and, like the
moon, destined to undergo no further change. The
interior lava will continue to shrink, and then we shall
have the beginning of the end. An interior world will
begin to disengage itself from the outer crust, but its
birth will be ushered in by such convulsions as the world
has never seen. The waters of the sea will then begin
to find their way into the chasm between the two; and,
coming down upon the incandescent world within, will
produce a rupture and an explosion sufficient to create a
lunar Tycho upon earth, with its radiating rents extending over half a hemisphere. But, as even this would not
provide sufficient outlet for the vapour generated, there
would be earthquakes in divers places, and the volcanoes
would begin to roar, as they discharged into the outer
world the superabundance of the vapour beneath. The

temperature of the atmosphere would alarmingly increase, and the sea would begin to sink from its present level. By-and-by, these changes, instead of subsiding, would rather assume a more aggravated form; and the atmosphere, increasing in temperature, would scorch all animal and vegetable life, and at length mount up to its former gigantic elevation many hundreds of miles in height. The ocean would at length altogether disappear, part of it retiring into the interior, the rest suspended in the atmosphere. This state of matters, however, would be only temporary. The atmosphere, as it cooled, would gradually re-deposit the water of the ocean; so that, after some time when there was sufficient room within, both ocean and atmosphere would retire into the interior below. The day is coming when a telescope directed to our ruined world will find a desolation upon earth exactly resembling that of the moon. The bed of the former ocean will probably be marked by a different colour, but no vestige of either ocean or atmosphere will appear.

This final catastrophe, however, will be preceded by a season of unexampled cosmical repose. The crust of the earth, having at last become rigid and self-supporting, will then cease to lie heavily on the interior lava; and the further shrinking produced by cold, will, for some time, be compensated by the expansion produced by the cessation of pressure. During this time, perhaps for a thousand years, volcanoes will cease to be active; and earthquakes, for the first time in the world's history, will be altogether unknown. It may be that thousands of years may transpire before these things come to pass, but it may be also that the commencement of them is even now at hand.

THE CREATION OF THE SUN ACCORDING TO LAW.

" And God said, Let there be lights in the firmament of the heaven to divide the day from the night, and let them be for signs and for seasons, and for days and years. And let them be for lights in the firmament of the heavens to give light upon the earth, and it was so. And God made two great lights, the greater light to rule the day, and the lesser light to rule the night. He made the stars also. And God set them in the firmament of the heaven to give light upon the earth, and to rule over the day and over the night, and to divide the light from the darkness : and God saw that it was good : and the evening and the morning were the fourth day."

Science has not yet attained such maturity as would enable us to pronounce very decidedly on the exact work of the fourth day. At present there seems abundant reason to suppose that the sun and moon were already in existence, presenting an appearance not greatly different from that which they at present wear. Of one thing only we are certain, that at that early period they never shone upon the earth; and if we may be allowed to interpret the word by the works of God, the fourth day's work consisted in the complete condensation of the atmosphere of steam ; leaving only the atmosphere proper, which is composed of nitrogen and oxygen, drawn by gravitation from the universal ether. This would take place, of course, when the temperature of both the earth and the atmosphere had been reduced to nearly its present state; and when the surface of the earth had begun to wear somewhat of its present appearance.

When the entire ocean was suspended round the earth in the form of vapour, the sun's rays would fall only upon the exterior regions of the atmosphere; which, like that of Jupiter, would reflect rather than absorb them. Not only would there be no sunshine,—even mid-day would be comparatively dark. Absolute darkness, there could be none; because, in an atmosphere towering upwards several thousands of miles, twilight would be universal. As for summer and winter, no possible difference could be experienced, where the heat of the earth itself was a hundred times greater than that derived from the sun. It may be, too, that the sun itself was smaller. Ten millions of years is not a long time in geologic reckoning, but ten millions of years ago the sun could not have attained the quarter of its present size. We must speak very cautiously, therefore, of the relations which the sun and moon bore to the earth at the close of the third day.

But even supposing that both sun and moon had attained maturity, and that the earth and moon revolved in their present orbits, we have sufficient correspondence between the actual result upon the earth's surface and the work recorded in Genesis. There could not at that time be any true division between day and night, or between summer and winter; and when, in the clear atmosphere, both sun and moon became visible, they might truly be represented as set for the first time in the firmament of the heavens, "to give light upon the earth; the sun to rule over the day, and the moon to rule over the night, to divide the light from the darkness, and to be for signs and for seasons, and for days and years." We may add, that the introduction of "the stars also," seems almost decisive of this interpretation.

The sun, which was once supposed to be a standing

miracle, or an unfathomable mystery, we have reason to believe is no mystery at all; for although there are some phenomena connected with it which we do not yet fully understand, the great secret of its constitution is now tolerably plain. Ever since the time when men began to use lamps and candles, they have had before them little models of the great lamp of day which God set in the firmament of heaven; and in fact, the sun may be regarded as a gigantic candle, constructed so as to hang unsupported in the heavens. Like the candle, it has its reservoir of fuel placed outside of the flame, and sending inward a constant supply to support the combustion. In both cases the fuel is first solid, then fluid, and then gaseous, before being burned; and in both cases the structure of the flame is identical; because in both, the outer envelope alone is luminous, the interior being filled with the unconsumed vapour which is to be burned.

Fig. 1.

If we were able to cut the flame of a candle into two halves, we should find that this is really its structure, whether we cut perpendicularly down (Fig. 1) or horizontally across (Fig. 2). The only luminous part of the flame is the outer envelope, where the inflammable vapour comes in contact with the surrounding atmosphere; and the whole space within the envelope of flame is occupied with the gas. This gas has been boiled, or rather

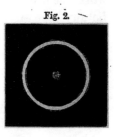

Fig. 2.

converted into vapour in the wick, which draws its supplies of liquid wax or tallow from the candle below.

A section of the sun would exhibit the very same arrangement. The outer surface of the sun, which is called the photosphere, is the only portion which is luminous; because it is there that the inflammable gas within comes in contact with the air without; and the interior nucleus is composed of the accumulated products of combustion, or, in other words, the oxides of the fuel that has been burned since it first was kindled. The nucleus or inner world, therefore, performs the same function for the sun that the wick does for the candle: it receives the meteoric matter that falls into it, melting and then vapourising it by its heat, so as to convert it into inflammable gas, to replenish the great gasometer within the flame.

The disc which we see and call the sun, is not the real body of the sun, but only the envelope of flame which surrounds it. The solid or liquid body of the sun we cannot see, and therefore we cannot tell its size. For anything that we can see, it may be of nearly the same size as the photosphere itself; so that, if the flame were extinguished, a white hot-ball would appear in its place; or it may be that the nucleus is so small as to be not much larger than Jupiter, and in that case, if the flame were extinguished, there would appear, in place of the sun, a small bright spot of molten lava. But although we cannot *see* the interior globe, which is surrounded by the flame, we can *weigh* it, and from its weight we can pretty nearly guess its size. In weight the sun is about 350 thousand times greater than the earth, but in bulk it is more than 1400 thousand times greater; so that, supposing the sun to be composed of the same materials as the earth, the real body of the sun cannot be even two-thirds of its apparent diameter,* the rest of the interior being composed of inflammable gas.

This is proved by the appearance of the solar spots as they approach the outer edge of the sun's disc. They continue to be seen in perspective without any appreciable refraction of the rays, showing that they come to us through a medium of equal density. This would not be the case if the body of the sun were immediately below the flame; because then there would be an increasing density of the atmosphere as it approached the surface, in consequence of the attraction increasing inversely as the square of the distance. It is true that for astronomical purposes we calculate from the centre; but with the atmosphere it is not so; because the surface, being nearest, has the greatest attraction. If the ratio counted from the centre, then the tropics, which are ten miles further from the centre than the poles, would be several miles above the line of perpetual snow. The body of the sun, therefore, must be many thousands of miles distant from the photosphere. The accompanying diagram will explain this. The central

* In all probability the real body of the sun is much smaller. The tabulated "Mass" of the sun includes all the matter, both inside and outside. But this leaves out of account the meteoric matter revolving round the sun which supplies it with fuel. For anything that we know, there may be as much as would make another sun.

white represents the sun's body; the depth of shading represents the density of the atmosphere, which decreases according to the distance; the white circular line represents the flame which we see. If the body of the sun were close to the flame, the density of the atmosphere above would rapidly diminish upwards; but as there is no perceptible inequality, the body of the sun must be at a great distance below.

When science enables us to measure the pressure of the gases at various distances from the surface of the photosphere, it will be found to be very much less than has hitherto been supposed.* The attraction upwards of the meteoric system outside, which is at present counted as part of the sun's mass, and the distance of the nucleus below, will both tend to diminish the pressure at the surface of the photosphere.

The great reservoir of fuel which supports the sun's combustion will, of course, consist of all kinds of meteoric substances; but in order to produce the effect which we see, it must consist chiefly, not of the lighter meteors, but of the heavy meteoric boulders, few of which now ever reach the earth. These, however, must be supplied in great abundance near the sun, and, besides being melted by its heat, will unite into larger masses before being precipitated into the flame. These agglomerated masses are sometimes so large as to be distinctly visible upon the sun's disc. Mr. Webb, in his "Celestial

* Since the above was written, the spectroscope has proved that the atmospheric pressure at the sun's surface "*is very far below the pressure of the earth's atmosphere.*" At one time it was said that the attraction was twenty-nine times greater than on the surface of the earth, and that a man would be "squeezed as flat as a pancake by his own weight." Now it appears that he would actually be lighter on the sun than on the earth.

Objects," has collected about twenty different records of such appearances, many of them as large as our own moon. One of them was believed to be a real planet, and received the name of Vulcan; but all of them have disappeared, and Vulcan itself has long since been converted into vapour, and is now, doubtless, supplying us with light and heat by its fall into the sun and its subsequent oxidation.

In two important respects, however, the action of the sun differs from that of a candle. In the first place, the products of combustion are different, and are differently disposed of. In a candle, the fuel is hydrogen and carbon, both of which, when burned, are converted into transparent vapours. The hydrogen is converted into steam or water, and the carbon into carbonic acid gas; and as both are invisible, and fly off to mingle with the atmosphere, they have the appearance of being altogether consumed or destroyed. It is very different with the fuel of the sun; the metals, when they are burned or oxidised, are not like wood or coal; because, instead of being sent off in the form of vapour, they are transformed into earthy substances, so that they actually become larger and heavier than they were before. For example, the metal calcium, when united to oxygen (that is to say, when it is burned), becomes lime, and, instead of flying off in vapour, falls down as a white powder, and, at the moment of combustion, becomes a Drummond light in every particle; because the Drummond light consists of pieces of lime heated to incandescence; the greater the heat the more brilliant is the flame. This peculiarity of the sun's fuel accounts for the excessive brightness of its rays; and it also explains why the products of combustion are to be found chiefly within the sun's photosphere. They are, in fact, the materials of which the sun's body is composed, the products of its combustion since it was first kindled.

The second point upon which the sun's action differs from that of a candle is, that the light and heat of the candle are caused by combustion only, whereas the light and heat of the sun are *almost entirely* due to friction, that is to say, they are produced chiefly by the *fall* of the meteorites rather than by their *combustion*. It has been calculated that one pound of meteoric fuel falling every five hours on every square foot of the sun's surface (supposing it to fall from an infinite distance), would be sufficient to produce all the light and heat of the sun, even though there were no combustion, and that it would require at least ten times the amount of fuel if the light and heat were produced by combustion only. This calculation is both an under-estimate and an over-estimate. It is an over-estimate, because the meteorites do not descend from an infinite distance; and it is an under-estimate, because we have to add the fall of the solidified oxygen which has been absorbed, descending nearly 200,000 miles from the flame to the nucleus.

This explains why the spectrum analysis of the sun's light exhibits black lines instead of bright lines. If the light of the sun were produced by the combustion of the gas, and had not to pass *through* part of the products of combustion, the lines would be bright, and not black; but because at least nine-tenths of the light is produced, not by the combustion of the gas, but by the incandescence of the earthy products—that is to say, as not one-tenth part is the light of combustion, and as more than nine-tenths are the light of incandescence (which has no spectrum lines, either bright or black); and as the whole light has to pass through the outer chromosphere, the feeble bright lines of combustion are neutralised, and the black lines alone remain.

At the same time, although the combustion adds comparatively little to the light and heat of the sun, it is indispensable to the continuity and uniformity of the flame. If the meteoric fuel were not capable of being converted into vapour and oxidised, there might not be much difference in the actual amount of light and heat; but there would be a very great difference in the appearance of the sun itself, and its usefulness to the worlds around. Not only would the disc be smaller, but the supply of light and heat would be very variable. At one time when the fall of meteorites was abundant, the whole effect would be given off at once; and at other times, when the fall was less abundant, there would be a season of comparative cold and darkness. Probably for some minutes there might be scarcely any light at all, but in a moment, by the fall of some great meteorite like Vulcan, there would be a tremendous flash, which would scorch not only our world, but the other planets. The appearance of the sun would not be, as at present, a continuous and equable flame, but a succession of sparks and flashes, produced by the fall of individual meteorites. By means of combustion, all this is avoided, the flame is equalised all around; and by means of the immense reservoir of gas, forming three-fourths of the sun's volume, the descent of even the planet Mercury would not be able to produce any perceptible effect. It would, no doubt, generate a very large amount of heat; and, if the planet could be converted into vapour, it would add to the bulk of the sun as it continued to be vaporised; but as the

No. I.—Section of the Sun, shewing the comparative magnitude of its real body, supposing it to be of the same specific gravity as that of the Earth.

No. II.—Magnified section of part of the photosphere, with the superincumbent chromosphere.

heat would be distributed over the whole expanse within the photosphere, it would really not be perceptible.

It will yet be discovered that the size of the sun is variable. What we see is only the outer surface of the interior atmosphere, where it comes in contact with the outer oxygen. The height of the photosphere, therefore, depends on the *average* supply of fuel, so that, although any temporary increase or decrease would not be observable, any change in the average fall of meteoric matter, for several successive centuries, could not fail to make an impression, which might be detected by very delicate measurements.

Mr. James Nasmyth has rendered great service to heliology by the discovery of what he calls the " willow leaf " structure of the sun's flame. It has not, like the flame of a candle, an equal plane of oxidation, but seems to consist of flames or tongues of fire rising from the unconsumed gas. It appears to be very like what would be produced by the setting on fire a layer of petroleum or naphtha upon the surface of a pond, on which the flames would rise in individual tongues of fire after some such fashion as this.

If the flames were wafted sideways by a wind passing over the lake, they would assume some such form as this, when looked down upon from above. Now this is not very unlike the actual appearance of the sun's photosphere as the flames are swept across its surface by tempests, compared with which the storms upon our planet are a

calm.   Each of the tongues of flame has been calculated to be about a thousand miles in length, and a hundred in breadth.   We can easily understand, therefore, why

their motion should not be observable, even though they were flying at the rate of a thousand miles an hour.
During a total eclipse of the sun, and while its disc is

entirely covered by the moon, we are enabled to see an immense atmosphere surrounding it, and extending to more than half-a-million of miles beyond.   This atmosphere reflects the sun's rays, and forms what is called the corona, or halo of light which surrounds the dark body of the moon during the eclipse.

Above the photosphere lies a cloudy envelope called the chromosphere, through which the light of the photosphere must pass.   It appears to consist of the products of combustion, tossed up from the flames as they ascend, and kept up, not by their intrinsic buoyancy, but by the perpetually-ascending currents from the photosphere below. It is this chromosphere which modifies the light as it passes through, producing the dark lines of the solar spectrum, and revealing the nature of the substances whose combustion constitutes the flame.

As this cloudy envelope is generated by the conflagration beneath, and would increase indefinitely, so that at length it would obscure the sun's rays, there must be some means by which it escapes downwards.   This in all probability is accomplished by means of those minute openings called " pores," which are observed in the telescope stippling the entire surface of the flame ; but it would appear that periodically there is need for supplementary discharges on a grander scale to prevent undue accumulation.   At such times the superabundant cloud, bursting through the flame, forms an opening, and discharges itself into the interior, forming what is called a " spot " upon the sun's disc.   When the equilibrium is restored, the flame again closes up, and the spot disappears.   This system of discharge appears to have a periodicity of about eleven years, indicating apparently a variation either in the quantity or the quality of the meteoric stream. Probably it may be due to other causes; but we must look for them, not in the interior, but in the exterior of the sun.

The following woodcut shows some of the forms which the spots assume; but the changes which take place are so rapid, that a few hours are sufficient to entirely alter their appearance.

Besides the products of combustion carried up with the flames, there must also be a continual fall of lava rain, which will commence its descent of nearly 200,000 miles from the photosphere to the body of the sun below. At first it will take the form of a fiery dew, but as it falls it will unite into drops, and then into spheres, whose descent will be accelerated to a velocity of prodigious power. The heat produced by their fall from such a height will be almost inconceivable.

The theory that the light of the sun is produced by the fall of meteoric metal to its surface, and not by the combustion of metallic gas was at one time generally received by scientific men; but it is now abandoned on account of its being inconsistent with actual facts. The fall of meteorites would have produced an irregular and dangerous succession of flames and flashes according to the quantity and quality of the meteorites that fell at every successive moment. But this is altogether unlike what we see on the sun's surface.

The nebular theory, therefore, has been again revived

as it can better account for the uniformity of the sun's light, and is not inconsistent with other astronomical phenomena which it is used to account for. It supposes that the whole solar system was originally a mass of nebulous matter, and that a gradual condensation of that matter has been going on, throwing off successive rings which ultimately became planets; first Neptune, then Uranus, then Saturn, then Jupiter, and so on, Mercury being the last. Being able to throw off no more, the heat of the sun is produced by its continual condensation.

But the nebular theory presupposes the existence of nebulous matter which is only an imaginary substance, nothing of the kind having ever been observed in nature. This theory also supposes that the external planets were formed first; but this is inconsistent with the fact that the interior planets are cold, while the exterior planets are still hot. In addition to this, the violent changes observable in the sun's disk could not be accounted for by any process of condensation. They can be produced only by external causes. In fact, all the objections to the theory of the meteoric fuel of the sun are removed by the supposition that the photosphere is produced by the *combustion* of the metallic gas. In no other way can we account for the fact that the materials of our planet are all oxides, while the materials without are all combustible and unoxidised.

THE CREATION OF THE MOON ACCORDING TO LAW.

Supposing the moon to have been formed in the same manner as that in which the sun is being formed now, and supposing it to be composed of the same kind of materials as those of which the earth is composed—that is to say, supposing that the moon was a miniature sun, and that it attained its present size by the accumulation of meteoric matter falling to its surface, there must have been a time when it also had its zodiacal system of meteorites, and was surrounded with an envelope of flame nearly twice as large as the present moon.

The time must have come, however, when the fuel being nearly exhausted, the flame would contract, and, after flickering around the white hot ball, would at length expire. It would then be succeeded by fitful blazes of larger or smaller extent, as the single meteorites descended, and, like lumps of wax thrown upon glowing embers, would raise conflagrations whenever they fell. These conflagrations would at first be of continual occurrence, sufficient to keep up, it might be for centuries, an incandescent surface on the moon; but by-and-by they would become less frequent, and at length altogether cease, yet not until they had written on its surface the story of their last visitation. So long as the outer skin was sufficiently plastic to receive the impressions, and, at the same time, sufficiently hard to retain them, their advent would continue to be recorded. In fact, the present appearance of the moon's surface seems to be the record of the period when it was in a transition state between the liquid and the solid.

Had the supply of meteoric fuel ceased suddenly—a supposition altogether improbable — the liquid ball would have been left to cool without anything to disturb the smoothness of its surface.   There was nothing within the molten globe which could possibly produce any change. As well might we expect volcanoes to arise in a pot of melted metal left to cool, as in the residuary oxides of the moon's formation.   Like a drop of melted lead falling from a shot-tower, it would retain the smoothness of its surface till it cooled; and the only disturbance that could take place must have been from without.   We have the most satisfactory evidence, therefore, that the supply of meteorites did not suddenly cease; because the disturbances which we see recorded on the moon's surface are exactly such as would be produced by the descent of these from time to time, while the outer crust was passing from the fluid to the solid state.   The different ring mountains, and other appearances which are usually ascribed to volcanic agency, may all be accounted for by the fall of meteorites, varying in size, their different chemical qualities, and their time of falling.

Perhaps it may appear to some that the ring mountains of the moon are too large to be produced by the fall of single meteorites; and, if the little stones which are preserved under glass in our museums were fair specimens of the meteorites that feed the sun, and went to the formation of the earth and the moon, the difficulty would be insurmountable; but when we remember that our orbit has long been cleared of this kind of fuel, we must be prepared to believe that these are but the residuary dust that occasionally falls after the supply has for thousands of years ceased in our orbit.   Besides, we are not without evidence that the meteoric boulders that go to the formation of the celestial spheres are much more formidable masses. The largest meteorite which has been discovered and preserved is one in Brazil, weighing 14,000 lbs.; but Mrs. Somerville mentions one which passed within twenty-five miles of the earth, and which was estimated to weigh 600,000 tons. Astronomers, moreover, have repeatedly observed immense masses crossing the sun's disk as large as the moon itself; and, as they never were seen again, they must have fallen to its surface. Probably they were accumulations which had amalgamated as they approached the sun; but whatever be their formation, it is certain that they must be *large* and comparatively *few*, otherwise they would be seen as a luminous ring during a total eclipse.

But we must also take into account the increased effect which such disturbances would produce, in consequence of gravitation being greatly less in the moon than upon our planet. The explosive power of the heat would get free play when the meteoric metal sank into the glowing interior. It would send up gigantic accumulations of gas, which, as they rose to the surface, and burst into flame, would fling outwards tremendous waves of liquid lava all around, to a height and to a distance that would be impossible on such a body as the earth. It is well known that diminished gravitation produces effects upon a grand scale, which otherwise would be produced upon a small scale. An elephant would be able to move about as nimbly as a dog on a world the size of the moon; and if there were an ocean upon its surface, the waves would rise under a storm to the height of real mountains. We should, therefore, make a great mistake if we estimated the size of the meteorites necessary to produce the ring mountains of the moon, by what would be necessary to produce them on such a world as our own.

At first, the descent of these gigantic boulders would leave no permanent impression whatever : because the liquid state of the moon's body would allow the commotion to subside without producing any change ; but when these visitations became less frequent, and when the outer surface had got time to cool and harden, the first permanent mark which a colossal meteorite would leave would be a great circular lake of lava, re-liquified by the burning of the meteorite where it fell, and having its borders raised by the dashing over of the liquid, wave after wave depositing each a thick coating of lava on the margin all around.   Let us imagine the descent of one of these, of the size, say, of Mont Blanc.   On plunging into the moon's body it would tear through the viscid covering of lava, producing by the percussion of its fall a heat far more intense than could be produced by its combustion.   The metal, being heavier than the lava, would continue to sink in the thin liquid to where the heat would be a thousand degrees greater than red heat ; and there it would begin to melt and then to boil, sending up great globes of inflammable gas, which would take fire on coming to the surface, and melt the lava all around. But besides remelting the viscid lava for leagues around, these immense bubbles, on rising to the surface, would raise mountain waves, driven outwards from the centre, and which, washing over the unmelted margin, would pile layer upon layer, like beds of lava flowing from the crater of a volcano.   These earliest formations, however, although they would be the most extensive, would have no high rampart around ; because the liquid upon which they were resting would not be able to support any great weight, and its distance from the centre would weaken the force of the wave in proportion to the increase of its

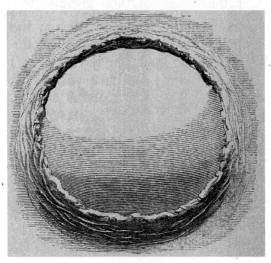

circumference. The accompanying diagram represents an ideal formation of the earliest type, and corresponds with those extensive areas called seas, such as Mare Imbrium, Mare Tranquillitatis, and Mare Serenitatis; and it will be observed, that in all these earliest formations, the level of the interior lava is not perceptibly lower than the level of the crust which had not been re-liquified.

When the crust was still further hardened, the fall of a colossal meteorite would produce a somewhat different effect. The circle would be very much smaller, but the surrounding hills would be higher in proportion; and a still more decisive evidence of its later date would be found in the lower level of the interior lava. The gradual cooling of the moon's mass would be accompanied with a corresponding diminution of its bulk; as in a pot of melted lead, the central part, which is latest in hardening, is that which gives most evidence of the lowering of the level. We find, accordingly, that in the later formations when the meteoric mass pierced the crust and melted the surrounding lava, the level of the interior liquid stands considerably lower than the surrounding plain; so that from these levels the comparative ages of the different formations might be ascertained.

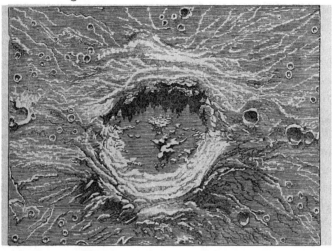

The accompanying woodcut is from a drawing by Mr. James Nasmyth, of Penhurst.   It represents the ring formation called Copernicus, one of the most interesting mountains of the moon; and around it are corresponding formations of every variety of dimensions corresponding with the size and quality of the meteorites which produced them.   Being comparatively a late formation, it shows signs of the upheaval of gas below, opening the outer crust in a *slit*, before heaping up the circular walls around by its ebullition.   The height of Copernicus itself is between two and three thousand feet, but the floor of the crater within is more than eight thousand feet *lower*

than the outside level of the moon. So far had the substance of the moon shrunk when Copernicus was formed.

In studying these formations, we are struck with the variety and yet the sameness of the phenomena, pointing to a common origin—viz., the disturbance produced by external violence, but varied according to the magnitude and chemical composition of the meteorite, as well as its period, and the state of the moon's surface when it fell. In some they appear like the fall of a pebble into thick mortar, in others like the radiating cracks of a pane of glass with a central ring, as if the perforation through which the meteorite was shot closed before the gas had had time to ascend. In some there seem to have been no waves, the meteorite burning on the surface, and merely melting down a circle till it reached the then level of the liquid within. Such appears to be the Mare Crisium. In others a peculiar effect appears to have been produced by the union of two very different kinds of metal in the same boulder. After the more fusible portion had exhausted itself in the formation of its circular mountain and central plain, the more refractory metal appears to have only then begun its tardy ebullition, sending up its scanty supply of gas and forming a small jet in the centre of the crater. The products of this later combustion appear in the formation of a central cone or obelisk, the vitreous oxide guttering down its sides from the flame above. We have also to add to all these the fall of meteorites at a time when they were unable to perforate the crust. In some cases the heat produced by their fall seems to have been sufficient to commence their combustion, but not to complete it; others are scattered about in detached masses, or in various stages of unfinished combustion, according to the nature of the substances of which they were composed.

During all this time there must have been an atmosphere of some considerable density, although not by any means equal to the atmosphere which surrounded the earth at its formation. Like the latter, it would consist partly of the atmospheric air drawn from the surrounding ether, and partly of the watery vapour produced by the combustion of hydrogen. We merely *infer* the existence of water from its presence in our own planet, as well as in the sun and in some of the fixed stars; but there is no uncertainty regarding the atmospheric air; because the moon must be composed of oxides, not of metallic substances; and also because the moon's surface presents the appearance of lava and not metallic formations. As in the case of the sun, we are also able to weigh the moon; and had it been composed of meteoric matter not oxidised, that is to say, if the metals had not been changed into earths, it would have been much heavier in proportion than our earth. It has been ascertained that our earth is six and a-half times heavier than water, but the moon is specifically nearly as light again. If, then, our earth is heavier, although it is oxidised, it must needs be that the moon's materials are oxidised also. How, then, could the meteorites of which the moon is composed, obtain their oxygen, except by means of an atmosphere, continually replenished with oxygen from the ether, as rapidly as it was consumed.

The question next arises, What has become of this atmosphere? In regard to the watery vapour generated by the combustion of hydrogen, when the temperature fell it would be deposited in the form of water on the side turned towards the sun, and in the form of snow on the other. It might be interesting to speculate on the effect which would be produced by an atmosphere of common air attracted by gravitation to the moon in connection with another atmosphere of watery vapour; but it is more interesting to notice that the gradual cooling of the moon's substance would produce effects which would ultimately make room for the atmosphere in its interior, so as to leave none of it visible on the outside at all.

So long as it is a law of nature that heat expands substances, and that cold makes them shrink in bulk, it was an absolute impossibility that the moon's atmosphere should continue on the outside after the outer crust had ceased to become smaller by cold. In the interior of all the craters we have a gauge of the shrinking process which was going on while they were being formed. In the earlier craters the level is high, in the later craters the level is low; but when the crust had become so hard that the meteorites were unable to pierce it, the shrinking would not stop, but must have continued; and, indeed, must even at the present moment be still going on. In that case the interior lava would very soon part company with the exterior crust, and an interval would be formed between them which must continually be increasing in extent, and into which the atmosphere and water would at length retreat, through the apertures on the surface (unless it had been hermetically sealed), leaving the outer crust entirely bare as we find it.

If the crust of the moon had been continually undergoing geologic changes like those which have been hitherto going on upon our own planet, the outer crust

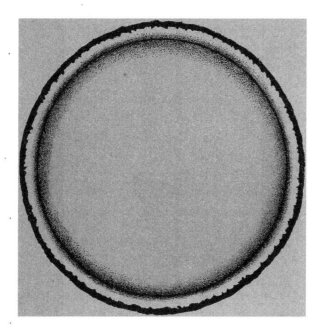

SECTION OF THE MOON.

With its interior atmosphere, shewing the extent to which it must have shrunk after the outer crust had become rigid, supposing its specific gravity to be the same as that of the Earth.

would have continued to lean upon the fluid lava beneath;. and although it would have been continually broken in consequence of its inability to find room to lie upon a bed which was always growing too narrow to hold it, still the atmosphere would have been found on the outside of the moon's disc. But as we know that the moon's crust is not undergoing any geologic changes, the cooling and shrinking process must have resulted sooner or later in the formation of such an interior vault as we have supposed; and the existence of an *exterior* atmosphere under such circumstances would have been more wonderful and unaccountable than its absence.

APPENDIX (C.)

THE EFFICACY OF PRAYER.

THE efficacy of prayer has been objected to, on the ground that it supposes a miraculous interference with the course of nature. Even though it were so, the argument against prayer would not be conclusive, because if God assures us that the prayer of faith shall be answered, what we have to do with is the promise, not the mode or the means by which the promise is fulfilled. But we have really no reason to suppose that the answer to prayer must necessarily be miraculous, any more than the fulfilment of prophecy or any other part of the providential administration of God's moral government. The difficulty arises from misunderstanding the difference between the Divine and human modes of action. When we pray, we do not pray to a mere creature floating down the same current of time with ourselves, but to God, who is above all sequences, to whom all time, past, present, and to come, is equally present, and who is therefore able to lay His hand upon the springs of action, wherever they lie. No man who has studied history, and observed the events that are taking place around him, can fail to be convinced, that besides the mere sequences of cause and effect, there is a Divine administration that overrules all events in the interests of truth and justice. Some of the most cardinal events in the world's history depended upon some little circumstance that, humanly speaking, was nothing more than an accident, so that the turning of a straw might have changed the current of a nation's destiny. Unless we are prepared to believe that there is no such thing as Providence, and that the universe is the sport of a blind and shapeless chance, which God does not or cannot overrule, we have no alternative but to conclude that all things are the subjects of His moral government, and that a sparrow cannot fall to the ground without its having been so arranged in harmony with all the events around. It is the *want* of miracle that makes this Providence so wonderful and so Divine; for, if instead of "all things working together for good," the object had been to be obtained by a direct interference when they were going wrong, there might be more obtrusive evidence of the hand of some overruling power, but it would not be so characteristic of a *Divine* administration.

Let us take as an illustration the death of Ahab, which was a political event, and which, though not an answer to prayer, was the fulfilment of a prophecy. When the arrow shot at a venture was to enter the joints of his harness, it was as easy for God to guide the hand of the archer, as to deflect the arrow in its course after it had been shot. But we go further, and we say that it was not more easy to guide the hand of the archer than to guide the course of events so as to make the archer shoot his arrow so *without any guidance*, all the circumstances of time and place having conspired to produce the designed effect. Of course, in each remove backwards, there would be the greater difficulty in calculating effects and securing accuracy, supposing the work to be done by human skill or human forethought; but in God's hands it is not so. It is as easy for God to pre-arrange the sequences of ten thousand objects for ten thousand years, with ten thousand complications, as for man to pre-arrange the contact of two bodies, whose distance and whose velocity are known.

With such a God the answer to prayer needs no miracle, and is most characteristic of His way of working without it. Take for illustration the case of Joshua's prayer, the answer to which is recorded by the inspired historian as it appeared to him. "Then spake Joshua to the Lord, in the day when the Lord delivered up the Amorites before the children of Israel : and he said in the sight of Israel, Sun, stand thou still upon Gibeon; and thou, moon, in the valley of Ajalon. And the sun stood still, and the moon stayed, until the people had avenged themselves upon their enemies."

Joshua's appeal to the sun and the moon was a *prayer*, which the Bible informs us was answered; but it was answered in God's own way. Joshua was not aware that it was the earth that moved, and not the sun and moon. Scientifically, therefore, his prayer was no prayer at all. And yet his prayer was answered *in effect*, as is always the case when God answers prayer. What Joshua evidently wanted was *light to pursue his enemies*, and God might have granted his request by arresting the earth's motion for a whole day, and then setting it again in motion at exactly the same rate as before. But God could have answered his prayer in another way: *foreknowing the prayer*, God might, in answer to his prayer, *at creation*, have planted a meteoric stratum, such as was needed to produce the effect, in such a position as that the earth, in its orbit, should cross it on *that very day;* and if the night happened to be cloudy, and the meteoric shower unusually bright, the sky would be lit up with mid-day splendour till the following morning, and, at the same time, shower down meteoric stones to slay the Canaanites. The prayer, in that case, was more than answered. A providential answer to prayer is more wonderful than a miraculous one. The calculation of an eclipse a century beforehand is not very easy; and the arrow of William Tell must have been finely drawn, when it smote the apple without killing the child; but if God, *at creation*, aimed heaven's artillery with such precision, that it struck down the Canaanites *that night,* by the action of the natural laws, without injuring their pursuers, it was much more wonderful than if it had been done by miracle. We do not say that this was the way in which Joshua's prayer was answered—perhaps it was not : but we do say that, *if it was,* God's hand was more wonderfully and more characteristically displayed than if, at Joshua's request, He had arrested the earth's motion on its axis without any one feeling the shock; and had, after an interval of rest, again communicated to it a velocity of a thousand miles an hour without strewing the cities of the earth in ruins.

Perhaps it will be objected, that, according to this view, the event would have taken place whether the prayer had been offered or not. The real meaning of that is, that

God might foresee what never came to pass, and might, therefore, make previous arrangements which would necessarily be inappropriate. But " known unto God are all His works, from the beginning of the world," and if " *all things* work together for good to them that love God," who will presume to say *when* it is that He begins to set the train in motion ? The flood was sent by God as a punishment upon a guilty world ; and the exact time when it came was determined by circumstances which were purely moral in their character. But we have no reason to suppose that it was miraculous, or that it was any thing more than one of those great cosmical catastrophes which must have been frequent in the early part of our planet's history, and which, by God's pre-arrangement, should purposely become due exactly at the time required in His moral government. We do not say that it was so ; it may have been otherwise : but if this was really the case, we say confidently that it would not have been less the act of God, nor less a part of His moral administration, than if He had first created, and then annihilated a new ocean of water.

Even in those cases where there was evidently a miracle in answer to prayer, we cannot tell to what extent it may have been aided by the operation of natural laws. We are told, for example, in regard to the plague of locusts, that " the Lord brought an east wind upon the land, all that day and all that night, and when it was morning the east wind brought the locusts." And again, when the Red Sea was divided, we are told that " the Lord caused the sea to go back by a strong east wind all that night." It may also have been by angelic power, or it may have been by other means, of which we at present can form no conception, that the miracle was accomplished ; but whatever were the means employed, the hand of God was as conspicuous in the fore-ordination of the natural causes, as in the employment of those abnormal agencies which were called into requisition for the purpose.

APPENDIX (D.)

THE SOUL AND THE SPIRIT.

WHEN Paul speaks so distinctively of the soul-body and the spirit-body, a very interesting question is opened up in regard to the difference between the soul and the spirit, which are generally regarded as synonymous. When he prayed for the Thessalonians that their whole *Spirit, Soul,* and *body,* should be preserved blameless unto the coming of the Lord Jesus Christ (1 Thess. v. 23), he evidently intimated that the soul and spirit are not the same. In Hebrews also (iv. 12) it is said that the Word "is quick and powerful and sharper than any two-edged sword, piercing even to the dividing asunder of the *Soul* and *Spirit.*"

The popular notion regarding the Soul is that it is that immaterial part of man that lives after death—that goes to hell or heaven till the resurrection; and if the question were asked, "And what becomes of the Spirit?" the answer would probably be, "The Soul is the Spirit, and the Spirit is the Soul."

There is reason to suspect, however, that we have ceased to recognise a distinction which was once universally acknowledged, and that soul and spirit are not synonyms. The Bible does not use them as such; and so marked is the distinction, that when we try to ignore it, we are surprised to discover that it is impossible. The Bible speaks of the danger of a man losing his soul, not of losing his spirit. The Bible speaks of God being a Spirit; we should be shocked were we to hear any one say that God is a soul. Nor is it only in English that the distinction is made, we find it also in every classic language, from Hebrew downwards.

When we examine the passages of Scripture in which the words occur, we at once discover that the words are used in a totally different sense, although, in consequence of the defects of our English translation, the distinction is not so evident. The word psuchē (soul) in the New Testament is sometimes translated life, as well as soul, meaning by life the life of the *body*, as distinguished from life generally (zoē).

" Therefore, I say unto you, Take no thought for your soul (psuchē), what ye shall eat, or what ye shall drink ; nor yet for your body, what ye shall put on " (Matt. vi. 25).

" He that findeth his soul (*psuchē*) shall lose it " (Matt. x. 30).

" The good shepherd giveth his soul (*psuchē*) for the sheep " (John x. 11).

" Is not the soul (*psuchē*) more than meat ?" (Luke xii. 23).

" Is it lawful to save the soul (*psuchē*) or to kill ? " (Mark iii. 4).

In all these and similar passages, the word is translated *life*, and is the same as that translated *soul* elsewhere. We, therefore, conclude that the true meaning of the word is to be found in a combination of the two ideas. It is not *life* as a state, but a *soul* as an immaterial substance, as when it is said (Matt. x. 28) : " Fear not them which kill the body ; but rather fear Him which

2 A

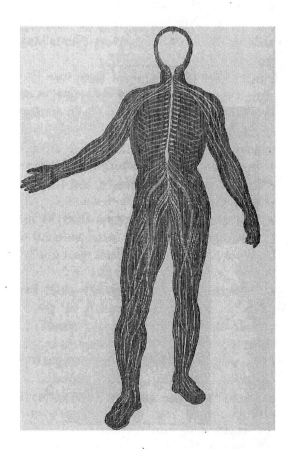

CEREBRO-SPINAL SYSTEM OF NERVES.
Ministry for Foreign Affairs.
(*Supposed Seat of the Spirit.*)

is able to destroy both soul (*psuchē*) and body in hell;" and, again (Acts ii. 27): "Thou wilt not leave my soul (*psuchē*) in hell (*hades*)."

In Latin the word for soul is "*anima,*" the animating principle of the body, and this really appears to be the true meaning of *soul,* as distinguished from *spirit* when spoken of in Scripture.

We find also in Scripture that the word Soul is used in a secondary sense, as the seat of the *emotional* part of our nature, as distinguished from the intellectual. It is the Soul that rejoices or is sorrowful, that longs for or that loathes, that loves or that hates, independent of the intellect.

Corresponding with this duality of soul and spirit, we find another duality in the nervous systems with which they are respectively *en rapport.* We have already noticed one of these systems, the cerebro-spinal, commencing with the brain, and reaching out to every part of the body by means of the spinal cord. But there is another and totally different system of nerves, called the ganglionic or sympathetic system, which attends to the domestic economy of life, and over which the spirit has no control. This great system of nerves is distributed over the trunk without having any central mass like the brain to give unity to its action. It has, however, numerous patches or ganglia, as they are called, in different parts of the body, so that whatever may be the use of the brain in the cerebro-spinal system, these ganglia perform corresponding duties in this. The advantage of this arrangement is evident. In the cerebro-spinal system unity of thought and concentration of attention are necessary; therefore, a single brain forms the metropolis of its operations; but in the other system, where

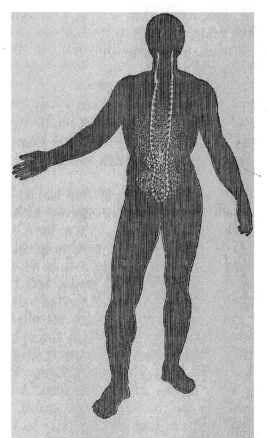

GANGLIONIC SYSTEM OF NERVES.
Ministry of the Interior.
(*Supposed Seat of the Soul.*)

the operations are so numerous and so varied, and where all must be going on at the same time, instead of there being only a single brain, the cares of office are distributed among many ganglia, which, like the municipal courts of a country, adapt their labours to local circumstances, and perform their subordinate functions without having to engage the attention of the central imperial government.

We find, then, two great nervous systems which divide between them the vitality and government of the body. One of them is in connection with, and inhabited by the spirit; and the question arises, What is the tenant of the other? The nervous matter is evidently a medium of communication between the body and the spirit in the cerebro-spinal system. Does it perform no similar duty in the ganglionic? And if there be a Soul distinct from the Spirit, must not this be its residence, in the same manner as the cerebro-spinal system is the residence of the Spirit?

In confirmation of this conjecture, we may notice how much the ganglionic system is connected with the emotional part of our nature. Distinct from the local pains which we feel when the sensitive nerves are injured in connection with the cerebro-spinal system; there is the suffering of sickness, which is sometimes even more distressing than local pain, and whose seat must be the ganglionic system. May it not be then that all our emotions and temperaments, elevations and depressions, are produced by the combined action of the two systems, and that it is the soul that is the subject of the emotions?

APPENDIX (E.)

THE EMPLOYMENTS OF THE REDEEMED
AFTER THE RESURRECTION.

UNTIL the day of the resurrection, the redeemed are represented as having entered into their rest, and fallen asleep in Jesus. After their resurrection, such a state of inaction would be unworthy of the high destiny to which they are called, and for which they will then be so gloriously equipped. If their present mortal bodies fit the spirit for high enterprise and active labour, how much more active must they be when that which is sown in weakness shall be raised in power! With bodies possessing all the attributes of material manhood, and, at the same time, all the spiritual immunities of angelic natures, there seems to be no end to the variety, as well as the grandeur of their occupations. Like Christ and the angels, they will be able to walk and to sit, to eat and to drink, on such worlds as this; but they will also be able to pass through material obstacles, or to mount through the air, and wing their way from star to star upon the errands of their Master. Gifted with noblest thought, and endowed with high intellectual powers, they will be able to fulfil their commissions in the distant worlds to which they may be sent. Happiness is produced by the exercise of our faculties; if, therefore, the faculties of the resurrection body be not exercised, a great source of pleasure will be lost; and it is only because our weak powers of imagination are unable to fathom the future glories of God's administration, that we feel at a loss when we attempt to anticipate the employments of the sons of God. Eye hath not seen, ear hath not heard, neither hath it entered into the heart of man to conceive what is laid up for those who shall be thought worthy to attain to the resurrection of the dead. We may, however, in im-agination, be able to realise, in part, the future history of our occupations, by accompanying such an one as Gabriel in one of his angelic pilgrimages. It was in the days of Darius the Mede, who reigned over Chaldea, more than five hundred years before the birth of our Saviour.

The captive Jews were, at that time, hanging their harps on the willows, beside the waters of Babylon, far from the loved land of their inheritance; but they had now nearly fulfilled the seventy years of their captivity, which had been predicted by the prophet Jeremiah. Daniel, who was one of them, and who had been elevated to the rank of one of the princes of the kingdom, had anxiously studied the prediction; and, finding that only about two years remained before the expected dawn of their deliverance, he resolved to prepare for this blessed consummation, by fasting, and supplication, and prayer. We are not informed regarding the length of the time thus devoted to his prayerful intercession before God; upon a subsequent occasion it occupied three full weeks, in which he ate no pleasant bread, and neither flesh nor wine entered his mouth; but upon this occasion, it appears to have lasted only one day, for we are told that the answer was received about the time of the evening sacri-fice. Had it been more than one day, we should have been told, as in the 4th verse of the 10th chapter, upon what day, rather than about what hour, he obtained the response from heaven.

" Whiles I was speaking," says he, " and praying, and

confessing my sin, and the sin of my people Israel, and presenting my supplications before the Lord my God for the holy mountain of my God ; yea, whiles I was speaking in prayer, even the man Gabriel, whom I had seen in the vision at the beginning, being caused to fly swiftly, touched me about the time of the evening oblation. And he informed me, and talked with me, and said, O Daniel, I am now come forth to give thee skill and understanding. At the beginning of thy supplications the commandment came forth, and I am come to show thee ; for thou art greatly beloved : therefore understand the matter, and consider the vision " (Dan. ix. 20-23).

At the beginning of his supplications, probably early in the morning of this memorable day of fasting and prayer, the commandment went forth to Gabriel from the throne of the Eternal, to fly swiftly to this earth on this errand of revelation. Swiftly he flew, no doubt in obedience to this high behest—so swiftly, that he arrived upon our planet that same day, occupying probably not more than six hours, or, at the very most, ten hours in his passage.

But here the question occurs, how far had he to travel, and from what place did he come ? We cannot answer the first question, but, in regard to the second, we may be assured that it was from some distant world in space. Was it from one of the sister planets of our own solar system, or was it from some other star, or rather some other system connected with our own Milky Way ! There is still one other alternative : may it not have been from beyond the confines of even this great galaxy—from some distant nebula that trembles in the field of our most powerful telescopes ?

If so, it would not be difficult to imagine the scenes

through which he passed in his stupendous flight.   After springing upwards from the orb on which he lived, and bending his eye on the far distant point towards which his flight must be directed, he would press onwards with increasing swiftness, rivalling at length the velocity of light.   In the first hour, he would have left behind him the firmament of his native world, and entered the great wilderness of the universe, where no single star was visible, and where the black vault above, beneath, and around, was sprinkled only with its distant nebulæ. Here he is alone with God ; and, probably, in the solemn silence of his solitary flight, is receiving upon his inmost spirit the prophetic message that he was to bear to earth.

For hours together the same dread grandeur of nebulous scenery would continue; and yet the inconceivable swiftness of his progress would produce, as it were, a moving panorama around him, the nebulæ in front opening and enlarging themselves before him, passing on each side at greater and less distances, according to the line of his flight, and finally closing up and disappearing in the distant wake.   Such would be the characteristic scenery of the greater part of his voyage.   Like the vessel that leaves its port, and, after passing through a forest of shipping, and witnessing for a few hours the surrounding scenery of its enclosing bay, enters at length the wide ocean, and continues sailing there, perhaps for weeks, before it sees the corresponding scenery of the port to which it is bound : so would Gabriel's flight be one of weary sameness during the greater part of its continuance.

Sometimes, no doubt, the strange outlines of the distant clusters would present interesting objects of study to the angelic astronomer. Ring-shaped nebulæ, contrasting with spherical or lenticular conformations; these would approach and enlarge, and, after decreasing again, would ultimately disappear. Grotesque arrangements of congregated stars, some like spiral comets, others like fringed crowns, some like tangled clouds, others like rocket showers, would appear to sail along the silent heavens as his flight bore on. Sometimes his way would lie so near their confines, that occasionally the form of some distant nebula would grow in brightness as it neared him, and when it sailed closely by, perhaps only a few quadrillions of miles distant, it would expand and resolve itself into myriads of little stars, till, being past, it would again gather up its glories into some new and strange outline, and at length fade away in the ethereal distance.

Towards the close of his voyage, his course is directed to one particular nebula, from which he swerves not either to the right hand or the left. It is evidently the sought-for object of his flight. It is our Milky Way, although, as yet, it is no more than a small speck in the distant night. By-and-by it grows in brightness and becomes more distinct in outline, like a small flat cloud split along one of its flanks. Onwards and onwards he flies towards this bourne, and, as he approaches, its outline gradually disappears, and the stars of which its dim light was composed disengage themselves, and open up on his field of view. Now he must gradually slacken his flight, because he is approaching the termination of his voyage. Like the ship entering the port of its destination, and passing through another forest of shipping, so would Gabriel find the stars of the Milky Way open out upon his view; and, gradually radiating from the central point towards which his flight is directed, they would at length brighten into a starry firmament around, such as meets our admiring gaze on a cloudless and moonless night.

Having entered the firmament of the Milky Way, his eye is now directed towards a feeble, undistinguished star, upon which all his interest is concentrated. Swift as the light he makes towards it, and, as it brightens before him, he can look round and notice the same well-known stars and constellations that we are accustomed to see, with no great difference in their arrangements. There is Sirius, brighter than all beside; there is Orion, with his cloudy sword; there are the Pleiades, that vast system of congregated suns, around which our own appears to be revolving; there is the Southern Cross; and there are the glorious Magellanic clouds, from which, it may be, his morning flight began. The sky is blacker than night, and the stars sparkle with a brilliancy that no mortal eye has ever seen.

Meantime his star has grown a sun—small, indeed, as the morning star, but dazzling with a light which no planet can ever equal. He has come within the orbit of Neptune, and there is Uranus with his moon, and there is Saturn with his moons and rings, and Jupiter, also with his bands and moons. He can even perceive, in close proximity to the enlarging sun, a red speck, which is the planet Mars. But where is the Earth, of which he is yet in search? It is still invisible, because it is yet immersed in the solar rays. Onward he flies, and, entering successively the orbits of Uranus and Saturn, his piercing eye can now detect a little speck emerging from the glowing sunshine in which it was previously lost— it is the Earth at last. It brightens into a small blue star, growing richer and larger as he enters successively the orbits of Jupiter and the Mero-planets; and when, at length he has reached the orbit of Mars, the disk of the earth has become visible, and the rich blue tint of our planet is conspicuous over all the others.

Onward and onward the pilgrim angel flies, keeping our little planet still before him until its growing disk expands into a gigantic moon; and, in a few minutes more dipping beneath the blue atmosphere that covers the Babylonian plains, he lays his hand upon the prostrate Daniel. It is the time of the evening oblation.

"Know ye not that ye shall judge angels?" (2 Cor. vi. 3).

THE END.

LORIMER AND GILLIES, PRINTERS, 31 ST. ANDREW SQUARE, EDINBURGH.

AN INTERPRETING CONCORDANCE.

OF

THE NEW TESTAMENT:

Being an English-Greek Concordance for those who know nothing of Greek.

By the Rev. JAMES GALL.

In One Vol. pp. 372, Imp. 8vo, Cloth lettered, 7s. 6d.

This Work gives—

First.—The Greek original for every word used in our English version.

Second.—A Glossary giving the derivation and meaning of every Greek word. (*The Greek words being in Roman letters.*)

Third.—Under each English heading, the passages classified according to the Greek word that is used.

Fourth.—The different translations that are given to each Greek word in our English version.

By this means the Bible student who knows nothing of Greek is placed nearly on a level with Greek scholars in the study of the New Testament.

OPINIONS OF THE PRESS.

"**This ought to be the third book in the library of every Christian unacquainted with the original language of the New Testament.** We do not transgress the limits of sobriety and truth in saying that, after the Bible and Cruden, the most necessary book to a Bible reader is a Greek or English-Greek Concordance. There is **no other book of the kind which, for simplicity of design, ease of reference, portability, and cheapness, can be compared** for its usefulness to the English Bible reader **with this Interpreting Concordance,** which we therefore cordially recommend to all who desire accurately to know the words which the Holy Ghost has used."—*Revival.*

"**This work is one of the most important helps to the thorough study of the New Testament,** by those who have no knowledge of the Greek language, **that has ever been produced.** The English student is enabled, by its use, to ascertain in any passage the very word used in the original, to detect its first signification, to trace it through various renderings, and to distinguish it from other words of different first-signification, which are represented by the same English word. *Most valuable assistance may be thus gained in clearing away obscurities from many passages of the authorised version, and in acquiring firmly the true meaning of a passage, not by lengthy and indirect explanation, but by face-to-face view of the words themselves. . . .* **A work which ought to be possessed before almost all others.**"—*The Nonconformist.*

"We welcome Mr. Gall's Concordance as a work of this kind, being persuaded that it will be found to be a great boon."—*The Literary Churchman.*

"The execution is good, no pains seem to have been spared; the work is full and accurate, embracing everything that comes within the purpose of the compiler."—*The Athenæum.*

Edinburgh : GALL & INGLIS, 20 Bernard Terrace.

Just Published, price Three Shillings and Sixpence.

THE SCIENCE OF MISSIONS.

The Evangelistic Baptism indispensable to the Church for the Conversion of the World.

BY THE REV. JAMES GALL.

————➤o◄————

"We have been thoroughly delighted, and greatly encouraged and stimulated by a perusal of this work. . . ."—*Independent Methodist Magazine.*

"A singularly earnest and stirring book. . . . Every page glows with the fire of an intense and overpowering conviction; . . . it is not, therefore, the theorizing of a student, but the experience of a soldier who has fought valiantly and successfully. . . . His words are like a clarion call to prayer and work."—*Baptist Magazine.*

"A work of rare excellence, interesting and valuable. It is eminently suggestive, and deserves and will amply repay a careful and repeated perusal. . . . It contains much that is new and striking : it is throughout evangelical in tone and sentiment ; and in the fulness and clearness with which it discusses the doctrines of the Trinity and the work of the Spirit, there is much to instruct and edify the church, and to animate christians to entire consecration for the conversion of the world. . . . We are thoroughly convinced that little or no progress will ever be made until the church cease to do the work by proxy. . . . The church should be stirred up to seek what the author so clearly exhibits and ably advocates,—the promised power of the Spirit. . . . The second part will be looked for with earnest interest."—*Original Secession Magazine.*

"This is a remarkable volume, as are indeed more than one other work of the author. . . . When we think of his special training and experience, as well as his peculiar talents, we must concede him the right to speak with authority on the subject. . . . We cannot help admiring the strength and conclusiveness of the argument advanced for the Evangelistic Baptism, and we must confess that it has considerably corrected our own views as to the duty of christian ministers and people. . . . His argument is clear and trenchant ; and we question if there is a view of christian duty which has been presented to the world in modern times, that can for a moment be compared with the one here discussed and enforced. . . . We cordially commend the work for its intellectual force, for its refreshing christian views, and above all for its striking illustration and enforcement of the great command, 'Go ye,' &c."—*Liverpool Courier.*

"A most practically sensible as well as stimulating treatise, which we earnestly recommend. . . . There are some wonderfully wise remarks on the spirit and manner in which christians should devote their money to God ; the chapter on Corban is especially good. . . . Even Methodists might learn much from these glowing pages."—*Wesleyan Methodist Magazine.*

"Whether we consider the spirit and purpose of the book, or the originality and masterly clearness with which the subject is handled, it is equally satisfactory. . . . It is alike creditable to his spiritual insight, his moral earnestness, and his mental power. . . . It should be read by all the churches, but by Methodists with especial interest."—*Primitive Methodist Magazine.*

"This is a remarkable book, and has the mark of genius. . . . It aims at nothing short of revolutionizing the views of the church in regard to the evangelization of the world. . . . Profound and far-reaching arguments ; . . .

deeply interesting and well-reasoned. . . . There is already some awakening to the fact that the world will not be gained over for Christ, till the *whole* church is doing evangelistic work. . This book will be most serviceable in stimulating and directing this movement. . . . No reader interested in the subject can begin it without reading with enjoyment to the end."—*The Christian Week.*

"This is a remarkable book, well worthy the perusal of all who take an interest in evangelism. . . . In answer to the question how to account for the comparative want of the propagative power of christianity, he shows that the old dispensation was not propagative, while the new is; but that the church has fallen back on the old. . . . He demolishes the principle of 'systematic giving,' and shows that the church will never do her work till every member is a worker. . . . The views are based upon a foundation of Scripture which, to our apprehension, seems conclusive."—*Perthshire Advertiser.*

"A compendium of the practical philosophy of mission work, containing the summary of fifty years' experience of the writer. . . . As might be expected, it is plain and practical, and yet so well and so ably written as to carry conviction of its wisdom to the reader. . . . His views, if adopted, would bring about a complete change in our present system of evangelism. Its great defect, he says, is that it proposes to regenerate the world without the church being itself revived. It is an awful mistake. . . . His clear and earnest reasoning puts the necessity of the Evangelistic Baptism of the church for the world's conversion before the minds of all who are privileged to read his words. May the second part be as good as the first."—*The Christian.*

"The author, from his long, wide, and hardly-earned experience, is well entitled to speak with authority on the subject. . . . He gives no uncertain sound, and what he says is well said and well reasoned. He would revive the old apostolic principle, that every christian is a missionary—and with this power he would evangelize the world. . . . We expect that these opinions will meet with opposition, but there is this to be said for them, they are advocated in a masterly way. . . . The author's refutation of the substitutes for the Evangelistic Baptism is able, and admirably illustrated."—*Aberdeen Journal.*

"To the theologian, the minister of the gospel, and others called to labour in Christ's cause, we commend the book for study, because of its earnestness, ability, and practical suggestiveness."—*British Messenger.*

"The aim of the writer is to prove that we want not one minister for each district, but hundreds of living christians to do the work of Christ. . . . The chapters devoted to the mission work of the apostles are extremely well done."—*English Churchman.*

"There is not a chapter in the volume which will not repay careful perusal, and when the second part is published, the christian church will be in possession of a work which discusses, as the subject deserves, the true science of missions."—*Ardrossan Herald.*

"Joined to a mature experience, the author possesses a highly cultivated mind. As a practical worker no less than a thinker the author is entitled to a high place; and all who have any interest in home-mission work should read this book."—*Oban Times.*

"Every christian should read it, and give it prayerful and thoughtful study."—*London Sunday-School Teacher.*

"An admirable chapter on what is called 'systematic liberality.'"—*Dumfries and Galloway Courier.*

"We cordially recommend the book to all who are interested in evangelistic work."—*Montrose Standard.*

"A genuine and healthy book, that will well repay perusal."—*Glasgow Herald.*

GALL & INGLIS : EDINBURGH AND LONDON.

CPSIA information can be obtained
at www.ICGtesting.com
Printed in the USA
BVHW090103180122
626439BV00010B/136